Readings in Western Civilization

ぴ **Vere dignum**

University of Chicago Readings in Western Civilization
John W. Boyer and Julius Kirshner, General Editors

1. **The Greek Polis**
   Edited by Arthur W. H. Adkins and Peter White

2. **Rome: Late Republic and Principate**
   Edited by Walter Emil Kaegi, Jr., and Peter White

3. **The Church in the Roman Empire**
   Edited by Karl F. Morrison

4. **Medieval Europe**
   Edited by Julius Kirshner and Karl F. Morrison

5. **The Renaissance**
   Edited by Eric Cochrane and Julius Kirshner

6. **Early Modern Europe: Crisis of Authority**
   Edited by Eric Cochrane, Charles M. Gray, and Mark A. Kishlansky

7. **The Ancien Régime and the French Revolution**
   Edited by Keith Michael Baker

8. **Nineteenth-Century Europe: Liberalism in an Age of Industrialization**
   Edited by Jan Goldstein and John W. Boyer

9. **Twentieth-Century Europe**
   Edited by John W. Boyer and Jan Goldstein

University of Chicago
Readings in Western Civilization

John W. Boyer and Julius Kirshner, General Editors

3
The Church in the Roman Empire

Edited by Karl F. Morrison

The University of Chicago Press

Chicago and London

Karl F. Morrison is the Ahmanson-Murphy Distinguished Professor of Medieval and Renaissance History at the University of Kansas. From 1965 to 1984, he was professor of history at the University of Chicago.

The University of Chicago Press, Chicago 60637
The University of Chicago Press, Ltd., London
© 1986 by The University of Chicago
All rights reserved. Published 1986
Printed in the United States of America

95 94 93 92 91 90 89 88 87 86   54321

Library of Congress Cataloging-in-Publication Data
Main entry under title:

University of Chicago readings in Western civilization.

    Includes bibliographies and indexes.
    Contents: —v. 3. The Church in the Roman
Empire / edited by Karl F. Morrison—v. 4. Medieval
Europe / edited by Julius Kirshner and Karl F. Morrison.
    1. Civilization, Occidental—History—Sources.
2. Europe—Civilization—Sources. I. Boyer, John W.
II. Kirshner, Julius.   III. Title: Readings in Western
civilization.
CB245.U64   1986   909'.09821   85-16328
ISBN 0-226-06934-6 (v. 1)
ISBN 0-226-06935-4 (pbk.: v. 1)

ISBN: 0-226-06938-9 (v. 3)
ISBN: 0-226-06939-7 (pbk.: v. 3)

Contents

Series Editors' Foreword

This series is the result of almost four decades of teaching the History of Western Civilization course at the College of the University of Chicago. The course was founded in its present form in the late 1940s by a group of young historians at Chicago, including William H. McNeill, Christian Mackauer, and Sylvia Thrupp, and has been sustained during the past twenty-five years by the distinguished teaching of Eric Cochrane, Hanna H. Gray, Charles M. Gray, and Karl J. Weintraub. In the beginning it served as a counterpoint to the antihistorical and positivistic thrust of the general education curriculum in the social sciences in the Hutchins College. Western Civilization has since been incorporated as a year-long course into different parts of the College program, from the first to the last year. It now forms part of the general intercivilizational requirement for sophomores and juniors. It is still taught, as it has been almost constantly since its inception, in discussion groups ranging from twenty to thirty students.

Although both the readings and the instructors of the course have changed over the years, its purpose has remained the same. It seeks not to provide students with morsels of Western culture, nor to nourish their moral and aesthetic sensitivities, and much less to attract recruits for the history profession. Its purpose instead is to raise a whole set of complex conceptual questions regarding the nature of time and change and the intended and unintended consequences of human action and consciousness. Students in this course learn to analyze past events and ideas by rigorously examining a variety of texts. This is in contrast to parallel courses in the social sciences, which teach students to deploy synchronic and quantitative techniques in analyzing society, usually without reference to historical context or process.

Ours is a history course that aims not at imparting relevant facts or exotic ideas but at providing students with the critical tools by which to ana-

lyze texts produced in the distant or near past. It also serves a related purpose: to familiarize students with major epochs of that Western historical
tradition to which most of them, albeit at times unknowingly, are heirs.
The major curricular vehicle of the course is the *Readings in Western Civilization*, a nine-volume series of primary sources in translation, beginning
with Periclean Athens and concluding with Europe in the twentieth century.
The series is not meant to be a comprehensive survey of Western history.
Rather, in each volume, we provide a large number of documents on specific themes in the belief that depth, not breadth, is the surest antidote to
superficiality. The very extensiveness of the documentation in each volume
allows for a variety of approaches to the same theme. At the same time the
concentrated focus of individual volumes makes it possible for them to
serve as source readings in more advanced and specialized courses.

Many people contributed to the publication of these volumes. The en-
thusiastic collaboration and labors of the members of the Western Civilization staff made it possible for these *Readings* to be published. We thank
Barbara Boyer for providing superb editorial direction to the project and
Mary Van Steenbergh for her dedication in creating beautifully text-edited
manuscripts. Steven Wheatley's advice in procuring funding for this project
was invaluable. Members of the University of Chicago Press have given
their unstinting support and guidance. We also appreciate the confidence
and support accorded by Donald N. Levine, the Dean of the College at the
University of Chicago. Above all, we are deeply grateful for the extraordinary dedication, energy, and erudition which our colleague and current
chairperson of the course, Eric Cochrane, has contributed to the *Readings
in Western Civilization*.

We are grateful to the National Endowment for the Humanities for
providing generous funding for the preparation and publication of the
volumes.

JOHN W. BOYER AND JULIUS KIRSHNER

General Introduction

The following collection of texts belongs to a series of anthologies that have been compiled for use in teaching a course at the University of Chicago: the History of Western Civilization. The principles of selection, exclusion, and arrangement that I have followed pertain to the specific needs of that course. Teaching proceeds largely by discussion of original documents in translation, and instructors in the course make a special effort, letting the documents speak for themselves, to provide an array of views on each topic for analysis and debate.

One salient characteristic of the enterprise is portrayal of the past as a shifting manifold, with false starts, regressions, and detours, rather than as a single narrative line. This approach naturally requires teachers to select and arrange texts as though they were case studies, witnesses clustered around common irritants, rather than beads on the string of narrative. Assuming that many crucial texts will be available elsewhere, they compile anthologies meant to extend the range of what is possible in class discussion. Efforts are made, through the selection of texts, to provide thematic links between earlier and later segments of the course.

The effects of these general guidelines are evident in the present anthology, *The Church in the Roman Empire*. It includes no documents concerning the earliest days of the Church: namely, the era of Jesus, the Apostles, and their immediate followers. The reason is that, in the Western Civilization course at the University of Chicago, primitive Christianity is approached through texts readily available in the New Testament. In compiling this collection, I assumed that the space available to me could best be devoted to the post-Apostolic Church: that is, to the Church between the third and the sixth centuries.

In the crucible of this age, an awesome transformation took place. Centuries before, Rome had overwhelmed Greece by force of arms, only to succumb to Greek culture by assimilation. Now again, Rome, waging wars of persecution against the Church, succumbed to the subculture of

Christianity, which, in time, became the official religion of the Empire. For its part, the Church too was assimilated to the Roman Empire that it had converted, and, even as it continued to preach contempt for the world, it was grafted onto dominant institutions of law, wealth, and power. A gulf—fateful for all later movements of reform—widened between the worldly magnificence of the Church, patterned on the imperial government, and the spiritual call of Christianity to renounce the world, the flesh, and the devil.

In selecting topics for discussion and gathering representative texts, I have been conscious of preparing materials for a general course in history, and not for more narrowly defined courses in theology or Church history. I have attempted to gather materials that would provide useful points of comparison, as the course progressed, with other pivotal moments in the formation of Europe. Some such topics are explicit. They figure in the table of contents. Others are implicit; they need to be ferreted out from the texts. For example, I have included in each topic documents illustrating the status of women, not as a distinct subject, but as a significant aspect of late Antique society at its most dramatic turning point.

Clearly, not all the topics, much less all the materials, in this volume will be studied in any single year. At Chicago, the number of class sessions devoted to this subject varies greatly from instructor to instructor, and, for each instructor, from year to year. For these reasons, I have gathered enough materials to allow flexibility in the subjects, methods, and levels of discussion. I also want to encourage intellectual prodding at the junctures of some topics, such as at the point where ideas about ascetic discipline overlapped with those about the relations between imperial and Church government, or at the point where abstract speculations about Church order intersected with pragmatic rulings on the status of men and women in the Church.

Of course, it is essential that students be able to place individual documents and topics against a broad historical background. To that end, parallel readings in general histories of the Church or of the late Roman Empire are strongly recommended.

A highly selective list of recommended books on various topics follows.

Select Bibliography

The field of study represented by this collection is large and ever expanding. To keep track of current publications, one needs to consult annual bibliographies such as those published by the *Archivium historiae pon-*

tificiae or the *Revue d'histoire ecclésiastique*, which inventory books and articles in every pertinent language.

Students who wish to learn about the antecedents and first stages of Christian history might enjoy reading Rudolf Bultmann, *Primitive Christianity in Its Contemporary Setting* (New York: Thames & Hudson, 1956). Through sheer good fortune two ancient libraries from non-Christian sects that shaped primitive Christianity have been discovered and published in comparatively recent times. Their intrinsic fascination and their importance for later religious history is evident in translations, which also describe the exciting discoveries of the libraries themselves. See James M. Robinson, ed., *The Nag Hammadi Library* (Leiden: E. J. Brill, 1977), and Geza Vermes, *The Dead Sea Scrolls in English* (Harmondsworth: Penguin, 1973). On the two most prominent figures of primitive Christianity, see the highly provocative study by Morton Smith, *Jesus the Magician* (New York: Harper & Row, 1978); and Michael Grant, *Saint Paul, the Man* (London: Weidenfeld & Nicolson, 1976). For those interested in cross-disciplinary studies, it might be useful to consult Howard Clark Kee, *Christian Origins in Sociological Perspective: Methods and Resources* (Philadelphia: Westminster, 1980), together with Kee's anthology, *The Origins of Christianity: Sources and Documents* (Englewood Cliffs, N.J.: Prentice-Hall, 1973).

For general treatments of the history of the age of the Fathers, the following books can be especially recommended: Henry Chadwick, *The Early Church*, The Pelican History of the Church, volume 1 (Harmondsworth: Penguin, 1967); Jaroslav Pelikan, *The Emergence of the Catholic Tradition (100–600)*, The Christian Tradition: A History of the Development of Doctrine, volume 1 (Chicago: University of Chicago, 1971); and Joseph Vogt, *The Decline of Rome*, translated by Janet Sondheimer (New York: New American Library, 1967.)

On the special topics treated in this collection, the following books may be helpful.

1. The Call to Conversion in a Hostile Environment

Jean Daniélou. *The Origins of Latin Christianity*. Translated by David Smith and John Austin Baker. A History of Early Christian Doctrine before the Council of Nicaea, volume 3. Philadelphia: Westminster, 1977.

A. D. Nock. *Conversion: The Old and the New in Religion from Alexander the Great to Augustine of Hippo*. Oxford: Oxford University Press, 1933.

2. From Persecuted to Persecutor

Peter Brown. *The Cult of the Saints: Its Rise and Function in Latin Christianity*. Chicago: University of Chicago Press, 1981.
W. H. C. Frend. *The Donatist Church: A Moment of Protest in Roman North Africa*. Oxford: Clarendon, 1952.
A. H. M. Jones. *Constantine and the Conversion of Europe*. London: Hodder & Staughton, 1948.

3. Relations between Church Government and Imperial Administration

Robert M. Grant. *Early Christianity and Society*. New York: Harper & Row, 1977.
Harold Mattingly. *Christianity in the Roman Empire*. New York: W. W. Norton, 1967.
Kenneth M. Setton. *Christian Attitude toward the Emperor in the Fourth Century*. New York: Columbia University Press, 1941.

4. Christianity and Paganism

E. R. Dodds. *Pagan and Christian in an Age of Anxiety*. Cambridge: Cambridge University Press, 1965.
H. Hagendahl. *Latin Fathers and the Classics. A Study in the Apologists, Jerome and Other Christian Writers*. Studia Graeca et Latina Gothoburgensia. Göteborg, 1958.
M. L. W. Laistner. *Christianity and Pagan Culture in the Later Roman Empire*. Ithaca, N.Y.: Cornell University Press, 1951.
R. A. Markus. *Christianity in the Roman World*. London: Thames & Hudson, 1974.
David Wagner, ed. *The Seven Liberal Arts in the Middle Ages*. Bloomington: Indiana University Press, 1983.

5. Asceticism

Louis Bouyer. *The Spirituality of the New Testament and the Fathers*. A History of Christian Spirituality, volume 1. New York: Desclee Co., 1963.
Helen Waddell. *The Desert Fathers*. Ann Arbor: University of Michigan Press, 1957.

6. Church Order

Elizabeth A. Clark. *Jerome, Chrysostom and Friends*. Studies in Women and Religion, volume 2. New York: Edwin Mellen Press, 1979.

Hans Lietzmann. *A History of the Early Church*. Volumes 3, 4. Translated by Bertram Lee Woolf. New York: Meridian, 1953.

1
The Call to Conversion in a Hostile Environment

The three texts in the following section illuminate the motives and the experience of conversion. They also testify to the predominately Greek character that the western Church retained well into the fourth century. The authors of two of the texts, a teacher from Palestine and his disciple from Syria, met in Rome, and the author of a segment of the third text may have been a Levantine whom a splinter group elected bishop of Rome. All three texts display the convert's zeal to discredit his former attachments and to magnify his new faith, and the thirst for conflict even—perhaps especially—if it led to martyrdom.

Justin Martyr (died about 165) was born into a non-Christian Greek family in the Palestinian city now known as Nablus. He was an avid student of philosophy, especially of Platonism, from a relatively early age. The decisive moment in his conversion came on the road to Ephesus when a mysterious old man revealed to him the immortality of the soul and directed him to the sacred writings of the Christians. Justin became an itinerant teacher, finally settling in Rome, where he was martyred. He is known to have written eight treatises, of which three survive. Two of these are apologies. The following selections come from his first apology, which was written about 150–55.

Tatian (flourished 170) was a widely traveled Syrian who became a disciple of Justin Martyr at Rome. Subsequently, he returned to the Near East, where he founded a Christian sect known for its esoteric doctrines and austere practices. His vehemence contrasts with Justin's even-tempered presentation.

The *Letter to Diognetus*, probably written late in the second century, appears to have been unknown in Antiquity. It survived in only one manuscript, which was destroyed in 1870. Its time and place of origin are unknown. Chapters 11 and 12 are unlike earlier chapters in the treatise.

6

They may come from another document, perhaps a sermon on Easter or the Epiphany. Some scholars have proposed that the author was the celebrated Hippolytus of Rome (died 235), who, like Justin and Tatian, was born in the Near East and traveled to Rome. He was a prolific writer. Distinguished by his learning and rigor, Hippolytus was elected pope by a faction in the Roman Church. He was subsequently reconciled with his opponents, and died in exile under persecution.

---

1. Justin Martyr, *First Apology*

1. Address

To the Emperor Titus Aelius Adrianus Antoninus Pius Augustus Caesar, and to his son Verissimus the philosopher, and to Lucius the philosopher, the natural son of Caesar, and the adopted son of Pius, a lover of learning, and to the sacred senate, with the whole people of the Romans, I, Justin, the son of Priscus and grandson of Bacchius, natives of Flavia Neapolis in Palestine, present this address and petition in behalf of those of all nations who are unjustly hated and wantonly abused, myself being one of them.

2. Justice Demanded

Reason directs those who are truly pious and philosophical to honour and love only what is true, declining to follow traditional opinions, if these be worthless. For not only does sound reason direct us to refuse the guidance of those who did or taught anything wrong, but it is incumbent on the lover of truth, by all means, and if death be threatened, even before his own life, to choose to do and say what is right. Do you, then, since ye are called pious and philosophers, guardians of justice and lovers of learning, give good heed, and hearken to my address; and if ye are indeed such, it will be manifested. For we have come, not to flatter you by this writing, nor please you by our address, but to beg that you pass judgment, after an accurate and searching investigation, not flattered by prejudice or by a desire of pleasing superstitious men, nor induced by irrational impulse or evil rumours which have long been prevalent, to give a decision which will prove to be against yourselves. For as for us, we reckon that no evil can be done us, unless we be convicted as evildoers, or be proved to be wicked men; and you, you can kill, but not hurt us.

From *Ante-Nicene Christian Library*, vol. 2, *Justin Martyr and Athenagoras*, translated by M. Dods, G. Reith, and B. P. Pratter (Edinburgh: T. & T. Clark, 1867).

3. Claim of Judicial Investigation

But lest any one think that this is an unreasonable and reckless utterance, we demand that the charges against the Christians be investigated, and that, if these be substantiated, they be punished as they deserve; [or rather, indeed, we ourselves will punish them.] But if no one can convict us of anything, true reason forbids you, for the sake of a wicked rumour, to wrong blameless men, and indeed rather yourselves, who think fit to direct affairs, not by judgment, but by passion. And every sober-minded person will declare this to be the only fair and equitable adjustment, namely, that the subjects render an unexceptionable account of their own life and doctrine; and that, on the other hand, the rulers should give their decision in obedience, not to violence and tyranny, but to piety and philosophy. For thus would both rulers and ruled reap benefit. For even one of the ancients somewhere said, "Unless both rulers and ruled philosophize, it is impossible to make states blessed." It is our task, therefore, to afford to all an opportunity of inspecting our life and teachings, lest, on account of those who are accustomed to be ignorant of our affairs, we should incur the penalty due to them for mental blindness; and it is your business, when you hear us, to be found, as reason demands, good judges. For if, when ye have learnt the truth, you do not what is just, you will be before God without excuse.

4. Christians Unjustly Condemned for Their Mere Name

By the mere application of a name, nothing is decided, either good or evil, apart from the actions implied in the name; and indeed, so far at least as one may judge from the name we are accused of, we are most excellent people. But as we do not think it just to beg to be acquitted on account of the name, if we be convicted as evil-doers, so, on the other hand, if we be found to have committed no offence, either in the matter of thus naming ourselves, or of our conduct as citizens, it is your part very earnestly to guard against incurring just punishment, by unjustly punishing those who are not convicted. For from a name neither praise nor punishment could reasonably spring, unless something excellent or base in action be proved. And those among yourselves who are accused you do not punish before they are convicted; but in our case you receive the name as proof against us, and this although, so far as the name goes, you ought rather to punish our accusers. For we are accused of being Christians, and to hate what is "excellent" (*Chrestian*) is unjust. Again, if any of the accused deny the name, and say that he is not a Christian, you acquit him, as having no evidence against him as a wrong-doer; but if any one acknowledge that he is a Christian, you punish him on account of the acknowledgment. Justice requires that you inquire into the life both of him who confesses and of him who denies, that by his deeds it may be apparent what kind of man each is. For as some who have been taught by the Master, Christ, not to deny Him, give encouragement to others when they are put to the question, so in all probability do those who lead wicked lives give occasion to those who, without consideration, take upon them to accuse all the Christians of impiety and wickedness. And this also is not right. For of philosophy, too, some assume the name and the garb who do nothing worthy of their profession; and you are well aware, that those of the ancients whose opinions and teachings were quite diverse, are yet all called by the one name of philosophers. And of these some taught atheism; and the poets who have flourished among you raise a laugh out of the uncleanness of Jupiter with his own children. And those who now adopt such instruction are not restrained by you; but, on the contrary, you bestow prizes and honours upon those who euphoniously insult the gods.

5. Christians Charged with Atheism

Why, then, should this be? In our case, who pledge ourselves to do no wickedness, nor to hold these atheistic opinions, you do not examine the charges made against us; but, yielding to unreasoning passion, and to the instigation of evil demons, you punish us without consideration or judgment. For the truth shall be spoken; since of old these evil demons, effecting apparitions of themselves, both defiled women and corrupted boys, and showed such fearful sights to men, that those who did not use their reason in judging of the actions that were done, were struck with terror; and being carried away by fear, and not knowing that these were demons, they called them gods, and gave to each the name which each of the demons chose for himself. And when Socrates endeavoured, by true reason and examination, to bring these things to light, and deliver men from the demons, then the demons themselves, by means of men who rejoiced in iniquity, compassed his death, as an atheist and a profane person, on the charge that "he was introducing new divinities;" and in our case they display a similar activity. For not only among the Greeks did reason (Logos) prevail to condemn these things through Socrates, but also among the Barbarians were they condemned by Reason (or the Word, the Logos) Himself, who took shape, and became man, and was called Jesus Christ; and in obedience to Him, we not only deny that they who did such things as these are gods, but assert that they are wicked and impious demons, whose actions will not bear comparison with those even of men desirous of virtue.

6. Charge of Atheism Refuted

Hence are we called atheists. And we confess that we are atheists, so far as gods of this sort are concerned, but not with respect to the most true God, the Father of righteousness and temperance and the other virtues, who is free from all impurity. But both Him, and the Son who came forth from Him and taught us these things, and the host of the other good angels who follow and are made like to Him, and the prophetic Spirit, we worship and adore, knowing them in reason and truth, and declaring without grudging to every one who wishes to learn, as we have been taught.

7. Each Christian Must Be Tried by His Own Life

But some one will say, Some have ere now been arrested and convicted as evil-doers. For you condemn many, many a time, after inquiring into the life of each of the accused severally, but not on account of those of whom we have been speaking. And this we acknowledge, that as among the Greeks those who teach such theories as please themselves are all called by the one name "Philosopher," though their doctrines be diverse, so also among the Barbarians this name on which accusations are accumulated is the common property of those who are and those who seem wise. For all are called Christians. Wherefore we demand that the deeds of all those who are accused to you be judged, in order that each one who is convicted may be punished as an evil-doer, and not as a Christian; and if it is clear that any one is blameless, that he may be acquitted, since by the mere fact of his being a Christian he does no wrong. For we will not require that you punish our accusers; they being sufficiently punished by their present wickedness and ignorance of what is right.

8. Christians Confess Their Faith in God

And reckon ye that it is for your sakes we have been saying these things; for it is in our power, when we are examined, to deny that we are Christians; but we would not live by telling a lie. For, impelled by the desire of the eternal and pure life, we seek the abode that is with God, the Father and Creator of all, and hasten to confess our faith, persuaded and convinced as we are that they who have proved to God by their works that they followed

Him, and loved to abide with Him where there is no sin to cause disturbance, can obtain these things. This, then, to speak shortly, is what we expect and have learned from Christ, and teach. And Plato, in like manner, used to say that Rhadamanthus and Minos would punish the wicked who came before them; and we say that the same thing will be done, but at the hand of Christ, and upon the wicked in the same bodies united again to their spirits which are now to undergo everlasting punishment; and not only, as Plato said, for a period of a thousand years. And if any one say that this is incredible or impossible, this error of ours is one which concerns ourselves only, and no other person, so long as you cannot convict us of doing any harm.

9. Folly of Idol Worship

And neither do we honour with many sacrifices and garlands of flowers such deities as men have formed and set in shrines and called gods; since we see that these are soulless and dead, and have not the form of God (for we do not consider that God has such a form as some say that they imitate to His honour), but have the names and forms of those wicked demons which have appeared. For why need we tell you who already know, into what forms the craftsmen, carving and cutting, casting and hammering, fashion the materials? And often out of vessels of dishonour, by merely changing the form, and making an image of the requisite shape, they make what they call a god; which we consider not only senseless, but to be even insulting to God, who, having ineffable glory and form, thus gets His name attached to things that are corruptible, and require constant service. And that the artificers of these are both intemperate, and, not to enter into particulars, are practiced in every vice, you very well know; even their own girls who work along with them they corrupt. What infatuation! that dissolute men should be said to fashion and make gods for your worship, and that you should appoint such men the guardians of the temples where they are enshrined; not recognizing that it is unlawful even to think or say that men are the guardians of gods.

10. How God Is to Be Served

But we have received by tradition that God does not need the material offerings which men can give, seeing, indeed, that He Himself is the provider of all things. And we have been taught, and are convinced, and do believe, that He accepts those only who imitate the excellences which reside in Him, temperance, and justice, and philanthropy, and as many virtues as are peculiar to a God who is called by no proper name. And we have been taught that He in the beginning did of His goodness, for man's sake, create all things out of unformed matter; and if men by their works show themselves worthy of this His design, they are deemed worthy, and so we have received-of reigning in company with Him, being delivered from corruption and suffering. For as in the beginning He created us when we were not, so do we consider that, in like manner, those who choose what is pleasing to Him are, on account of their choice, deemed worthy of incorruption and of fellowship with Him. For the coming into being at first was not in our own power; and in order that we may follow those things which please Him, choosing them by means of the rational faculties He has Himself endowed us with, He both persuades us and leads us to faith. And we think it for the advantage of all men that they are not restrained from learning these things, but are even urged thereto. For the restraint which human laws could not effect, the Word, inasmuch as He is divine, would have effected, had not the wicked demons, taking as their ally the lust of wickedness which is in every man, and which draws variously to all manner of vice, scattered many false and profane accusations, none of which attach to us.

17. Christ Taught Civil Obedience

And everywhere we, more readily than all men, endeavor to pay to those appointed by you the taxes both ordinary and extraordinary, as we have been taught by Him; for at that time some came to Him and asked Him, if one ought to pay tribute to Caesar; and He answered, "Tell me, whose image does this coin bear?" And they said, "Caesar's"; And again He answered them, "Render therefore to Caesar the things that are Caesar's, and to God the things that are God's." Whence to God alone we render worship, but in other things we gladly serve you, acknowledging you as kings and rulers of men, and praying that with your kingly power you be found to possess also sound judgment. But if you pay no regard to our prayers and frank explanations, we shall suffer no loss, since we believe (or rather, indeed, are persuaded) that every man will suffer punishment in eternal fire according to the merit of his deed, and will render account according to the power he has received from God, as Christ intimated when He said, "To whom God has given more, of him shall more be required."

18. Proof of Immortality and the Resurrection

For reflect upon the end of each of the preceding kings, how they died the death common to all, which, if it issued in insensibility, would be a godsend to all the wicked. But since sensation remains to all who have ever lived, and eternal punishment is laid up (i.e. for the wicked), see that ye neglect not to be convinced, and to hold as your belief, that these things are true. For let even necromancy, and the divinations you practise by immaculate children, and the evoking of departed human souls, and those who are called among the magi, Dream-senders and Assistant-spirits (Familiars), and all that is done by those who are skilled in such matters—let these persuade you that even after death souls are in a state of sensation; and those who are seized and cast about by the spirits of the dead, whom all call demoniacs or madmen; and what you repute as oracles, both of Amphilochus, Dodona, Pytho, and as many other such as exist; and the opinions of your authors, Empedocles and Pythagoras, Plato and Socrates, and the pit of Homer, and the descent of Ulysses to inspect these things, and all that has been uttered of a like kind. Such favor as you grant to these, grant also to us, who not less but more firmly than they believe in God; since we expect to receive again our own bodies, though they be dead and cast into the earth, for we maintain that with God nothing is impossible.

19. The Resurrection Possible

And to any thoughtful person would anything appear more incredible, than, if we were not in the body, and some one were to say it was possible that from a small drop of human seed bones and sinews and flesh be formed into a shape such as we see? For let this now be said hypothetically: if you yourselves were not such as you now are, and born of such parents [and causes], and one were to show you human seed and a picture of a man, and were to say with confidence that from such a substance such a being could be produced, would you believe before you saw the actual production? No one will dare to deny [that such a statement would surpass belief]. In the same way, then, you are now incredulous because you have never seen a dead man rise again. But as at first you would not have believed it possible that such persons could be produced from the small drop, and yet now you see them thus produced, so also judge ye that it is not impossible that the bodies of men, after they have been dissolved, and like seeds resolved into earth, should in God's appointed time rise again and put on incorruption. For what power worthy of God those imagine who say, that each thing returns to that from which it was produced, and that beyond this not even God Himself can do anything, we are unable to conceive; but this we see clearly, that they would not have believed it possible that they could have become such and produced from such materials, as they now see both themselves and the whole world to be. And that it is better to believe even what is impossible to our own nature and to men, than to be unbelieving like the rest of the world, we have learned; for we know that our master Jesus Christ said, that "what is impossible with men is possible with God,"[1] and "Fear not them that kill you, and after that can do no more; but fear Him who after death is able to cast both soul and body into hell."[2] And hell is a place where those are to be punished who have lived wickedly, and who do not believe that those things which God has taught us by Christ will come to pass.

20. Heathen Analogies to Christian Doctrine

And the Sibyl and Hystaspes said that there should be a dissolution by God of things corruptible. And the philosophers called Stoics teach that even God Himself shall be resolved into fire, and they say that the world is to be formed anew by this revolution; but we understand that God, the creator of all things, is superior to the things that are to be changed. If, therefore, on some points we teach the same things as the poets and philosophers whom you honour, and on other points are fuller and more divine in our teaching, and if we alone afford proof of what we assert, why are we unjustly hated more than all others? For while we say that all things have been produced and arranged into a world by God, we shall seem to utter the doctrine of Plato; and while we say that there will be a burning up of all, we shall seem to utter the doctrine of the Stoics; and while we affirm that the souls of the wicked, being endowed with sensation even after death, are punished, and that those of the good being delivered from punishment spend a blessed existence, we shall seem to say the same things as the poets and philosophers; and while we maintain that men ought not to worship the works of their hands, we say the very things which have been said by the comic poet Menander, and other similar writers, for they have declared that the workman is greater than the work.

21. Analogies to the History of Christ

And when we say also that the Word, who is the first-birth of God, was produced without sexual union, and that He, Jesus Christ, our teacher, was crucified and died, and rose again, and ascended into heaven, we propound nothing different from what you believe regarding those whom you esteem sons of Jupiter. For you know how many sons your esteemed writers ascribe to Jupiter: Mercury, the interpreting word and teacher of all; Aescu-

---

1. Matt. 19:26.   2. Matt. 10:28.

lapius, who though he was a great physician, was struck by a thunderbolt, and so ascended to heaven; and Bacchus too, after he had been torn limb from limb; and Hercules, when he had committed himself to the flames to escape his toils; and the sons of Leda, the Dioscuri; and Perseus, son of Danae; and Bellerophon, who, though sprung from mortals, rose to heaven on the horse Pegasus. For what shall I say of Ariadne, and those who, like her, have been declared to be set among the stars? And what of the emperors who die among yourselves, whom you deem worthy of deification, and in whose behalf you produce some one who swears he has seen the burning Caesar rise to heaven from the funeral pyre? And what kind of deeds are recorded of each of these reputed sons of Jupiter, it is needless to tell to those who already know. This only shall be said, that they are written for the advantage and encouragement of youthful scholars; for all reckon it an honourable thing to imitate the gods. But far be such a thought concerning the gods from every well-conditioned soul, as to believe that Jupiter himself, the governor and creator of all things, was both a parricide and the son of a parricide, and that being overcome by the love of base and shameful pleasures, he came in to Ganymede and those many women whom he violated, and that his sons did like actions. But, as we said above, wicked devils perpetrated these things. And we have learned that those only are deified who have lived near to God in holiness and virtue; and we believe that those who live wickedly and do not repent are punished in everlasting fire.

22. Analogies to the Sonship of Christ

Moreover, the Son of God called Jesus, even if only a man by ordinary generation, yet, on account of His wisdom, is worthy to be called the Son of God; for all writers call God the Father of men and gods. And if we assert that the Word of God was born of God in a peculiar manner, different from ordinary generation, let this, as said above, be no extraordinary thing to you, who say that Mercury is the angelic word of God. But if any one objects that He was crucified, in this also He is on a par with those reputed sons of Jupiter of yours, who suffered as we have now enumerated. For their sufferings at death are recorded to have been not all alike, but diverse; so that not even by the peculiarity of His suffering does He seem to be inferior to them; but on the contrary, as we promised in the preceding part of this discourse, we will now prove Him superior—or rather have already proved Him to be so—for the superior is revealed by His actions. And if we even affirm that He was born of a virgin, accept this in common with what you accept of Perseus. And in that we say that He made whole the lame, the paralytic, and those born blind, we seem to say what is very similar to the deeds said to have been done by Aesculapius.

23. The Argument

And that this may now become evident to you—(firstly) that whatever we assert in conformity with what has been taught us by Christ, and by the prophets who preceded Him, are alone true, and are older than all the writers who have existed, that we claim to be acknowledged, not because we say the same things as these writers said, but because we say true things: and (secondly) that Jesus Christ is the only proper Son who has been begotten by God, being His Word and first-begotten, and power; and, becoming man according to His will, He taught us these things for the conversion and restoration of the human race: and (thirdly) that before He became a man among men, some influenced by the demons before mentioned, related beforehand, through the instrumentality of the poets, those circumstances as having really happened, which, having fictitiously devised, they narrated, in the same manner as they have caused to be fabricated the scandalous reports against us of infamous and impious actions, of which there is neither witness nor proof—we shall bring forward the following proof.

24. Varieties of Heathen Worship

In the first place we furnish proof, because, though we say things similar to what the Greeks say, we only are hated on account of the name of Christ, and though we do no wrong, are put to death as sinners; other men in other places worshipping trees and rivers, and mice and cats and crocodiles, and many irrational animals. Nor are the same animals esteemed by all; but in one place one is worshipped, and another in another, so that all are profane in the judgment of one another; on account of their not worshipping the same objects. And this is the sole accusation you bring against us, that we do not reverence the same gods as you do, nor offer to the dead libations and the savour of fat, and crowns for their statues, and sacrifices. For you very well know that the same animals are with some esteemed gods, with others wild beasts, and with others sacrificial victims.

25. False Gods Abandoned by Christians

And, secondly, because we—who, out of every race of men, used to worship Bacchus the son of Semele, and Apollo the son of Latona (who in their loves with men did such things as it is shameful even to mention), and

Proserpine and Venus (who were maddened with love of Adonis, and whose mysteries also you celebrate), or Aesculapius, or some one or other of those who are called gods—have now, through Jesus Christ, learned to despise these, though we be threatened with death for it, and have dedicated ourselves to the unbegotten and impassible God; of whom we are persuaded that never was he goaded by lust of Antiope, or such other women, or of Ganymede, nor was rescued by that hundred-handed giant whose aid was obtained through Thetis, nor was anxious on this account that her son Achilles should destroy many of the Greeks because of his concubine Briseis. Those who believe these things we pity, and those who invented them we know to be devils.

26. Magicians Not Trusted by Christians

And, thirdly, because after Christ's ascension into heaven the devils put forward certain men who said that they themselves were gods; and they were not only not persecuted by you, but even deemed worthy of honours. There was a Samaritan, Simon, a native of the village called Gitto, who in the reign of Claudius Caesar, and in your royal city of Rome, did mighty acts of magic, by virtue of the art of the devils operating in him. He was considered a god, and as a god was honoured by you with a statue, which statue was erected on the river Tiber, between the two bridges, and bore this inscription, in the language of Rome:

"Simoni Deo Sancto,"
"To Simon the holy God"

and almost all the Samaritans, and few even of other nations, worship him, and acknowledge him as the first god; and a woman, Helena, who went about with him at that time, and had formerly been a prostitute, they say is the first idea generated by him. And a man, Menander, also a Samaritan, of the town Capparetaea, a disciple of Simon, and inspired by devils, we know to have deceived many while he was in Antioch by his magical art. He persuaded those who adhered to him that they should never die, and even now there are some living who hold this opinion of his. And there is Marcion, a man of Pontus, who is even at this day alive, and teaching his disciples to believe in some other god greater than the Creator. And he, by the aid of the devils, has caused many of every nation to speak blasphemies, and to deny that God is the maker of this universe, and to assert that some other, being greater than He, has done greater works. All who take their opinions from these men, are as we before said, called Christians; just as also those who do not agree with the philosophers in their doctrines, have yet in common with them the name of philosophers given to them. And whether they perpetrate those fabulous and shameful deeds—the upsetting of the lamp, and promiscuous intercourse, and eating human flesh—we know not; but we do know that they are neither persecuted nor put to death by you, at least on account of their opinions. But I have a treatise against all the heresies that have existed already composed, which, if you wish to read it, I will give you.

27. Guilt of Exposing Children

But as for us, we have been taught that to expose newly-born children is the part of wicked men; and this we have been taught lest we should do any one an injury, and lest we should sin against God, first, because we see that almost all so exposed (not only the girls, but also the males) are brought up to prostitution. And as the ancients are said to have reared herds of oxen, or goats, or sheep, or grazing horses, so now we see you rear children only for this shameful use; and for this pollution a multitude of females and hermaphrodites, and those who commit unmentionable iniquities, are found in every nation. And you receive the hire of these, and duty and taxes from them, whom you ought to exterminate from your realm. And any one who uses such persons, besides the godless and infamous and impure intercourse, may possibly be having intercourse with his own child, or relative, or brother. And there are some who prostitute even their own children and wives, and some are openly mutilated for the purpose of sodomy; and they refer these mysteries to the mother of the gods, and along with each of those whom you esteem gods there is painted a serpent, a great symbol and mystery. Indeed, the things which you do openly and with applause, as if the divine light were overturned and extinguished these you lay to our charge; which, in truth, does no harm to us who shrink from doing any such things, but only to those who do them and bear false witness against us.

28. God's Care for Men

For among us the prince of the wicked spirits is called the serpent, and Satan, and the devil, as you can learn by looking into our writings. And that he would be sent into the fire with his host, and the men who follow him, and would be punished for an endless duration, Christ foretold. For the reason why God has delayed to do this, is His regard for the human race. For He foreknows that some are to be saved by repentance, some even that are perhaps not yet born. In the beginning He made the human race with the power of thought and of choosing the truth and doing right, so that all men are without excuse before God; for they have been born rational and contemplative. And if any one disbelieves that God cares for these things, he will thereby either insinuate that God does not exist, or he will assert that though He exists He delights in vice, or exists like a stone, and that neither virtue nor vice are anything, but only in the opinion of men these things are reckoned good or evil. And this is the greatest profanity and wickedness.

29. Continence of Christians

And again [we fear to expose children], lest some of them be not picked up, but die, and we become murderers. But whether we marry, it is only that we may bring up children; or whether we decline marriage, we live continently. And that you may understand that promiscuous intercourse is not one of our mysteries, one of our number a short time ago presented to Felix the governor in Alexandria a petition, craving that permission might be given to a surgeon to make him an eunuch. For the surgeons there said that they were forbidden to do this without the permission of the governor. And when Felix absolutely refused to sign such a permission, the youth remained single, and was satisfied with his own approving conscience, and the approval of those who thought as he did. And it is not out of place, we think, to mention here Antinous, who was alive but lately, and whom all were prompt, through fear, to worship as a god, though they knew both who he was and what was his origin.

43. Responsibility Asserted

But lest some suppose, from what has been said by us, that we say that whatever happens, happens by a fatal necessity, because it is foretold as known beforehand, this too we explain. We have learned from the prophets, and we hold it to be true, that punishments, and chastisements, and good rewards, are rendered according to the merit of each man's actions. Since if it be not so, but all things happen by fate, neither is anything at all in our own power. For if it be fated that this man, e.g., be good, and this other evil, neither is the former meritorious nor the latter to be blamed. And again, unless the human race have the power of avoiding evil and choosing good by free choice, they are not accountable for their actions, of whatever kind they be. But that it is by free choice they both walk uprightly and stumble, we thus demonstrate. We see the same man making a transition to opposite things. Now, if it had been fated that he were to be either good or bad, he could never have been capable of both the opposites, nor of so many transitions. But not even would some be good and others bad, since we thus make fate the cause of evil, and exhibit her as acting in opposition to herself; or that which has been already stated would seem to be true, that neither virtue nor vice is anything, but that things are only reckoned good or evil by opinion; which, as the true word shows, is the greatest impiety and wickedness. But this we assert is inevitable fate, that they who choose the good have worthy rewards, and they who choose the opposite have their merited awards. For not like other things, as trees and quadrupeds, which cannot act by choice, did God make man: for neither would he be worthy of reward or praise did he not of himself choose the good, but were created for this end; nor, if he were evil, would he be worthy of punishment, not being evil of himself, but being able to be nothing else than what he was made.

44. Not Nullified by Prophecy

And the holy Spirit of prophecy taught us this, telling us by Moses that God spoke thus to the man first created: "Behold, before thy face are good and evil: choose the good." [3] And again, by the other prophet Isaiah, that the following utterance was made as if from God the Father and Lord of all: "Wash you, make you clean; put away evils from your souls; learn to do well; judge the orphan, and plead for the widow: and come and let us reason together, saith the Lord: And if your sins be as scarlet, I will make them white as wool; and if they be red like as crimson, I will make them white as snow. And if ye be willing and obey me, ye shall eat the good of the land; but if ye do not obey me, the sword shall devour you: for the mouth of the Lord hath spoken it." [4] And that expression, "The sword shall devour you," does not mean that the disobedient shall be slain by the sword, but the sword of God is fire, of which they who choose to do wickedly become the fuel. Wherefore He says, "The sword shall devour you: for the mouth of the Lord hath spoken it." And if He had spoken concerning a sword that cuts and at once despatches, He would not have said, "shall devour." And so, too, Plato, when he says, "The blame is his who chooses, and God is blameless" [5] took this from the prophet Moses and uttered it. For Moses is more ancient than all the Greek writers. And whatever both philosophers and poets have said concerning the immortality of the soul, or punishments after death, or contemplation of things heavenly, or doctrines of the like kind, they have received such suggestions from the prophets as have enabled them to understand and interpret these things. And hence there seem to be seeds of truth among all men; but they are

3. Deut. 30:15, 19.   5. Plato, Rep. 10.
4. Isa. 1:16, etc.

charged with not accurately understanding [the truth] when they assert contradictories. So that what we say about future events being foretold, we do not say it as if they came about by all men, and it being His decree that the future actions of men shall all be recompensed according to their several values, He foretells by the Spirit of prophecy that He will bestow meet rewards according to the merit of the actions done, always urging the human race to effort and recollection, showing that He cares and provides for men. But by the agency of the devils death has been decreed against those who read the books of Hystaspes, or of the Sibyl, or of the prophets, that through fear they may prevent men who read them from receiving the knowledge of the good, and may retain them in slavery to themselves; which, however, they could not always effect. For not only do we fearlessly read them, but, as you see, bring them for your inspection, knowing that their contents will be pleasing to all. And if we persuade even a few, our gain will be very great; for, as good husbandmen, we shall receive the reward from the Master.

51. The Majesty of Christ

And that the Spirit of prophecy might signify to us that He who suffers these things has an ineffable origin and rules His enemies, He spake thus: "His generation who shall declare? because His life is cut off from the earth: for their transgressions He comes to death. And I will give the wicked for His burial, and the rich for His death; because He did no violence, neither was any deceit in His mouth. And the Lord is pleased to cleanse Him from the stripe. If He be given for sin, your soul shall see His seed prolonged in days. And the Lord is pleased to deliver His soul from grief, to show Him light, and to form Him with knowledge, to justify the righteous who richly serveth many. And He shall bear our iniquities. Therefore He shall inherit many, and He shall divide the spoil of the strong; because His soul was delivered to death: and He was numbered with the transgressors; and He bore the sins of many, and He was delivered up for their transgressions." [6] Hear, too, how He was to ascend into heaven according to prophecy. It was thus spoken: "Lift up the gates of heaven; be ye opened, that the King of glory may come in. Who is this King of glory? The Lord, strong and mighty." [7] And how also He should come again out of heaven with glory, hear what was spoken in reference to this by the prophet Jeremiah. [8] His words are: "Behold, as the Son of man He cometh in the clouds of heaven, and His angels with Him." [9]

6. Isa. 53:8–12.

7. Ps. 24:7.

8. This prophecy occurs, not in Jeremiah, but in Dan. 7:13.

9. Dan. 7:13.

52. Certain Fulfillment of Prophecy

Since, then, we prove that all things which have already happened had been predicted by the prophets before they came to pass, we must necessarily believe also that those things which are in like manner predicted, but are yet to come to pass, shall certainly happen. For as the things which have already taken place came to pass when foretold, and even though unknown, so shall the things that remain, even though they be unknown and disbelieved, yet come to pass. For the prophets have proclaimed two advents of His: the one, that which is already past, when He came as a dishonoured and suffering man; but the second, when according to prophecy, He shall come from heaven with glory, accompanied by His angelic host, when also He shall raise the bodies of all men who have lived, and shall clothe those of the wicked endued with eternal sensibility, into everlasting fire with the wicked devils. And that these things also have been foretold as yet to be, we will prove. By Ezekiel the prophet it was said: "Joint shall be joined to joint, and bone to bone, and flesh shall grow again; and every knee shall bow to the Lord, and every tongue shall confess Him." [10] And in what kind of sensation and punishment the wicked are to be, hear from what was said in like manner with reference to this; it is as follows: "Their worm shall not rest, and their fire shall not be quenched;" [11] and then shall they repent, when it profits them not. And what the people of the Jews shall say and do, when they see Him coming in glory, has been thus predicted by Zechariah the prophet: "I will command the four winds to gather the scattered children; I will command the north wind to bring them, and the south wind, that it keep not back. And then in Jerusalem there shall be great lamentation, not the lamentation of mouths or of lips, but the lamentation of the heart; and they shall rend not their garments, but their hearts. Tribe by tribe they shall mourn, and then they shall look on Him whom they have pierced; and they shall say, Why, O Lord, hast Thou made us to err from Thy way? The glory which our fathers blessed, has for us been turned into shame." [12]

53. Summary of the Prophecies

Though we could bring forward many other prophecies, we forbear, judging these sufficient for the persuasion of those who have ears to hear and understand; and considering also that those persons are able to see that we do not make mere assertions without being able to produce proof, like those fables that are told of the so-called sons of Jupiter. For with what

10. Ezek. 37:7, 8; Isa. 45:24.   12. Zech. 12:3–14; Isa. 63:17, 64:11.
11. Isa. 66:24.

reason should we believe of a crucified man that He is the first-born of the Unbegotten God, and Himself will pass judgment on the whole human race, unless we had found testimonies concerning Him published before He came and was born as man, and unless we saw that things had happened accordingly—the devastation of the land of the Jews, and men of every race persuaded by His teaching through the apostles, and rejecting their old habits, in which, being deceived, they had had their conversation; yea, seeing ourselves too, and knowing that the Christians from among the Gentiles are both more numerous and more true than those from among the Jews and Samaritans? For all the other human races are called Gentiles by the Spirit of prophecy; but the Jewish and Samaritan races are called the tribe of Israel, and the house of Jacob. And the prophecy in which it was predicted that there should be more believers from the Gentiles than from the Jews and Samaritans, we will produce: it ran thus: "Rejoice, O barren, thou that dost not bear; break forth and shout, thou that dost not travail, because many more are the children of the desolate than of her that hath an husband." [13] For all the Gentiles were "desolate" of the true God, serving the works of their hands; but the Jews and Samaritans, having the word of God delivered to them by the prophets, and always expecting the Christ, did not recognise Him when He came except some few, of whom the Spirit of prophecy by Isaiah had predicted that they should be saved. He spoke as from their person: "Except the Lord had left us a seed, we should have been as Sodom and Gomorrah." [14] For Sodom and Gomorrah are related by Moses to have been cities of ungodly men, which God burned with fire and brimstone, and overthrew, no one of their inhabitants being saved except a certain stranger, a Chaldaean by birth, whose name was Lot; with whom also his daughters were rescued. And those who care may yet see their whole country desolate and burned, and remaining barren. And to show how those from among the Gentiles were foretold as more true and more believing, we will cite what was said by Isaiah [15] the prophet; for he spoke as follows: "Israel is uncircumcised in heart, but the Gentiles are uncircumcised in the flesh." So many things, therefore, as these, when they are seen with the eye, are enough to produce conviction and belief in those who embrace the truth, and are not bigoted in their opinions, nor are governed by their passions.

61. Christian Baptism

I will also relate the manner in which we dedicated ourselves to God when we had been made new through Christ; lest, if we omit this, we seem to be

---

13. Isa. 54:1.
14. Isa. 1:9.

15. The following words are found, not in Isaiah, but in Jer. 9:26.

unfair in the explanation we are making. As many as are persuaded and believe that what we teach and say is true, and undertake to be able to live accordingly, are instructed to pray and to entreat God with fasting, for the remission of their sins that are past, we praying and fasting with them. Then they are brought by us where there is water, and are regenerated in the same manner in which we were ourselves regenerated. For, in the name of God, the Father and Lord of the universe, and of our Saviour Jesus Christ, and of the Holy Spirit, they then receive the washing with water. For Christ also said, "Except ye be born again, ye shall not enter into the kingdom of heaven." [16] Now, that it is impossible for those who have once been born to enter into their mothers' wombs, is manifest to all. And how those who have sinned and repent shall escape their sins, is declared by Isaiah the prophet, as I wrote above; [17] he thus speaks: "Wash you, make you clean; put away the evil of your doings from your souls; learn to do well; judge the fatherless, and plead for the widow: and come and let us reason together, saith the Lord. And though your sins be as scarlet, I will make them white like wool; and though they be as crimson, I will make them white as snow. But if ye refuse and rebel, the sword shall devour you: for the mouth of the Lord hath spoken it." [18]

And for this [rite] we have learned from the apostles this reason. Since at our birth we were born without our own knowledge or choice, by our parents coming together, and were brought up in bad habits and wicked training; in order that we may not remain the children of necessity and of ignorance, but may become the children of choice and knowledge, and may obtain in the water the remission of sins formerly committed, there is pronounced over him who chooses to be born again, and has repented of his sins, the name of God the Father and Lord of the universe; he who leads to the laver the person that is to be washed calling him by this name alone. For no one can utter the name of the ineffable God; and if any one dare to say that there is a name, he raves with a hopeless madness. And this washing is called illumination, because they who learn these things are illuminated in their understandings. And in the name of Jesus Christ, who was crucified under Pontius Pilate, and in the name of the Holy Ghost, who through the prophets foretold all things about Jesus, he who is illuminated is washed.

62. Its Imitation by Demons

And the devils, indeed, having heard this washing published by the prophet, instigated those who enter their temples, and are about to approach them

16. John 3:5.

17. Chap. 44.

18. Isa. 1:16–20.

with libations and burnt-offerings, also to sprinkle themselves; and they cause them also to wash themselves entirely, as they depart [from the sacrifice], before they enter into the shrines in which their images are set. And the command, too, given by the priests to those who enter and worship in the temples, that they take off their shoes, the devils, learning what happened to the above-mentioned prophet Moses, have given in imitation of these things. For at that juncture, when Moses was ordered to go down into Egypt and lead out the people of the Israelites who were there, and while he was tending the flocks of his maternal uncle in the land of Arabia, our Christ conversed with him under the appearance of fire from a bush, and said, "Put off thy shoes, and draw near and hear." And he, when he had put off his shoes and drawn near, heard that he was to go down into Egypt and lead out the people of the Israelites there; and he received mighty power from Christ, who spoke to him in the appearance of fire, and went down and led out the people, having done great and marvellous things; which, if you desire to know, you will learn accurately from his writings.

63. How God Appeared to Moses

And all the Jews even now teach that the nameless God spake to Moses; whence the Spirit of prophecy, accusing them by Isaiah the prophet mentioned above, said, "The ox knoweth his owner, and the ass his master's crib; but Israel doth not know me, and my people do not understand." [19] And Jesus the Christ, because the Jews knew not what the Father was, and what the Son, in like manner accused them; and Himself said, "No one knoweth the Father, but the Son; nor the Son, but the Father, and they to whom the Son revealeth Him." [20] Now the Word of God is His Son, as we have before said. And He is called Angel and Apostle; for He declares whatever we ought to know, and is sent forth to declare whatever is revealed; as our Lord Himself says, "He that heareth me, heareth Him that sent me." [21] From the writings of Moses also this will be manifest; for thus it is written in them, "And the Angel of God spake to Moses, in a flame of fire out of the bush, and said, I am that I am, the God of Abraham, the God of Isaac, the God of Jacob, the God of thy fathers; go down into Egypt, and bring forth my people." [22] And if you wish to learn what follows, you can do so from the same writings; for it is impossible to relate the whole here. But so much is written for the sake of proving that Jesus the Christ is the Son of God and His apostle, being of old the Word, and appearing sometimes in the form of fire, and sometimes in the likeness of angels; but now,

19. Isa. 1:3.
20. Matt. 11:27.
21. Luke 10:16.
22. Ex. 3:6.

by the will of God, having become man for the human race, He endured all the sufferings which the devils instigated the senseless Jews to inflict upon Him; who though they have it expressly affirmed in the writings of Moses, "And the angel of God spake to Moses in a flame of fire in a bush, and said, I am that I am, the God of Abraham, and the God of Isaac, and the God of Jacob," yet maintain that He who said this was the Father and Creator of the universe. Whence also the Spirit of prophecy rebukes them, and says, "Israel doth not know me, my people hath not understood me." [23] And again, Jesus, as we have already shown, while He was with them, said, "No one knoweth the Father, but the Son; nor the Son, but the Father, and those to whom the Son will reveal Him." [24] The Jews, accordingly, being throughout of opinion that it was the Father of the universe who spake to Moses, though He who spake to him was indeed the Son of God, who is called both Angel and Apostle, are justly charged, both by the Spirit of prophecy and by Christ Himself, with knowing neither the Father nor the Son. For they who affirm that the Son is the Father, are proved neither to have become acquainted with the Father, nor to know that the Father of the universe has a Son; who also, being the first-begotten Word of God, is even God. And of old He appeared in the shape of fire and in the likeness of an angel to Moses and to the other prophets; but now in the times of your reign, having, as we before said, become man by a virgin, according to the counsel of the Father, for the salvation of those who believe on Him, He endured both to be set at nought and to suffer, that by dying and rising again He might conquer death. And that which was said out of the bush to Moses, "I am that I am, the God of Abraham, and the God of Isaac, and the God of Jacob, and the God of your fathers," [25] this signified that they, even though dead, are yet in existence, and are men belonging to Christ Himself. For they were the first of all men to busy themselves in the search after God; Abraham being the father of Isaac, and Isaac of Jacob, as Moses wrote.

64. Further Misrepresentations of the Truth

From what has been already said, you can understand how the devils, in imitation of what was said by Moses, asserted that Proserpine was the daughter of Jupiter, and instigated the people to set up an image of her under the name of Kore [Cora, i.e. the maiden or daughter] at the spring-heads. For, as we wrote above, Moses said, "In the beginning God made the heaven and the earth. And the earth was without form, and unfur-

23. Isa. 1:3.   25. Chap. 59.
24. Matt. 11:27.

nished: and the Spirit of God moved upon the face of the waters." In imitation, therefore, of what is here said of the Spirit of God moving on the waters, they said that Proserpine [or Cora] was the daughter of Jupiter." And in like manner also they craftily feigned that Minerva was the daughter of Jupiter, not by sexual union, but, knowing that God conceived and made the world by the Word, they say that Minerva is the first conception [ennoia]; which we consider to be very absurd, bringing forward the form of the conception in a female shape. And in like manner the actions of those others who are called sons of Jupiter sufficiently condemn them.

65. Administration of the Sacraments

But we, after we have thus washed him who has been convinced and has assented to our teaching, bring him to the place where those who are called brethren are assembled, in order that we may offer hearty prayers in common for ourselves and the baptized [illuminated] person, and for all others in every place, that we may be counted worthy, now that we have learned the truth, by our works also to be found good citizens and keepers of the commandments, so that we may be saved with an everlasting salvation. Having ended the prayers, we salute one another with a kiss. There is then brought to the president of the brethren bread and a cup of wine mixed with water; and he taking them, gives praise and glory to the Father of the universe, through the name of the Son and of the Holy Ghost, and offers thanks at considerable length for our being counted worthy to receive these things at His hands. And when he has concluded the prayers and thanksgiving, all the people present express their assent by saying Amen. This word Amen answers in the Hebrew language to [so be it]. And when the president has given thanks, and all the people have expressed their assent, those who are called by us deacons give to each of those present to partake of the bread and wine mixed with water over which the thanksgiving was pronounced, and to those who are absent they carry away a portion.

66. Of the Eucharist

And this food is called among us "Eucharistia,"[26] [the Eucharist], of which no one is allowed to partake but the man who believes that the things which we teach are true and who has been washed with the washing that is for the remission of sins, and unto regeneration, and who is so living as Christ has

---

26. Literally, thanksgiving. See Matt. 26:27.

enjoined. For not as common bread and common drink do we receive these; but in like manner as Jesus Christ our Saviour, having been made flesh by the word of God, had both flesh and blood for our salvation, so likewise have we been taught that the food which is blessed by the prayer of His word, and from which our blood and flesh by transmutation are nourished, is the flesh and blood of that Jesus who was made flesh. For the apostles, in the memoirs composed by them, which are called Gospels, have thus delivered unto us what was enjoined upon them; that Jesus took bread, and when He had given thanks, said "This do ye in remembrance of me,[27] this is my body;" and that, after the same manner, having taken the cup and given thanks, He said, "This is my blood"; and gave it to them alone. Which the wicked devils have imitated in the mysteries of Mithras, commanding the same thing to be done. For, that bread and a cup of water are placed with certain incantations in the mystic rites of one who is being initiated, you either know or can learn.

67. Weekly Worship of the Christians

And we afterwards continually remind each other of these things, and the wealthy among us help the needy; and we always keep together; and for all things wherewith we are supplied, we bless the Maker of all through His Son Jesus Christ, and through the Holy Ghost. And on the day called Sunday, all who live in cities or in the country gather together to one place, and the memoirs of the apostles or the writings of the prophets are read, as long as time permits; then, when the reader has ceased, the president verbally instructs, and exhorts to the imitation of these good things. Then we all rise together and pray, and, as we before said, when our prayer is ended, bread and wine and water are brought, and the president in like manner offers prayers and thanksgivings, according to his ability, and the people assent, saying Amen; and there is a distribution to each, and a participation of that over which thanks have been given, and to those who are absent a portion is sent by the deacons. And they who are well to do, and willing, give what each thinks fit; and what is collected is deposited with the president, who succours the orphans and widows, and those who, through sickness or any other cause, are in want, and those who are in bonds, and the strangers sojourning among us, and in a word takes care of all who are in need. But Sunday is the day on which we all hold our common assembly, because it is the first day on which God, having wrought a change in the darkness and matter, made the world; and Jesus Christ our Saviour on the

27. Luke 22:19.

same day rose from the dead. For He was crucified on the day before that of Saturn (Saturday); and on the day after that of Saturn, which is the day of the Sun, having appeared to His apostles and disciples, He taught them these things, which we have submitted to you also for your consideration.

68. Conclusion

And if these things seem to you to be reasonable and true, honour them; but if they seem nonsensical, despise them as nonsense, and do not decree death against those who have done no wrong, as you would against enemies. For we forewarn you, that you shall not escape the coming judgment of God, if you continue in your injustice; and we ourselves will invite you to do that which is pleasing to God.

2. Tatian, *Address to the Greeks*

1. The Greeks Claim, without Reason, the Invention of the Arts

Be not, O Greeks, so very hostilely disposed towards the Barbarians, nor look with ill will on their opinions. For which of your institutions has not been derived from the Barbarians? The most eminent of the Telmessians invented the art of divining by dreams; the Carians, that of prognosticating by the stars; the Phrygians and the most ancient Isaurians, augury by the flight of birds; the Cyprians, the art of inspecting victims. To the Babylonians you owe astronomy; to the Persians, magic; to the Egyptians, geometry; to the Phoenicians, instruction by alphabetic writing. Cease, then, to miscall these imitations inventions of your own. Orpheus, again, taught you poetry and song; from him, too, you learned the mysteries. The Tuscans taught you the plastic art; from the annals of the Egyptians you learned to write history; you acquired the art of playing the flute from Marsyas and Olympus,—these two rustic Phrygians constructed the harmony of the shepherd's pipe. The Tyrrhenians invented the trumpet; the Cyclopes, the smith's art; and a woman who was formerly a queen of the Persians, as Hellanicus tells us, the method of joining together epistolary tablets: her name was Atossa. Wherefore lay aside this conceit, and be not ever boasting of your elegance of diction; for, while you applaud yourselves, your own people will of course side with you. But it becomes a man

Address to the Greeks, chaps. 1–4, 21–30, 34–35, 40, 42, reprinted from *The Ante-Nicene Fathers*, vol. 2 (New York: Christian Literature Co., 1890), pp. 65–66, 74–77, 79–80, 81–82.

of sense to wait for the testimony of others, and it becomes men to be of one accord also in the pronunciation of their language. But, as matters stand, to you alone it has happened not to speak alike even in common intercourse; for the way of speaking among the Dorians is not the same as that of the inhabitants of Attica, nor do the Aeolians speak like the Ionians. And, since such a discrepancy exists where it ought not to be, I am at a loss whom to call a Greek. And, what is strangest of all, you hold in honour expressions not of native growth, and by the intermixture of barbaric words have made your language a medley. On this account we have re-nounced your wisdom, though I was once a great proficient in it; for, as the comic poet says,—

> These are gleaners' grapes and small talk,—
> Twittering places of swallows, corrupters of art.

Yet those who eagerly pursue it shout lustily, and croak like so many ravens. You have, too, contrived the art of rhetoric to serve injustice and slander, selling the free power of your speech for hire, and often representing the same thing at one time as right, at another time as not good. The poetic art, again, you employ to describe battles, and the amours of the gods, and the corruption of the soul.

2. The Vices and Errors of the Philosophers

What noble thing have you produced by your pursuit of philosophy? Who of your most eminent men has been free from vain boasting? Diogenes, who made such a parade of his independence with his tub, was seized with a bowel complaint through eating a raw polypus, and so lost his life by gluttony. Aristippus, walking about in a purple robe, led a profligate life, in accordance with his professed opinions. Plato, a philosopher, was sold by Dionysius for his gormandizing propensities. And Aristotle, who absurdly placed a limit to Providence and made happiness to consist in the things which give pleasure, quite contrary to his duty as a preceptor flattered Alexander, forgetful that he was but a youth; and he, showing how well he had learned the lessons of his master, because his friend would not worship him shut him up and carried him about like a bear or a leopard. He in fact obeyed strictly the precepts of his teacher in displaying manliness and courage by feasting, and transfixing with his spear his intimate and most beloved friend, and then, under a semblance of grief, weeping and starving himself, that he might not incur the hatred of his friends. I could laugh at those also who in the present day adhere to his tenets,—people who say that sublunary things are not under the care of Providence; and so, being nearer the earth than the moon, and below its orbit, they themselves look after what is thus left uncared for; and as for those who have neither beauty, nor wealth, nor bodily strength, nor high birth, they have no happiness, according to Aristotle. Let such men philosophize, for me!

3. Ridicule of the Philosophers

I cannot approve of Heraclitus, who, being self-taught and arrogant, said, "I have explored myself." Nor can I praise him for hiding his poem in the temple of Artemis, in order that it might be published afterwards as a mystery; and those who take an interest in such things say that Euripides the tragic poet came there and read it and, gradually learning it by heart, carefully handed down to posterity this darkness of Heraclitus. Death, however, demonstrated the stupidity of this man; for, being attacked by dropsy, as he had studied the art of medicine as well as philosophy, he plastered himself with cow-dung, which, as it hardened, contracted the flesh of his whole body, so that he pulled in pieces, and thus died. Then, one cannot listen to Zeno, who declares that at the conflagration the same man will rise again to perform the same actions as before; for instance, Anytus and Miletus to accuse, Busiris to murder his guests, and Hercules to repeat his labours; and in this doctrine of the conflagration he introduces more wicked than just persons—one Socrates and a Hercules, and a few more of the same class, but not many, for the bad will be found far more numerous than the good. And according to him the Deity will manifestly be the author of evil, dwelling in sewers and worms, and in the perpetrators of impiety. The eruptions of fire in Sicily, moreover, confute the empty boasting of Empedocles, in that, though he was no god, he falsely almost gave himself out for one. I laugh, too, at the old wife's talk of Pherecydes, and the doctrine inherited from him by Pythagoras, and that of Plato, an imitation of his, though some think otherwise. And who would give his approval to the cynogamy of Crates, and not rather, repudiating the wild and tumid speech of those who resemble him, turn to the investigation of what truly deserves attention? Wherefore be not led away by the solemn assemblies of philosophers who are no philosophers, who dogmatize one against the other, though each one vents but the crude fancies of the moment. They have, moreover, many collisions among themselves; each one hates the other; they indulge in conflicting opinions, and their arrogance makes them eager for the highest places. It would better become them, moreover, not to pay court to kings unbidden, nor to flatter men at the head of affairs, but to wait till the great ones come to them.

4. The Christians Worship God Alone

For what reason, men of Greece, do you wish to bring the civil powers, as in a pugilistic encounter, into collision with us? And, if I am not disposed to comply with the usages of some of them, why am I to be abhorred as a vile miscreant? Does the sovereign order the payment of tribute, I am ready to render it. Does my master command me to act as a bondsman and to serve, I acknowledge the serfdom. Man is to be honoured as a fellow-man; God alone is to be feared,—He who is not visible to human eyes, nor comes within the compass of human art. Only when I am commanded to deny Him, will I not obey, but will rather die than show myself false and ungrateful. Our God did not begin to be in time: He alone is without beginning, and He Himself is the beginning of all things. God is a Spirit,[1] not pervading matter, but the Maker of material spirits, and of the forms that are in matter; He is invisible, impalpable, being Himself the Father of both sensible and invisible things. Him we know from His creation, and apprehend His invisible power by His works.[2] I refuse to adore that workmanship which He has made for our sakes. The sun and moon were made for us: how, then, can I adore my own servants? How can I speak of stocks and stones as gods? For the Spirit that pervades matter is inferior to the more divine spirit; and this, even when assimilated to the soul, is not to be honoured equally with the perfect God. Nor even ought the ineffable God to be presented with gifts; for He who is in want of nothing is not to be misrepresented by us as though He were indigent. But I will set forth our views more distinctly.

21. Doctrines of the Christians and Greeks Respecting God Compared

We do not act as fools, O Greeks, nor utter idle tales, when we announce that God was born in the form of a man. I call on you who reproach us to compare your mythical acounts with our narrations. Athené, as they say, took the form of Deïphobus for the sake of Hector, and the unshorn Phoebus for the sake of Admetus fed the trailing-footed oxen, and the spouse of Zeus came as an old woman to Semelé. But, while you treat seriously such things, how can you deride us? Your Asclepios died, and he who ravished fifty virgins in one night at Thespiae lost his life by delivering himself to the devouring flame. Prometheus, fastened to Caucasus, suffered punishment for his good deeds to men. According to you, Zeus is envious, and hides the dream from men, wishing their destruction. Wherefore, looking

---

1. John 4:24.   2. Rom. 1:20.

at your own memorials, vouchsafe us your approval, though it were only as dealing in legends similar to your own. We, however, do not deal in folly, but your legends are only idle tales. If you speak of the origin of the gods, you also declare them to be mortal. For what reason is Hera now never pregnant? Has she grown old? or is there no one to give you information? Believe me now, O Greeks, and do not resolve your myths and gods into allegory. If you attempt to do this, the divine nature as held by you is over-thrown by your own selves; for, if the demons with you are such as they are said to be, they are worthless as to character; or, if regarded as symbols of the powers of nature, they are not what they are called. But I cannot be persuaded to pay religious homage to the natural elements, nor can I under-take to persuade my neighbour. And Metrodorus of Lampsacus, in his treatise concerning Homer, has argued very foolishly, turning everything into allegory. For he says that neither Hera, nor Athené, nor Zeus are what those persons suppose who consecrate to them sacred enclosures and groves, but parts of nature and certain arrangements of the elements. Hector also, and Achilles, and Agamemnon, and all the Greeks in general, and the Barbarians with Helen and Paris, being of the same nature, you will of course say are introduced merely for the sake of the machinery of the poem; not one of these personages having really existed. But these things we have put forth only for argument's sake; for it is not allowable even to compare our notion of God with those who are wallowing in matter and mud.

22. Ridicule of the Solemnities of the Greeks

And of what sort are your teachings? Who must not treat with contempt your solemn festivals, which, being held in honour of wicked demons, cover men with infamy? I have often seen a man—and have been amazed to see, and the amazement has ended in contempt, to think how he is one thing internally, but outwardly counterfeits what he is not—giving himself excessive airs of daintiness and indulging in all sorts of effeminacy; some-times darting his eyes about; sometimes throwing his hands hither and thither, and raving with his face smeared with mud; sometimes personating Aphrodité, sometimes Apollo; a solitary accuser of all the gods, an epit-ome of superstition, a vituperator of heroic deeds, an actor of murders, a chronicler of adultery, a storehouse of madness, a teacher of cynaedi, an instigator of capital sentences;—and yet such a man is praised by all. But I have rejected all his falsehoods, his impiety, his practices,—in short, the man altogether. But you are led captive by such men, while you revile those who do not take a part in your pursuits. I have no mind to stand agape at a number of singers, nor do I desire to be affected in sympathy with a man when he is winking and gesticulating in an unnatural manner. What wonderful or extraordinary thing is performed among you? They utter ribaldry in affected tones, and go through indecent movements; your daughters and your sons behold them giving lessons in adultery on the stage. Admirable places, forsooth, are your lecture-rooms, where every base action perpetrated by night is proclaimed aloud, and the hearers are regaled with the utterance of infamous discourses! Admirable, too, are your mendacious poets, who by their fictions beguile their hearers from the truth!

23. Of the Pugilists and Gladiators

I have seen men weighed down by bodily exercise, and carrying about the burden of their flesh, before whom rewards and chaplets are set, while the adjudicators cheer them on, not to deeds of virtue, but to rivalry in violence and discord; and he who excels in giving blows is crowned. These are the lesser evils; as for the greater, who would not shrink from telling them? Some, giving themselves up to idleness for the sake of profligacy, sell themselves to be killed; and the indigent barters himself away, while the rich man buys others to kill him. And for these the witnesses take their seats, and the boxers meet in single combat, for no reason whatever, nor does any one come down into the arena to succour. Do such exhibitions as these redound to your credit? He who is chief among you collects a legion of blood-stained murderers, engaging to maintain them; and these ruffians are sent forth by him, and you assemble at the spectacle to be judges, partly of the wickedness of the adjudicator, and partly of that of the men who engage in the combat. And he who misses the murderous exhibition is grieved, because he was not doomed to be a spectator of wicked and impious and abominable deeds. You slaughter animals for the purpose of eating their flesh, and you purchase men to supply a cannibal banquet for the soul, nourishing it by the most impious bloodshedding. The robber commits murder for the sake of plunder, but the rich man purchases gladiators for the sake of their being killed.

24. Of the Other Public Amusements

What advantage should I gain from him who is brought on the stage by Euripides raving mad, and acting the matricide of Alcmaeon; who does not even retain his natural behaviour, but with his mouth wide open goes about sword in hand, and, screaming aloud, is burned to death, habited in a robe unfit for man? Away, too, with the mythical tales of Acusilaus, and Menander, a versifier of the same class! And why should I admire the mythic piper? Why should I busy myself about the Theban Antigenides, like Aristoxenus? We leave you to these worthless things; and do you either believe our doctrines, or, like us, give up yours.

25. Boastings and Quarrels of the Philosophers

What great and wonderful things have your philosophers effected? They leave uncovered one of their shoulders; they let their hair grow long; they cultivate their beards; their nails are like the claws of wild beasts. Though they say that they want nothing, yet, like Proteus, they need a currier for their wallet, and a weaver for their mantle, and a wood-cutter for their staff, and the rich, and a cook also for their gluttony. O man competing with the dog, you know not God, and so have turned to the imitation of an irrational animal. You cry out in public with an assumption of authority, and take upon you to avenge your own self; and if you receive nothing, you indulge in abuse, and philosophy is with you the art of getting money. You follow the doctrines of Plato, and a disciple of Epicurus lifts up his voice to oppose you. Again, you wish to be a disciple of Aristotle, and a follower of Democritus rails at you. Pythagoras says that he was Euphorbus, and he is the heir of the doctrine of Pherecydes; but Aristotle impugns the immortality of the soul. You who receive from your predecessors doctrines which clash with one another, you the inharmonious, are fighting against the harmonious. One of you asserts that God is body, but I assert that He is without body; that the world is indestructible, but I say that it is to be destroyed; that a conflagration will take place at various times, but I say that it will come to pass once for all; that Minos and Rhadamanthus are judges, but I say that God Himself is Judge; that the soul alone is endowed with immortality, but I say that the flesh also is endowed with it. What injury do we inflict upon you, O Greeks? Why do you hate those who follow the word of God, as if they were the vilest of mankind? It is not we who eat human flesh—they among you who assert such a thing have been suborned as false witnesses; it is among you that Pelops is made a supper for the gods, although beloved by Poseidon, and Kronos devours his children, and Zeus swallows Metis.

26. Ridicule of the Studies of the Greeks

Cease to make a parade of sayings which you have derived from others, and to deck yourselves like the daw in borrowed plumes. If each state were to take away its contribution to your speech, your fallacies would lose their power. While inquiring what God is, you are ignorant of what is in yourselves; and while staring all agape at the sky, you stumble into pitfalls. The reading of your books is like walking through a labyrinth, and their readers resemble the cask of the Danaïds. Why do you divide time, saying that one part is past, and another present, and another future? For how can the future be passing when the present exists? As those who are sailing imagine in their ignorance, as the ship is borne along, that the hills are in motion, so you do not know that it is you who are passing along, but that time remains present as long as the Creator wills it to exist. Why am I called to account for uttering my opinions, and why are you in such haste to put them all down? Were not you born in the same manner as ourselves, and placed under the same government of the world? Why say that wisdom is with you alone, who have not another sun, nor other risings of the stars, nor a more distinguished origin, nor a death preferable to that of other men? The grammarians have been the beginning of this idle talk; and you who parcel out wisdom are cut off from the wisdom that is according to truth, and assign the names of the several parts to particular men; and you know not God, but in your fierce contentions destroy one another. And on this account you are all nothing worth. While you arrogate to yourselves the sole right of discussion, you discourse like the blind man with the deaf. Why do you handle the builder's tools without knowing how to build? Why do you busy yourselves with words, while you keep aloof from deeds, puffed up with praise, but cast down by misfortunes? Your modes of acting are contrary to reason, for you make a pompous appearance in public, but hide your teaching in corners. Finding you to be such men as these, we have abandoned you, and no longer concern ourselves with your tenets, but follow the word of God. Why, O man, do you set the letters of the alphabet at war with one another? Why do you, as in a boxing match, make their sounds clash together with your mincing Attic way of speaking, whereas you ought to speak more according to nature? For if you adopt the Attic dialect though not an Athenian, pray why do you not speak like the Dorians? How is it that one appears to you more rugged, the other more pleasant for intercourse?

27. The Christians Are Hated Unjustly

And if you adhere to their teaching, why do you fight against me for choosing such views of doctrine as I approve? Is it not unreasonable that, while the robber is not to be punished for the name he bears, but only when the truth about him has been clearly ascertained, yet we are to be assailed with abuse on a judgment formed without examination? Diagoras was an Athenian, but you punished him for divulging the Athenian mysteries; yet you who read his Phrygian discourses hate us. You possess the commentaries of

Leo, and are displeased with our refutations of them; and having in your hands the opinions of Apion concerning the Egyptian gods, you denounce us as most impious. The tomb of Olympian Zeus is shown among you, though some one says that the Cretans are liars. Your assembly of many gods is nothing. Though their despiser Epicurus acts as a torch-bearer, I do not any the more conceal from the rulers that view of God which I hold in relation to His government of the universe. Why do you advise me to be false to my principles? Why do you who say that you despise death exhort us to use art in order to escape it? I have not the heart of a deer; but your zeal for dialectics resembles the loquacity of Thersites. How can I believe one who tells me that the sun is a red-hot mass and the moon an earth? Such assertions are mere logomachies, and not a sober exposition of truth. How can it be otherwise than foolish to credit the books of Herodotus relating to the history of Hercules, which tell of an upper earth from which the lion came down that was killed by Hercules? And what avails the Attic style, the sorites of philosophers, the plausibilities of syllogisms, the measurements of the earth, the positions of the stars, and the course of the sun? To be occupied in such inquiries is the work of one who imposes opinions on himself as if they were laws.

28. Condemnation of the Greek Legislation

On this account I reject your legislation also; for there ought to be one common polity for all; but now there are as many different codes as there are states, so that things held disgraceful in some are honourable in others. The Greeks consider intercourse with a mother as unlawful, but this practice is esteemed most becoming by the Persian Magi; paederasty is condemned by the Barbarians, but by the Romans, who endeavour to collect herds of boys like grazing horses, it is honoured with certain privileges.

29. Account of Tatian's Conversion

Wherefore, having seen these things, and moreover also having been admitted to the mysteries, and having everywhere examined the religious rites performed by the effeminate and the pathic, and having found among the Romans their Latiarian Jupiter delighting in human gore and the blood of slaughtered men, and Artemis not far from the great city sanctioning acts of the same kind, and one demon here and another there instigating to the perpetration of evil,—retiring by myself, I sought how I might be able to discover the truth. And, while I was giving my most earnest attention to the matter, I happened to meet with certain barbaric writings, too old to be compared with the opinions of the Greeks, and too divine to be compared with their errors; and I was led to put faith in these by the unpretending cast of the language, the inartificial character of the writers, the foreknowledge displayed of future events, the excellent quality of the precepts, and the declaration of the government of the universe as centred in one Being. And, my soul being taught of God, I discern that the former class of writings lead to condemnation, but that these put an end to the slavery that is in the world, and rescue us from a multiplicity of rulers and ten thousand tyrants, while they give us, not indeed what we had not before received, but what we had received but were prevented by error from retaining.

30. How He Resolved to Resist the Devil

Therefore, being initiated and instructed in these things, I wish to put away my former errors as the follies of childhood. For we know that the nature of wickedness is like that of the smallest seeds; since it has waxed strong from a small beginning, but will again be destroyed if we obey the words of God and do not scatter ourselves. For He has become master of all we have by means of a certain "hidden treasure," which while we are digging for we are indeed covered with dust, but we secure it as our fixed possession. He who receives the whole of this treasure has obtained command of the most precious wealth. Let these things, then, be said to our friends. But to you Greeks what can I say, except to request you not to rail at those who are better than yourselves, nor if they are called Barbarians to make that an occasion of banter? For, if you are willing, you will be able to find out the cause of men's not being able to understand one another's language; for to those who wish to examine our principles I will give a simple and copious account of them.

34. Ridicule of the Statues Erected by the Greeks

Worthy of very great honour, certainly, was the tyrant Bhalaris, who devoured sucklings, and accordingly is exhibited by the workmanship of Polystratus the Ambraciot, even to this day, as a very wonderful man! The Agrigentines dreaded to look on that countenance of his, because of his cannibalism; but people of culture now make it their boast that they behold him in his statue! Is it not shameful that fratricide is honoured by you who look on the statues of Polynices and Eteocles, and that you have not rather buried them with their maker Pythagoras? Destroy these memorials of iniquity! Why should I contemplate with admiration the figure of the woman who bore thirty children, merely for the sake of the artist Periclymenus? One ought to turn away with disgust from one who bore off the fruits of great incontinence, and whom the Romans compared to a sow, which also on a like account, they say, was deemed worthy of a mystic worship. Ares committed adultery with Aphrodité, and Andron made an image of their offspring Harmonia. Sophron, who committed to writing trifles and absurdities, was more celebrated for his skill in casting metals, of which specimens exist even now. And not only have his tales kept the fabulist Aesop in everlasting remembrance, but also the plastic art of Aristodemus has increased his celebrity. How is it then that you, who have so many poetesses whose productions are mere trash, and innumerable courtesans, and worthless men, are not ashamed to slander the reputation of our women? What care I to know that Euanthé gave birth to an infant in the Peripatus, or to gape with wonder at the art of Callistratus, or to fix my gaze on the Neaera of Calliades? For she was a courtesan. Laïs was a prostitute, and Turnus made her a monument of prostitution. Why are you not ashamed of the fornication of Hephastion, even though Philo has represented him very artistically? And for what reason do you honour the hermaphrodite Ganymede by Leochares, as if you possessed something admirable? Praxiteles even made a statue of a woman with the stain of impurity upon it. It behoved you, repudiating everything of this kind, to seek what is truly worthy of attention, and not to turn with disgust from our mode of life while receiving with approval the shameful productions of Philaenis and Elephantis.

35. Tatian Speaks as an Eye-Witness

The things which I have thus set before you I have not learned at second hand. I have visited many lands; I have followed rhetoric, like yourselves; I have fallen in with many arts and inventions; and finally, when sojourning in the city of the Romans, I inspected the multiplicity of statues brought thither by you: for I do not attempt, as is the custom with many, to strengthen my own views by the opinions of others, but I wish to give you a distinct account of what I myself have seen and felt. So, bidding farewell to the arrogance of Romans and the idle talk of Athenians, and all their ill-connected opinions, I embraced our barbaric philosophy. I began to show how this was more ancient than your institutions, but left my task unfinished, in order to discuss a matter which demanded more immediate attention; but now it is time I should attempt to speak concerning its doctrines. Be not offended with our teaching, nor undertake an elaborate reply filled with trifling and ribaldry, saying, "Tatian, aspiring to be above the Greeks, above the infinite number of philosophic inquirers, has struck out a new path, and embraced the doctrines of Barbarians." For what grievance is it, that men manifestly ignorant should be reasoned with by a man of like nature with themselves? Or how can it be irrational, according to your own sophist, to grow old always learning something?

36. Testimony of the Chaldeans to the Antiquity of Moses

But let Homer be not later than the Trojan war; let it be granted that he was contemporary with it, or even that he was in the army of Agamemnon, and if any so please, that he lived before the invention of letters. The Moses before mentioned will be shown to have been many years older than the taking of Troy, and far more ancient than the building of Troy, or than Tros and Dardanus. To demonstrate this I will call in as witnesses the Chaldeans, the Phoenicians, and the Egyptians. And what more need I say? For it behoves one who professes to persuade his hearers to make his narrative of events very concise. Berosus, a Babylonian, a priest of their god Belus, born in the time of Alexander, composed for Antiochus, the third after him, the history of the Chaldeans in three books; and narrating the acts of the kings, he mentions one of them, Nabuchodonosor by name, who made war against the Phoenicians and the Jews,—events which we know were announced by our prophets, and which happened much later than the age of Moses, seventy years before the Persian empire. But Berosus is a very trustworthy man, and of this Juba is a witness, who, writing concerning the Assyrians, says that he learned the history from Berosus: there are two books of his concerning the Assyrians.

37. Testimony of the Phoenicians

After the Chaldeans, the testimony of the Phoenicians is as follows. There were among them three men, Theodotus, Hypsicrates, and Mochus; Chaitus translated their books into Greek, and also composed with exactness the lives of the philosophers. Now, in the histories of the aforesaid writers it is shown that the abduction of Europa happened under one of the kings, and an account is given of the coming of Menelaus into Phoenicia, and of the matters relating to Chiramus, who gave his daughter in marriage to Solomon the king of the Jews, and supplied wood of all kind of trees for the building of the temple. Menander of Pergamus composed a history concerning the same things. But the age of Chiramus is somewhere about the Trojan war; but Solomon, the contemporary of Chiramus, lived much later than the age of Moses.

38. The Egyptians Place Moses in the Reign of Inachus

Of the Egyptians also there are accurate chronicles. Ptolemy, not the king, but a priest of Mendes, is the interpreter of their affairs. This writer, narrating the acts of the kings, says that the departure of the Jews from Egypt to the places whither they went occurred in the time of king Amosis, under the leadership of Moses. He thus speaks: "Amosis lived in the time of king Inachus." After him, Apion the grammarian, a man most highly esteemed, in the fourth book of his Aegyptiaca (there are five books of his), besides many other things, says that Amosis destroyed Avaris in the time of the Argive Inachus, as the Mendesian Ptolemy wrote in his annals. But the time from Inachus to the taking of Troy occupies twenty generations. The steps of the demonstration are the following:—

39. Catalog of the Argive Kings

The kings of the Argives were these: Inachus, Phoroneus, Apis, Criasis, Triopas, Argeius, Phorbas, Crotopas, Sthenelaus, Danaus, Lynceus, Proetus, Abas, Acrisius, Perseus, Sthenelaus, Eurystheus, Atreus, Thyestes, and Agamemnon, in the eighteenth year of whose reign Troy was taken. And every intelligent person will most carefully observe that, according to the tradition of the Greeks, they possessed no historical composition; for Cadmus, who taught them letters, came into Boetia many generations later. But after Inachus, under Phoroneus, a check was with difficulty given to their savage and nomadic life, and they entered upon a new order of things. Wherefore, if Moses is shown to be contemporary with Inachus, he is four hundred years older than the Trojan war. But this is demonstrated from the succession of the Attic, [and of the Macedonian, the Ptolemaic, and the Antiochian] kings. Hence, if the most illustrious deeds among the Greeks were recorded and made known after Inachus, it is manifest that this must have been after Moses. In the time of Phoroneus, who was after Inachus, Ogygus is mentioned among the Athenians, in whose time was the first deluge; and in the time of Phorbas was Actaeus, from whom Attica was called Actaea; and in the time of Triopas were Prometheus, and Epimetheus, and Atlas, and Cecrops of double nature, and Io; in the time of Crotopas was the burning of Phaëthon and the flood of Deucalion; in the time of Sthenelus was the reign of Amphictyon and the coming of Danaus into Peloponnesus, and the founding of Dardania by Dardanus, and the return of Europa from Phoenicia to Crete; in the time of Lynceus was the abduction of Koré, and the founding of the temple in Eleusis, and the husbandry of Triptolemus, and the coming of Cadmus to Thebes, and the reign of Minos; in the time of Proetus was the war of Eumolpus against the Athenians; in the time of Acrisius was the coming over of Pelops from Phrygia, and the coming of Ion to Athens, and the second Cecrops, and the deeds of Perseus and Dionysus, and Musaeus, the disciple of Orpheus; and in the reign of Agamemnon Troy was taken.

40. Moses More Ancient and Credible than the Heathen Heroes

Therefore, from what has been said it is evident that Moses was older than the ancient heroes, wars, and demons. And we ought rather to believe him, who stands before them in point of age, than the Greeks, who, without being aware of it, drew his doctrines [as] from a fountain. For many of the sophists among them, stimulated by curiosity, endeavoured to adulterate whatever they learned from Moses, and from those who have philoso- phized like him, first that they might be considered as having something of their own, and secondly, that covering up by a certain rhetorical artifice whatever things they did not understand, they might misrepresent the truth as if it were a fable. But what the learned among the Greeks have said con- cerning our polity and the history of our laws, and how many and what kind of men have written of these things, will be shown in the treatise against those who have discoursed of divine things.

41

But the matter of principal importance is to endeavour with all accuracy to make it clear that Moses is not only older than Homer, but than all the writers that were before him—older than Linus, Philammon, Thamyris, Amphion, Musaeus, Orpheus, Demodocus, Phemius, Sibylla, Epimenides of Crete, who came to Sparta, Arestaeus of Proconnesus, who wrote the Arimaspia, Asbolus the Centaur, Isatis, Drymon, Euclus the Cyprian, Horus the Samian, and Pronapis the Athenian. Now, Linus was the teacher of Hercules, but Hercules preceded the Trojan war by one generation; and this is manifest from his son Tlepolemus, who served in the army against Troy. And Orpheus lived at the same time as Hercules; moreover, it is said that all the works attributed to him were composed by Onomacritus the Athenian, who lived during the reign of the Pisistratids, about the fiftieth Olympiad. Musaeus was a disciple of Orpheus. Amphion, since he pre- ceded the siege of Troy by two generations, forbids our collecting further particulars about him for those who are desirous of information. Demod- ocus and Phemius lived at the very time of the Trojan war; for the one re- sided with the suitors, and the other with the Phaeacians. Thamyris and Philammon were not much earlier than these. Thus, concerning their several performances in each kind, and their times and the record of them, we have written very fully, and, as I think, with all exactness. But, that we may complete what is still wanting, I will give my explanation respecting the men who are esteemed wise. Minos, who has been thought to excel in every kind of wisdom, and mental acuteness, and legislative capacity, lived in the time of Lynceus, who reigned after Danaus in the eleventh generation after Inachus. Lycurgus, who was born long after the taking of Troy, gave laws to the Lacedemonians. Draco is found to have lived about the thirty-ninth Olympiad, Solon about the forty-sixth, and Pythagoras about the sixty-second. We have shown that the Olympiads commenced 407 years after the taking of Troy. These facts being demonstrated, we shall briefly remark concerning the age of the seven wise men. The oldest of these, Thales, lived about the fiftieth Olympiad; and I have already spoken briefly of those who came after him.

42. Concluding Statement as to the Author

These things, O Greeks, I Tatian, a disciple of the barbarian philosophy, have composed for you. I was born in the land of the Assyrians, having been first instructed in your doctrines, and afterwards in those which I now undertake to proclaim. Henceforward, knowing who God is and what is His work, I present myself to you prepared for an examination concerning my doctrines, while I adhere immoveably to that mode of life which is according to God.

3. *Letter to Diognetus*

1. Introduction

Since I perceive, most excellent Diognetus, that you are exceedingly zealous to learn the religion of the Christians and are asking very clear and careful questions concerning them, both who is the God in whom they believe, and how they worship him, so that all disregard the world and despise death, and do not reckon as Gods those who are considered to be so by the Greeks, nor keep the superstition of the Jews, and what is the love which they have for one another, and why this new race or practice has come to life at this time, and not formerly; I indeed welcome this zeal in you, and I ask from God who bestows on us the power both of speaking and

From *Letter to Diognetus*, chaps. 1–6, 10–12, in *The Apostolic Fathers*, vol. 2, translated by Kirsopp Lake (Cambridge, Mass.: Harvard University Press, 1913), pp. 350–63, 370–79. Reprinted by permission of the publishers and the Loeb Classical Library.

of hearing, that it may be granted to me so to speak that you may benefit so much as possible by your hearing, and to you so to hear that I may not be made sorry for my speech.

2. Discussion of the Gods of the Heathen

1. Come then, clear yourself of all the prejudice which occupies your mind, and throw aside the custom which deceives you, and become as it were a new man from the beginning, as one, as you yourself also admitted, who is about to listen to a new story. Look, not only with your eyes, but also with your intelligence, what substance or form they chance to have whom you call gods and regard as such. 2. Is not one a stone, like that on which we walk, another bronze, no better than the vessels which have been forged for our use, another wood already rotten, another silver, needing a man to guard it against theft, another iron, eaten by rust, another earthenware, not a whit more comely than that which is supplied for the most ordinary service? 3. Are not all these of perishable material? Were they not forged by iron and fire? Did not the wood-carver make one, the brass-founder another, the silversmith another, the potter another? Before they were moulded by their arts, into the shapes which they have, was it not possible and does it not still remain possible, for each of them to have been given a different shape? Might not vessels made out of the same material, if they met with the same artificers, be still made similar to such as they? 4. Again, would it not be possible, for these, which are now worshipped by you, to be made by men into vessels like any others? Are they not all dumb? Are they not blind? Are they not without souls? Are they not without feeling? Are they not without movement? Are not they all rotting? Are they not all decaying? 5. Do you call these things gods? Are these what you serve? Are these what you worship and in the end become like them? 6. Is this the reason why you hate the Christians—that they do not think that these are gods? 7. For is it not you, who, though you think and believe that you are praising the gods, are much more despising them? Are you not much rather mocking and insulting them, when you worship those of stone and earthenware without guarding them; but lock up at night and in the daytime place guards over those of silver and gold, that they be not stolen away? 8. And, if they have powers of perception, by the honours which you think to pay them you are rather punishing them, and, if they are without perception, you are refuting them by worshipping them with blood and burnt fat. 9. Let one of you suffer these things, let him endure that it should be done to him. Why, there is not a single man who would willingly endure this punishment, for he has perception and reason. But the stone endures, for it has no perception. Do you not then refute its perception? 10. I could

say much more as to the refusal of Christians to serve such gods, but if any one find these arguments insufficient, I think it useless to say more.

3. The Difference between Jews and Christians

1. In the next place I think that you are especially anxious to hear why the Christians do not worship in the same way as the Jews. 2. The Jews indeed, by abstaining from the religion already discussed, may rightly claim that they worship the one God of the Universe, and regard him as master, but in offering service to him in like manner to those already dealt with they are quite wrong. 3. For just as the Greeks give a proof of foolishness by making offerings to senseless and deaf images, so the Jews ought rather to consider that they are showing foolishness, not reverence, by regarding God as in need of these things. 4. For "He who made heaven and earth and all that is in them,"[1] and bestows on all of us that which we need, would not himself have need of any of these things which he himself supplies to those who think that they are giving them. 5. For after all, those who think that they are consecrating sacrifices to him by blood and burnt fat, and whole burnt offerings, and that they are reverencing him by these honours, seem to me to be in no way better than those who show the same respect to deaf images. For it seems that the one offer to those who cannot partake of the honour, the others to him who is in need of nothing.

4

1. Moreover I do not suppose that you need to learn from me that, after all, their scruples about food and superstition about the Sabbath, and their pride in circumcision and the sham of their fasting and feast of the new moon, are ridiculous and unworthy of any argument. 2. For how can it be anything but unlawful to receive some of the things created by God for the use of man as if well created, and to reject others as if useless and superfluous? 3. And what can it be but impious falsely to accuse God of forbidding that a good deed should be done on the Sabbath day? 4. And what does it deserve but ridicule to be proud of the mutilation of the flesh as a proof of election, as if they were, for this reason, especially beloved by God? 5. And their attention to the stars and moon, for the observance of months and days, and for their arbitrary distinctions between the changing seasons ordained by God, making some into feasts, and others into occasions of mourning;—who would regard this as a proof of piety, and not much more of foolishness? So then I think that you have learnt sufficiently

---

1. Exod. 20:11; Ps. 146:6; Acts 14:15.

that the Christians do rightly in abstaining from the general silliness and deceit and fussiness and pride of the Jews. But do not suppose that you can learn from man the mystery of the Christians' own religion.

5. The True Distinction of Christians

1. For the distinction between Christians and other men, is neither in country nor language nor customs. 2. For they do not dwell in cities in some place of their own, nor do they use any strange variety of dialect, nor practise an extraordinary kind of life. 3. This teaching of theirs has not been discovered by the intellect or thought of busy men, nor are they the advocates of any human doctrine as some men are. 4. Yet while living in Greek and barbarian cities, according as each obtained his lot, and following the local customs, both in clothing and food and in the rest of life, they show forth the wonderful and confessedly strange character of the constitution of their own citizenship. 5. They dwell in their own fatherlands, but as if sojourners in them; they share all things as citizens, and suffer all things as strangers. Every foreign country is their fatherland, and every fatherland is a foreign country. 6. They marry as all men, they bear children, but they do not expose their offspring. 7. They offer free hospitality, but guard their purity. 8. Their lot is cast "in the flesh," but they do not live "after the flesh." 9. They pass their time upon the earth, but they have their citizenship in heaven.[2] 10. They obey the appointed laws, and they surpass the laws in their own lives. 11. They love all men and are persecuted by all men. 12. They are unknown and they are condemned. They are put to death and they gain life. 13. "They are poor and make many rich"; they lack all things and have all things in abundance. 14. They are dishonoured, and are glorified in their dishonour, they are spoken evil of and are justified. 15. "They are abused and give blessing," they are insulted and render honour.[3] 16. When they do good they are buffeted as evil-doers, when they are buffeted they rejoice as men who receive life. 17. They are warred upon by the Jews as foreigners and are persecuted by the Greeks, and those who hate them cannot state the cause of their enmity.

6. The World and Christians

1. To put it shortly what the soul is in the body, that the Christians are in the world. 2. The soul is spread through all members of the body, and Christians throughout the cities of the world. 3. The soul dwells in the

2. 2 Cor. 10:3; Rom. 8:12–13; Philipp. 3:18–20.

3. 2 Cor. 6:9; 2 Cor. 6:10; 1 Cor. 4:12; 2 Cor. 6:10.

body, but is not of the body, and Christians dwell in the world, but are not of the world. 4. The soul is invisible, and is guarded in a visible body, and Christians are recognised when they are in the world, but their religion remains invisible. 5. The flesh hates the soul, and wages war upon it, though it has suffered no evil, because it is prevented from gratifying its pleasures, and the world hates the Christians though it has suffered no evil, because they are opposed to its pleasures. 6. The soul loves the flesh which hates it and the limbs, and Christians love those that hate them. 7. The soul has been shut up in the body, but itself sustains the body; and Christians are confined in the world as in a prison, but themselves sustain the world. 8. The soul dwells immortal in a mortal tabernacle, and Christians sojourn among corruptible things, waiting for the incorruptibility which is in heaven. 9. The soul when evil treated in food and drink becomes better, and Christians when buffeted day by day increase more. 10. God has appointed them to so great a post and it is not right for them to decline it.

10. The Benefits of Conversion

1. If you also desire this faith, and receive first complete knowledge of the Father. . . . 2. For God loved mankind for whose sake he made the world, to whom he subjected all things which are in the earth, to whom he gave reason, to whom he gave mind, on whom alone he enjoined that they should look upward to him, whom he made in his own image, to whom he sent his only-begotten Son, to whom he promised the kingdom in heaven,— and he will give it to them who loved him. 3. And when you have this full knowledge, with that joy do you think that you will be filled, or how greatly will you love him who thus first loved you? 4. But by your love you will imitate the example of his goodness. And do not wonder that it is possible for man to be the imitator of God; it is possible when he will. 5. For happiness consists not in domination over neighbours, nor in wishing to have more than the weak, nor in wealth, and power to compel those who are poorer, nor can anyone be an imitator of God in doing these things, but these things are outside his majesty. 6. But whoever takes up the burden of his neighbour, and wishes to help another, who is worse off in that in which he is the stronger, and by ministering to those in need the things which he has received and holds from God becomes a god to those who receive them,—this man is an imitator of God. 7. Then, though your lot be placed on earth you will see that God lives in heaven, then you will begin to speak of the mysteries of God, then you will both love and admire those who are being punished because they will not deny God, then you will condemn the deceit and error of the world, when you know what is the true life of heaven, when you despise the apparent death of this world, when you fear

the death which is real, which is kept for those that shall be condemned to
the everlasting fire, which shall punish up to the end those that were delivered to it. 8. Then you will marvel at those who endure for the sake of
righteousness the fire which is for a season, and you will count them
blessed when you know that other fire.

11. Conclusion

1. My speech is not strange, nor my inquiry unreasonable, but as a disciple
of apostles I am becoming a teacher of the heathen. I administer worthily
that which has been handed down to those who are becoming disciples of
the truth. 2. For who that has been properly taught, and has become a lover
of the word does not seek to learn plainly the things which have been
clearly shown by the word to disciples, to whom the Word appeared and
revealed them, speaking boldly, not being perceived by the unbelieving, but
relating them to disciples, who were held by him to be faithful and gained
knowledge of the mysteries of the Father? 3. And for his sake he sent the
Word to appear to the world, who was dishonoured by the chosen people,
was preached by apostles, was believed by the heathen. 4. He was from the
beginning, and appeared new, and was proved to be old, and is ever young,
as he is born in the hearts of the saints. 5. He is the eternal one, who to-day
is accounted a Son, through whom the Church is enriched, and grace is
unfolded and multiplied among the saints, who confers understanding,
manifests mysteries, announces seasons, rejoices in the faithful, is given to
them that seek, that is, to those by whom the pledges of faith are not broken, nor the decrees of the Fathers transgressed. 6. Then is the fear of the
Law sung, and the grace of the Prophets known, the faith of the Gospels is
established, and the tradition of apostles is guarded, and the grace of the
Church exults. 7. And if you do not grieve this grace you will understand
what the word says through the agents of his choice, when he will. 8. For in
all things which we were moved by the will of him who commands us to
speak with pain, we become sharers with you through love of the things
revealed to us.

12

1. If you consider and listen with zeal to these truths you will know what
things God bestows on those that love him rightly, who are become "a
Paradise of delight," raising up in themselves a fertile tree with all manner
of fruits, and are adorned with divers fruits.[4] 2. For in this garden has been

---

4. Gen. 2:15; 3:24.

planted "the tree of knowledge and the tree of life," but the tree of knowledge does not kill, but disobedience kills.[5] 3. For that which was written is quite plain, that God in the beginning planted "a tree of knowledge and a tree of life in the midst of Paradise," and showed that life is through knowledge. But those who did not use it in purity were in the beginning deprived of it by the deceit of the serpent; 4. for neither is there life without knowledge, nor sound knowledge without true life; wherefore both are planted together. 5. And when the apostle saw the force of this, he blamed the knowledge which is exercised apart from the truth of the injunction which leads to life and said; "Knowledge puffeth up, but love edifieth."[6] 6. For he who thinks that he knows anything without knowledge which is true and testified to by life, does not know, but is deceived by the serpent, not loving life. But he who has full knowledge with fear and seeks after life plants in hope, looking for fruit. 7. Let your heart be knowledge, and your life the true and comprehended word. 8. And if you bear the tree of this and pluck its fruit you will ever enjoy that which is desired by God, which the serpent does not touch, and deceit does not infect, and Eve is not corrupted but a virgin is trusted, 9. and salvation is set forth, and apostles are given understanding, and the Passover of the Lord advances, and the seasons are brought together, and are harmonised with the world, and the Word teaches the saints and rejoices, and through it the Father is glorified; to whom be glory for ever. Amen.

5. Gen. 2:9.   6. 1 Cor. 8:1.

2
From Persecuted to Persecutor

As the Empire assimilated the Church, the Church also assimilated the Empire. One dramatic measure of this two-fold movement was the change of Christians from persecuted sect to persecuting Church. The following documents pinpoint moments during that transition. They also underscore a growing tension between Christianity—the evangelical faith that professed not to be of this world—and the Church—the structure of authority that united with imperial power in the task of coercion. This tension is apparent even in Augustine's defense of persecution, which became the authoritative statement on the subject for later canonists and theologians.

The documents included in this section display a feature of Church history that our selection of apologetic writings also manifested: namely, the slow emergence of Latin Christianity and the dominance of Greek in the early centuries of the Church. With two exceptions, all the documents in this section were written in the Greek East. Though written in Latin, the official language of imperial administration, even the decree *On the Catholic Faith* was issued to the people of Constantinople. A further trait of early Church history is indicated by the fact that the two exceptions come from North Africa, a peripheral area of the Latin West.

The single-minded zeal of early apologists (such as Justin Martyr and Tatian) gave the theme of conflict pride of place. In fact, that theme, present throughout the Scriptures, dominated the ways in which Christians through the centuries have defined themselves, their relations with one another, and their mission in the world.

The texts in the following section illustrate the theme of conflict with regard to persecution. The first two documents (the *Martyrdom of Saint Perpetua* and Eusebius of Caesarea's account of martyrdoms that he, as a Christian, witnessed) concern the persecution of Christians by a hostile, unbelieving world. The subsequent texts tell the more complex story of how, in the passage of time, Christians persecuted one another, how they were persecuted by a formerly Christian emperor who reconverted to paganism, and how a theological defense of persecution was eventually worked out by Augustine of Hippo, a defense that Augustine applied to professed Christians whom he regarded as cut off from the true Church but that could also be applied to non-Christians.

The *Martyrdom of Saint Perpetua* belongs to a fascinating genre of early Christian literature: the testimonies and memoirs of martyrs. Perpetua was a Christian woman executed in Carthage in the year 202. This memoir, allegedly composed by Perpetua herself, is an important testimony to the effects of conversion on family ties and on the response of the community to conversion. The motif of conflict is especially well developed.

Eusebius of Caesarea (about 263–c. 340), was born in Palestine and educated in a library-school founded at Caesarea by the Alexandrine Church Father, Origen. He became bishop of Caesarea about 313, and entered the court of Constantine the Great, the first emperor to recognize Christianity as a legal religion. Eusebius is best known as the father of Church history, but he was also a prolific writer of apologies, Scriptural commentaries, and polemical treatises. His devotion to the cult of martyrs (and his own evasion of martyrdom) is illustrated by the following account of an execution that he witnessed in 303.

Bishop Athanasius of Alexandria (295–373) was one of the greatest theologians, controversialists, and ecclesiastical politicians of his day. He was present at the first ecumenical council, the Council of Nicaea, which Constantine the Great convened in 325, and he was a dominant figure in disputes from that time until his death. By virtue of two banishments (335, 340) and his writings (especially the *Life of Saint Anthony*; see document 27 below), he became a major conduit of monastic discipline from Egypt to the West. The *History of the Arians*, excerpted below, recounts events leading up to his third exile (356), when he fled from persecution by the Arian Emperor Constantius II (337–61). The account begins with the Synod of Milan (355), which Constantius coerced into deposing Athanasius. Athanasius also describes measures that Constantius took against the old Bishop Hosius of Cordova (256–357/8), who had been a bulwark of orthodoxy during the reign of Constantine the Great.

Sozomen, a lawyer in Constantinople, wrote a continuation of Eusebius's *Ecclesiastical History* for the period 324–423. He wrote between 439 and 450. In the selection below, Sozomen describes events under the emperor Julian (361–63). A nephew of Constantine the Great and cousin

of his son and successor, Constantius II, Julian rejected Christianity, repelled by the cruelty of his imperial relatives and the bitter conflicts
among Christians. He embraced a philosophical religion drawn from
pagan sources. In 362, he launched the legal persecution of Christians
described in the selection below, including the banishment of bishops
from their sees and the exclusion of Christians from public teaching
positions.

Bishop Augustine of Hippo (354–430) was the first Latin theologian,
and the first Christian writer to frame a fully developed philosophy of
history. His death, while the North African city of Hippo was under siege
by the Vandals, symbolizes the gradual disintegration of the Roman Empire and the corresponding infiltration of the Roman world by barbarian
peoples. The letter to Boniface, the imperial count of Africa, a portion of
which is reproduced here, was written about 417. The Donatists, against
whom Augustine invoked persecution, had formed as a sect in a disputed
election of the bishop of Carthage in 312. The theological issue from the
beginning was whether personal impurity of a priest could invalidate sacraments performed by him, as the Donatists alleged. Their position naturally raised serious problems for the Donatists regarding ecclesiastical
obedience. A century of relentless conflict destroyed every chance of
compromise. Imperial laws (412, 414) deprived the Donatists of civil and
ecclesiastical rights, and Augustine called for the strict execution of the
laws. Despite all the measures against them, the Donatists continued to
exist in North Africa almost until the region was engulfed by Islam in the
seventh century.

---

4. *The Martyrdom of Saint Perpetua*

<u>1</u>

If the ancient examples of faith, such as both testified to the grace of God,
and wrought the edification of man, have for this cause been set out in writing that the reading of them may revive the past, and so both God be
glorified and man strengthened, why should not new examples be set out
equally suitable to both those ends? For these in like manner will some day
be old and needful for posterity, though in their own time because of the
veneration secured to antiquity they are held in less esteem. But let them
see to this who determine the one power of the one Spirit by times and

From "The Passion of Ss. Perpetua and Felicitas," in *Some Authentic Acts of the Early
Martyrs*, translated by E. C. E. Owen (Oxford: Oxford University Press, 1927), pp. 74–85.

seasons: since the more recent things should rather be deemed the greater, as being "later than the last." This follows from the pre-eminence of grace promised at the last lap of the world's race. For "In the last days, saith the Lord, I will pour forth of My Spirit upon all flesh, and their sons and their daughters shall prophesy: and on my servants and on my handmaidens will I pour forth of My Spirit: and their young men shall see visions, and their old men shall dream dreams." And so we who recognize and hold in honour not new prophecies only but new visions as alike promised, and count all the rest of the powers of the Holy Spirit as intended for the equipment of the Church, to which the same Spirit was sent bestowing all gifts upon all as the Lord dealt to each man, we cannot but set these out and make them famous by recital to the glory of God. So shall no weak or despairing faith suppose that supernatural grace, in excellency of martyrdoms or revelations, was found among the ancients only; for God ever works what He has promised, to unbelievers a witness, to believers a blessing. And so "what we have heard and handled declare we unto you also," brothers and little children, "that ye also" who were their eyewitnesses may be reminded of the glory of the Lord, and you who now learn by the ear "may have fellowship with" the holy martyrs, and through them with the Lord Jesus Christ, to whom belong splendour and honour for ever and ever. Amen.

2

Certain young catechumens were arrested, Revocatus and his fellow-slave Felicitas, Saturninus, and Secundulus. Among these also Vibia Perpetua, well-born, liberally educated, honourably married, having father and mother, and two brothers, one like herself a catechumen, and an infant son at the breast. She was about twenty-two years of age. The whole story of her martyrdom is from this point onwards told by herself, as she left it written, hand and conception being alike her own.

3

"When I was still," she says, "with my companions, and my father in his affection for me was endeavouring to upset me by arguments and overthrow my resolution, 'Father,' I said, 'Do you see this vessel for instance lying here, waterpot or whatever it may be?' 'I see it,' he said. And I said to him, 'Can it be called by any other name than what it is?' And he answered, 'No.' 'So also I cannot call myself anything else than what I am, a Christian.'

Then my father, furious at the word 'Christian,' threw himself upon me as though to pluck out my eyes; but he was satisfied with annoying me; he

was in fact vanquished, he and his devil's arguments. Then I thanked the
Lord for being parted for a few days from my father, and was refreshed by
his absence. During those few days we were baptized, and the Holy Spirit
bade me make no other petition after the holy water save for bodily endurance. A few days after we were lodged in prison; and I was in great fear,
because I had never known such darkness. What a day of horror! Terrible
heat, thanks to the crowds! Rough handling by the soldiers! To crown all I
was tormented there by anxiety for my baby. Then Tertius and Pomponius,
those blessed deacons who were ministering to us, paid for us to be removed for a few hours to a better part of the prison and refresh ourselves.
Then all went out of the prison and were left to themselves. [My baby was
brought to me,] and I suckled him, for he was already faint for want of
food. I spoke anxiously to my mother on his behalf, and strengthened my
brother, and commended my son to their charge. I was pining because I
saw them pine on my account. Such anxieties I suffered for many days; and
I obtained leave for my baby to remain in the prison with me; and I at once
recovered my health, and was relieved of my trouble and anxiety for my
baby; and my prison suddenly became a palace to me, and I would rather
have been there than anywhere else.

4

Then my brother said to me: 'Lady sister, you are now in great honour, so
great indeed that you may well pray for a vision and may well be shown
whether suffering or release be in store for you.' And I who knew myself to
have speech of the Lord, for whose sake I had gone through so much, gave
confident promise in return, saying: 'To-morrow I will bring you word.'
And I made request, and this was shown me. I saw a brazen ladder of wondrous length reaching up to heaven, but so narrow that only one could ascend at once; and on the sides of the ladder were fastened all kinds of iron
weapons. There were swords, lances, hooks, daggers, so that if any one
went up carelessly or without looking upwards he was mangled and his
flesh caught on the weapons. And just beneath the ladder was a dragon
couching of wondrous size who lay in wait for those going up and sought to
frighten them from going up. Now Saturus went up first, who had given
himself up for our sakes of his own accord, because our faith had been of
his own building, and he had not been present when we were seized. And
he reached the top of the ladder, and turned, and said to me: 'Perpetua, I
await you; but see that the dragon bite you not.' And I said: 'In the name of
Jesus Christ he will not hurt me.' And he put out his head gently, as if
afraid of me, just at the foot of the ladder; and as though I were treading on
the first step, I trod on his head. And I went up, and saw a vast expanse of

garden, and in the midst a man sitting with white hair, in the dress of a shepherd, a tall man, milking sheep; and round about were many thousands clad in white. And he raised his head, and looked upon me, and said: 'You have well come, my child.' And he called me, and gave me a morsel of the milk which he was milking and I received it in my joined hands, and ate; and all they that stood around said: 'Amen.' And at the sound of the word I woke, still eating something sweet. And at once I told my brother, and we understood that we must suffer, and henceforward began to have no hope in this world.

5

After a few days a rumour ran that we were to be examined. Moreover, my father arrived from the city, worn with trouble, and came up the hill to see me, that he might overthrow my resolution, saying: 'Daughter, pity my white hairs! Pity your father, if I am worthy to be called father by you; if with these hands I have brought you up to this your prime of life, if I have preferred you to all your brothers! Give me not over to the reproach of men! Look upon your brothers, look upon your mother and your mother's sister, look upon your son who cannot live after you are gone! Lay aside your pride, do not ruin all of us, for none of us will ever speak freely again, if anything happen to you!' So spoke my father in his love for me, kissing my hands, and casting himself at my feet; and with tears called me by the name not of daughter but of lady. And I grieved for my father's sake, because he alone of all my kindred would not have joy in my suffering. And I comforted him, saying, 'It shall happen on that platform as God shall choose; for know well that we lie not in our own power but in the power of God.' And full of sorrow he left me.

6

On another day when we were having our midday meal, we were suddenly hurried off to be examined; and we came to the market-place. Forthwith a rumour ran through the neighbouring parts of the market-place, and a vast crowd gathered. We went up on to the platform. The others on being questioned confessed their faith. So it came to my turn. And there was my father with my child, and he drew me down from the step, beseeching me: 'Have pity on your baby.' And the procurator Hilarian, who had then received the power of life and death in the room of the late proconsul Minucius Timinianus, said to me: 'Spare your father's white hairs; spare the tender years of your child. Offer a sacrifice for the safety of the Emperors.' And I answered: 'No.' 'Are you a Christian!' said Hilarian. And I answered: 'I am.' And when my father persisted in trying to overthrow my resolution, he was ordered by Hilarian to be thrown down, and the judge struck him with his rod. And I was grieved for my father's plight, as if I had been struck myself, so did I grieve for the sorrow that had come on his old age. Then he passed sentence on the whole of us, and condemned us to the beasts; and in great joy we went down into the prison. Then because my baby was accustomed to take the breast from me, and stay with me in prison, I sent at once the deacon Pomponius to my father to ask for my baby. But my father refused to give him. And as God willed, neither had he any further wish for my breasts, nor did they become inflamed; that I might not be tortured by anxiety for the baby and pain in my breasts.

7

After a few days, while we were all praying, suddenly in the middle of the prayer I spoke, and uttered the name of Dinocrates; and I was astonished that he had never come into mind till then; and I grieved thinking of what had befallen him. And I saw at once that I was entitled, and ought, to make request for him. And I began to pray much for him, and make lamentation to the Lord. At once on this very night this was shown me. I saw Dinocrates coming forth from a dark place, where there were many other dark places, very hot and thirsty, his countenance pale and squalid; and the wound which he had when he died was in his face still. This Dinocrates had been my brother according to the flesh, seven years old, who had died miserably of a gangrene in the face, so that his death moved all to loathing. For him then I had prayed; and there was a great gulf between me and him, so that neither of us could approach the other. There was besides in the very place where Dinocrates was a font full of water, the rim of which was above the head of the child; and Dinocrates stood on tiptoe to drink. I grieved that the font should have water in it and that nevertheless he could not drink because of the height of the rim. And I woke and recognized that my brother was in trouble. But I trusted that I could relieve his trouble, and I prayed for him every day until we were transferred to the garrison prison, for we were to fight with the beasts at the garrison games on the Caesar Geta's birthday. And I prayed for him day and night with lamentations and tears that he might be given me.

8

During the daytime, while we stayed in the stocks, this was shown me. I saw that same place which I had seen before, and Dinocrates clean in body, well-clothed and refreshed; and where there had been a wound, I saw a scar; and the font which I had seen before had its rim lowered to the child's waist; and there poured water from it unceasingly; and on the rim a golden bowl full of water. And Dinocrates came forward and began to drink from it, and the bowl failed not. And when he had drunk enough of the water, he came forward being glad to play as children will. And I awoke. Then I knew that he had been released from punishment.

9

Then after a few days Pudens the adjutant, who was in charge of the prison, who began to show us honour perceiving that there was some great power within us, began to admit many to see us, that both we and they might be refreshed by one another's company. Now when the day of the games approached, my father came in to me worn with trouble, and began to pluck out his beard and cast it on the ground, and to throw himself on his face, and to curse his years, and to say such words as might have turned the world upside down. I sorrowed for the unhappiness of his old age.

10

On the day before we were to fight, I saw in a vision Pomponius the deacon come hither to the door of the prison and knock loudly. And I went out to him, and opened to him. Now he was clad in a white robe without a girdle, wearing shoes curiously wrought. And he said to me: 'Perpetua, we are waiting for you; come.' And he took hold of my hand, and we began to pass through rough and broken country. Painfully and panting did we arrive at last at an amphitheatre, and he led me into the middle of the arena. And he said to me: 'Fear not; I am here with you, and I suffer with you.' And he departed. And I saw a huge crowd watching eagerly. And because I knew that I was condemned to the beasts, I marvelled that there were no beasts let loose on me. And there came out an Egyptian, foul of look, with his attendants to fight against me. And to me also there came goodly young men to be my attendants and supporters. And I was stripped and was changed into a man. And my supporters began to rub me down with oil, as they are wont to do before a combat; and I saw the Egyptian opposite rolling in the sand. And there came forth a man wondrously tall so that he rose above the top of the amphitheatre, clad in a purple robe without a girdle with two stripes, one on either side, running down the middle of the breast, and wearing shoes curiously wrought made of gold and silver; carrying a wand, like a trainer, and a green bough on which were golden apples. And he asked for silence, and said: 'This Egyptian, if he prevail over her, shall kill her with a sword; and, if she prevail over him, she shall receive this

bough.' And he retired. And we came near to one another and began to use
our fists. My adversary wished to catch hold of my feet, but I kept on striking his face with my heels. And I was lifted up into the air, and began to
strike him in such fashion as would one that no longer trod on earth. But
when I saw that the fight lagged, I joined my two hands, linking the fingers
of the one with the fingers of the other. And I caught hold of his head, and
he fell on his face; and I trod upon his head. And the people began to
shout, and my supporters to sing psalms. And I came forward to the
trainer, and received the bough. And he kissed me, and said to me: 'Peace
be with thee, my daughter.' And I began to go in triumph to the Gate of
Life. And I awoke. And I perceived that I should not fight with beasts but
with the Devil; but I knew the victory to be mine. Such were my doings up
to the day before the games. Of what was done in the games themselves let
him write who will.''

5. Eusebius of Caesarea, *The Ecclesiastical History*, Book 8

The Egyptians That Suffered in Phoenice

We are already acquainted with those of them that shone conspicuous in
Palestine, and know also those in Tyre and Phoenice; and at the sight of
whom, who would not himself be struck with astonishment at the numberless blows inflicted, and the perseverance of those truly admirable
wrestlers for the true religion? Who can behold, without amazement, all
this: their conflicts, after scourging, with bloody beasts of prey, when they
were cast as food to leopards and bears, wild boars and bulls, goaded with
fire, and branded with glowing iron against them? And in each of these,
who can fail to admire the wonderful patience of these noble martyrs? At
these scenes we have been present ourselves, when we also observed the
divine power of our Lord and Saviour Jesus Christ himself present, and
effectually displayed in them; when, for a long time, the devouring wild
beasts would not dare either to touch or to approach the bodies of these
pious men, but directed their violence against others that were any where
stimulating them from without. But they would not even touch the holy
wrestlers standing naked and striking at them with their hands, as they
were commanded, in order to irritate the beasts against them. Sometimes,
indeed, they would also rush upon them, but, as if repulsed by some divine
power, they again retreated.

From Eusebius of Caesarea, *The Ecclesiastical History*, translated by Christian Frederick
Cruse (1850; reprint ed., Grand Rapids, Mich.: Baker Books, 1955), Book 8, chap. 7,
pp. 325–26.

This continuing, also, for a long time, created no little wonder to the spectators; so that now again on account of the failure in the first instance, they were obliged to let loose the beast a second and a third time upon one and the same martyr. One could not help being astonished at the intrepid perseverance of these holy men, and the firm and invincible mind of those, also, whose bodies were but young and tender. For you could have seen a youth of scarcely twenty years, standing unbound, with his arms extended, like a cross, but with an intrepid and fearless earnestness, intensely engaged in prayer to God, neither removing nor declining from the spot where he stood, whilst bears and leopards breathed rage and death, and almost touched his very flesh, and yet I know not how, by a divine and inscrutable power, they had their mouths in a manner bridled, and again retreated in haste. And such was he of whom we now speak.

Again, you might have seen others, for they were five in all, cast before a wild bull, who indeed seized others, that approached from without, with his horns, and tossed them in the air, leaving them to be taken up half dead, but only rushing upon the saints with rage and menaces; for the beast was not able even to approach them, but beating the earth with his feet, and pushing with his horns hither and thither, and from the irritation excited by the brands of glowing iron, he breathed madness and death, yet was drawn back again by a divine interposition.

6. Athanasius, *History of the Arians*

33. Persecution Is from the Devil

Now if it was altogether unseemly in any of the Bishops to change their opinions merely from fear of these things, yet it was much more so, and not the part of men who have confidence in what they believe, to force and compel the unwilling. In this manner it is that the Devil, when he has no truth on his side, attacks and breaks down the doors of them that admit him with axes and hammers. But our Saviour is so gentle that He teaches thus, "If any man wills to come after Me," and, "Whoever wills to be My disciple;"[1] and coming to each He does not force them, but knocks at the door and says, "Open unto Me, My sister, My spouse;"[2] and if they open to Him, He enters in, but if they delay and will not, He departs from them. For the truth is not preached with swords or with darts, nor by means of soldiers; but by persuasion and counsel. But what persuasion is there

From *History of the Arians*, chaps. 33–34, 42–45, in *Nicene and Post-Nicene Fathers*, 2d ser., vol. 4 (New York: Christian Literature Co., 1892), pp. 281–82, 284–87.

1. Matt. 16:24.   2. Cant. 5:2.

where fear of the Emperor prevails? or what counsel is there, when he who withstands them receives at last banishment and death? Even David, although he was a king, and had his enemy in his power, prevented not the soldiers by an exercise of authority when they wished to kill his enemy, but, as the Scripture says, David persuaded his men by arguments, and suffered them not to rise up and put Saul to death.[3] But he, being without arguments of reason, forces all men by his power, that it may be shewn to all, that their wisdom is not according to God, but merely human, and that they who favour the Arian doctrines have indeed no king but Caesar; for by his means it is that these enemies of Christ accomplish whatsoever they wish to do. But while they thought that they were carrying on their designs against many by his means, they knew not that they were making many to be confessors, of whom are those who have lately made so glorious a confession, religious men, and excellent Bishops, Paulinus Bishop of Treveri, the metropolis of the Gauls, Lucifer, Bishop of the metropolis of Sardinia, Eusebius of Vercelli in Italy, and Dionysius of Milan, which is the metropolis of Italy. These the Emperor summoned before him, and commanded them to subscribe against Athanasius, and to hold communion with the heretics; and when they were astonished at this novel procedure, and said that there was no ecclesiastical canon to this effect, he immediately said, "Whatever I will, be that esteemed a Canon; the 'Bishops' of Syria let me thus speak. Either then obey, or go into banishment."

34. Banishment of the Western Bishops Spread the Knowledge of the Truth

When the Bishops heard this they were utterly amazed, and stretching forth their hands to God, they used great boldness of speech against him, teaching him that the kingdom was not his, but God's, who had given it to him, Whom also they bid him fear, lest He should suddenly take it away from him. And they threatened him with the day of judgment, and warned him against infringing ecclesiastical order, and mingling Roman sovereignty with the constitution of the Church, and against introducing the Arian heresy into the Church of God. But he would not listen to them, nor permit them to speak further, but threatened them so much the more, and drew his sword against them, and gave orders for some of them to be led to execution; although afterwards, like Pharaoh, he repented. The holy men therefore shaking off the dust, and looking up to God, neither feared the threats of the Emperor, nor betrayed their cause before his drawn sword; but received their banishment, as a service pertaining to their ministry. And as

3. 1 Sam. 26:9.

they passed along, they preached the Gospel in every place and city, although they were in bonds, proclaiming the orthodox faith, anathematizing the Arian heresy, and stigmatizing the recantation of Ursacius and Valens. But this was contrary to the intention of their enemies; for the greater was the distance of their place of banishment, so much the more was the hatred against them increased, while the wanderings of these men were but the heralding of their impiety. For who that saw them as they passed along, did not greatly admire them as Confessors, and renounce and abominate the others, calling them not only impious men, but executioners and murderers, and everything rather than Christians?

42. Persecution and Lapse of Hosius

But although they had done all this, yet these impious men thought they had accomplished nothing, so long as the great Hosius escaped their wicked machinations. And now they undertook to extend their fury to that great old man. They felt no shame at the thought that he is the father of the Bishops; they regarded not that he had been a Confessor; they reverenced not the length of his Episcopate, in which he had continued more than sixty years; but they set aside everything, and looked only to the interests of their heresy, as being of a truth such as neither fear God, nor regard man.[4] Accordingly they went to Constantius, and again employed such arguments as the following: "We have done everything; we have banished the Bishop of the Romans; and before him a very great number of other Bishops, and have filled every place with alarm. But these strong measures of yours are as nothing to us, nor is our success at all more secure, so long as Hosius remains. While he is in his own place, the rest also continue in their Churches, for he is able by his arguments and his faith to persuade all men against us. He is the president of Councils, and his letters are everywhere attended to. He it was who put forth the Nicene Confession, and proclaimed everywhere that the Arians were heretics. If therefore he is suffered to remain, the banishment of the rest is of no avail, for our heresy will be destroyed. Begin then to persecute him also and spare him not, ancient as he is. Our heresy knows not to honour even the hoary hairs of the aged."

43. Brave Resistance of Hosius

Upon hearing this, the Emperor no longer delayed, but knowing the man, and the dignity of his years, wrote to summon him. And although Constantius wrote frequently, sometimes flattering him with the title of Father,

4. Luke 18:2.

and sometimes threatening and recounting the names of those who had been banished, and saying, "Will you continue the only person to oppose the heresy? Be persuaded and subscribe against Athanasius; for whoever subscribes against him thereby embraces with us the Arian cause;" still Hosius remained fearless, and while suffering these insults, wrote an answer in such terms as these. We have read the letter, which is placed at the end.

44

"Hosius to Constantius the Emperor sends health in the Lord.

I was a Confessor at the first, when a persecution arose in the time of your grandfather Maximian; and if you shall persecute me, I am ready now, too, to endure anything rather than to shed innocent blood and to betray the truth. But I cannot approve of your conduct in writing after this threatening manner. Cease to write thus; adopt not the cause of Arius, nor listen to those in the East, nor give credit to Ursacius, Valens and their fellows. For whatever they assert, it is not on account of Athanasius, but for the sake of their own heresy. Believe my statement, O Constantius, who am of an age to be your grandfather. I was present at the Council of Sardica, when you and your brother Constans of blessed memory assembled us all together; and on my own account I challenged the enemies of Athanasius, when they came to the church where I abode, that if they had anything against him they might declare it; desiring them to have confidence, and not to expect otherwise than that a right judgment would be passed in all things. This I did once and again, requesting them, if they were unwilling to appear before the whole Council, yet to appear before me alone; promising them also, that if he should be proved guilty, he should certainly be rejected by us; but if he should be found to be blameless, and should prove them to be calumniators, that if they should then refuse to hold communion with him, I would persuade him to go with me into the Spains. Athanasius was willing to comply with these conditions, and made no objection to my proposal; but they, altogether distrusting their cause, would not consent. And on another occasion Athanasius came to your Court, when you wrote for him, and his enemies being at the time in Antioch, he requested that they might be summoned either altogether or separately, in order that they might either convict him, or be convicted, and might either in his presence prove him to be what they represented, or cease to accuse him when absent. To this proposal also you would not listen, and they equally rejected it. Why then do you still give ear to them that speak evil of him? How can you endure Valens and Ursacius, although they have retracted, and made a written confession of their calumnies? For it is not true, as they pretend, that they were forced to confess; there were no soldiers at hand to influence them; your brother was not cognizant of the matter. No, such things were not done under his government, as are done now; God forbid. But they voluntarily went up to Rome, and in the presence of the Bishop and Presbyters wrote their recantation, having previously addressed to Athanasius a friendly and peaceable letter. And if they pretend that force was employed towards them, and acknowledge that this is an evil thing, which you also disapprove of; then do you cease to use force; write no letters, send no Counts; but release those that have been banished, lest while you are complaining of violence, they do but exercise greater violence. When was any such thing done by Constans? What Bishop suffered banishment? When did he appear as arbiter of an ecclesiastical trial? When did any Palatine of his compel men to subscribe against any one, that Valens and his fellows should be able to affirm this? Cease these proceedings, I beseech you, and remember that you are a mortal man. Be afraid of the day of judgment, and keep yourself pure thereunto. Intrude not yourself into ecclesiastical matters, neither give commands unto us concerning them; but learn them from us. God has put into your hands the kingdom; to us He has entrusted the affairs of His Church; and as he who would steal the empire from you would resist the ordinance of God, so likewise fear on your part lest by taking upon yourself the government of the Church, you become guilty of a great offence. It is written, "Render unto Caesar the things that are Caesar's, and unto God the things that are God's." [5] Neither therefore is it permitted unto us to exercise an earthly rule, nor have you, Sire, any authority to burn incense. These things I write unto you out of a concern for your salvation. With regard to the subject of your letters, this is my determination; I will not unite myself to the Arians; I anathematize their heresy. Neither will I subscribe against Athanasius, whom both we and the Church of the Romans and the whole Council pronounced to be guiltless. And yourself also, when you understood this, sent for the man, and gave him permission to return with honour to his country and his Church. What reason then can there be for so great a change in your conduct? The same persons who were his enemies before, are so now also; and the things they now whisper to his prejudice (for they do not declare them openly in his presence), the same they spoke against him, before you sent for him; the same they spread abroad concerning him when they come to the Council. And when I required them to come forward, as I have before said, they were unable to produce their proofs; had they possessed any, they would not have fled so disgracefully. Who then persuaded you so long after to forget your own letters and declarations? Forbear, and be not influenced by evil men,

5. Matt. 22:21.

lest while you act for the mutual advantage of yourself and them, you render yourself responsible. For here you comply with their desires, hereafter in the judgment you will have to answer for doing so alone. These men desire by your means to injure their enemy, and wish to make you the minister of their wickedness, in order that through your help they may sow the seeds of their accursed heresy in the Church. Now it is not a prudent thing to cast one's self into manifest danger for the pleasure of others. Cease then, I beseech you, O Constantius, and be persuaded by me. These things it becomes me to write, and you not to despise.''

45. Lapse of Hosius, Due to Cruel Persecution

Such were the sentiments, and such the letter, of the Abraham-like old man, Hosius, truly so called. But the Emperor desisted not from his designs, nor ceased to seek an occasion against him; but continued to threaten him severely, with a view either to bring him over by force, or to banish him if he refused to comply. And as the Officers and Satraps of Babylon,[6] seeking an occasion against Daniel, found none except in the law of his God; so likewise these present Satraps of impiety were unable to invent any charge against the old man (for this true Hosius, and his blameless life were known to all), except the charge of hatred to their heresy. They therefore proceeded to accuse him; though not under the same circumstances as those others accused Daniel to Darius, for Darius was grieved to hear the charge, but as Jezebel accused Naboth, and as the Jews applied themselves to Herod. And they said, "He not only will not subscribe against Athanasius, but also on his account condemns us; and his hatred to the heresy is so great, that he also writes to others, that they should rather suffer death, than become traitors to the truth. For, he says, our beloved Athanasius also is persecuted for the Truth's sake, and Liberius, Bishop of Rome, and all the rest, are treacherously assailed.'' When this patron of impiety, and Emperor of heresy, Constantius, heard this, and especially that there were others also in the Spains of the same mind as Hosius, after he had tempted them also to subscribe, and was unable to compel them to do so, he sent for Hosius, and instead of banishing him, detained him a whole year in Sirmium. Godless, unholy, without natural affection, he feared not God, he regarded not his father's affection for Hosius, he reverenced not his great age, for he was now a hundred years old; but all these things this modern Ahab, this second Belshazzar of our times, disregarded for the sake of impiety. He used such violence towards the old man, and

6. Dan. 6:5.

confined him so straitly, that at last, broken by suffering, he was brought, though hardly, to hold communion with Valens, Ursacius, and their fellows, though he would not subscribe against Athanasius. Yet even thus he forgot not his duty, for at the approach of death, as it were by his last testament, he bore witness to the force which had been used towards him, and anathematized the Arian heresy, and gave strict charge that no one should receive it.

7. Sozomen, *Ecclesiastical History*, Book 5

1. Apostasy of Julian, the Traitor. Death of the Emperor Constantius

Such were the transactions which took place in the Eastern Church. In the meantime, however, Julian, the Caesar, attacked and conquered the barbarians who dwelt on the banks of the Rhine; many he killed, and others he took prisoners. As the victory added greatly to his fame, and as his moderation and gentleness had endeared him to the troops, they proclaimed him Augustus. Far from making an excuse to Constantius for this act, he exchanged the officers who had been elected by Constantius, and industriously circulated letters wherein Constantius had solicited the barbarians to enter the Roman territories, and aid him against Magnentius. He then suddenly changed his religion, and although he had previously confessed Christianity, he declared himself high-priest, frequented the pagan temples, offered sacrifices, and invited his subjects to adopt that form of worship. . . .

A little while after the decease of Constantius, Julian, who had already made himself master of Thrace, entered Constantinople and was proclaimed emperor. Pagans assert that diviners and demons had predicted the death of Constantius, and the change in affairs, before his departure for Galatia, and had advised him to undertake the expedition. This might have been regarded as a true prediction, had not the life of Julian been terminated so shortly afterwards, and when he had only tasted the imperial power as in a dream. But it appears to me absurd to believe that, after he had heard the death of Constantius predicted, and had been warned that it would be his own fate to fall in battle by the hands of the Persians, he should have leaped into manifest death,—offering him no other fame in the world than that of lack of counsel, and poor generalship, and who, had he lived, would probably have suffered the greater part of the Roman ter-

From *Ecclesiastical History*, bk. 5, chaps. 1, 3–5, in *Nicene and Post-Nicene Fathers*, 2d ser., vol. 2 (New York: Christian Literature Co., 1890), pp. 327–30.

ritories to fall under the Persian yoke. This observation, however, is only inserted lest I should be blamed for omitting it. I leave every one to form his own opinion. . . .

3. Julian, on His Settlement in the Empire, Began Quietly to Stir Up Opposition to Christianity, and to Introduce Paganism Artfully.

When Julian found himself sole possessor of the empire, he commanded that all the pagan temples should be reopened throughout the East; that those which had been neglected should be repaired; that those which had fallen into ruins should be rebuilt, and that the altars should be restored. He assigned considerable money for this purpose; he restored the customs of antiquity and the ancestral ceremonies in the cities, and the practice of offering sacrifice.

He himself offered libations openly and publicly sacrificed; bestowed honors on those who were zealous in the performance of these ceremonies; restored the initiators and the priests, the hierophants and the servants of the images, to their old privileges; and confirmed the legislation of former emperors in their behalf; he conceded exemption from duties and from other burdens as was their previous right; he restored the provisions, which had been abolished, to the temple guardians, and commanded them to be pure from meats, and to abstain from whatever according to pagan saying was befitting him who had announced his purpose of leading a pure life.

He also ordered that the nilometer and the symbols and the former ancestral tablets should be cared for in the temple of Serapis, instead of being deposited, according to the regulation, established by Constantine, in the church. He wrote frequently to the inhabitants of those cities in which he knew paganism was nourished, and urged them to ask what gifts they might desire. Towards the Christians, on the contrary, he openly manifested his aversion, refusing to honor them with his presence, or to receive their deputies who were delegated to report about grievances.

When the inhabitants of Nisibis sent to implore his aid against the Persians, who were on the point of invading the Roman territories, he refused to assist them because they were wholly Christianized, and would neither reopen their temples nor resort to the sacred places; he threatened that he would not help them, nor receive their embassy, nor approach to enter their city before he should hear that they had returned to paganism.

He likewise accused the inhabitants of Constantia in Palestine, of attachment to Christianity, and rendered their city tributary to that of Gaza. Constantia, as we stated before, was formerly called Majuma, and was used as a harbor for the vessels of Gaza; but on hearing that the majority of its inhabitants were Christians, Constantine elevated it to the dignity of a city, and conferred upon it the name of his own son, and a separate form of government; for he considered that it ought not to be dependent on Gaza, a city addicted to pagan rites. On the accession of Julian, the citizens of Gaza went to law against those of Constantia. The emperor himself sat as judge, and commanded that Constantia should be an appendage to that city, although it was situated at a distance of twenty stadia.

Its former name having been abolished by him, it has since been denominated the maritime region of Gaza. They have now the same city magistrates, military officers, and public regulations. With respect to ecclesiastical concerns, however, they may still be regarded as two cities. They have each their own bishop and their own clergy; they celebrate festivals in honor of their respective martyrs, and in memory of the priests who successively ruled them; and the boundaries of the adjacent fields by which the altars belonging to the bishops are divided, are still preserved.

It happened within our own remembrance that an attempt was made by the bishop of Gaza, on the death of the president of the church at Majuma, to unite the clergy of that town with those under his own jurisdiction; and the plea he advanced was, that it was not lawful for two bishops to preside over one city. The inhabitants of Majuma opposed this scheme, and the council of the province took cognizance of the dispute, and ordained another bishop. The council decided that it was altogether right for those who had been deemed worthy of the honors of a city on account of their piety, not to be deprived of the privilege conferred upon the priesthood and rank of their churches, through the decision of a pagan emperor, who had taken a different ground of action.

But these events occurred at a later period than that now under review.

4. Julian Inflicted Evils upon the Inhabitants of Caesarea. Bold Fidelity of Maris, Bishop of Chalcedon.

About the same time, the emperor erased Caesarea, the large and wealthy metropolis of Cappadocia, situated near Mount Argeus, from the catalogue of cities, and even deprived it of the name of Caesarea, which had been conferred upon it during the reign of Claudius Caesar, its former name having been Mazaca. He had long regarded the inhabitants of this city with extreme aversion, because they were zealously attached to Christianity, and had formerly destroyed the temple of the ancestral Apollo and that of Jupiter, the tutelar deity of the city. The temple dedicated to Fortune, the only one remaining in the city, was overturned by the Christians after his accession; and on hearing of the deed, he hated the entire city intensely and could scarce endure it. He also blamed the pagans, who were few in number, but who ought, he said, to have hastened to the temple, and, if necessary, to have suffered cheerfully for Fortune. He caused all possessions and money belonging to the churches of the city and suburbs of Caesarea to be rigorously sought out and carried away; about three hundred pounds of gold, obtained from this source, were conveyed to the public treasury. He also commanded that all the clergy should be enrolled among the troops under the governor of the province, which is accounted the most arduous and least honorable service among the Romans.

He ordered the Christian populace to be numbered, women and children inclusive, and imposed taxes upon them as onerous as those to which villages are subjected.

He further threatened that, unless their temples were speedily re-erected, his wrath would not be appeased, but would be visited on the city, until none of the Galileans remained in existence; for this was the name which, in derision, he was wont to give to the Christians. There is no doubt but that his menaces would have been fully executed had not death quickly intervened.

It was not from any feeling of compassion towards the Christians that he treated them at first with greater humanity than had been evinced by former persecutors, but because he had discovered that paganism had derived no advantage from their tortures, while Christianity had been especially increased, and had become more honored by the fortitude of those who died in defense of the faith.

It was simply from envy of their glory, that instead of employing fire and the sword against them, and maltreating their bodies like former persecutors, and instead of casting them into the sea, or burying them alive in order to compel them to a change of sentiment, he had recourse to argument and persuasion, and sought by these means to reduce them to paganism; he expected to gain his ends more easily by abandoning all violent measures, and by the manifestation of unexpected benevolence. It is said that on one occasion, when he was sacrificing in the temple of Fortune at Constantinople, Maris, bishop of Chalcedon, presented himself before him, and publicly rebuked him as an irreligious man, an atheist, and an apostate. Julian had nothing in return to reproach him with except his blindness, for his sight was impaired by old age, and he was led by a child. According to his usual custom of uttering blasphemies against Christ, Julian afterward added in derision, "The Galilean, thy God, will not cure thee." Maris replied, "I thank God for my blindness, since it prevents me from beholding one who has fallen away from our religion." Julian passed on without giving a reply, for he considered that paganism would be more advanced by a personal and unexpected exhibition of patience and mildness towards Christians.

5. Julian Restores Liberty to the Christians, in Order to Execute Further Troubles in the Church. The Evil Treatment of Christians He Devised.

It was from these motives that Julian recalled from exile all Christians who, during the reign of Constantius, had been banished on account of their religious sentiments, and restored to them their property that had been confiscated by law. He charged the people not to commit any act of injustice against the Christians, not to insult them, and not to constrain them to offer sacrifice unwillingly. He commanded that if they should of their own accord desire to draw near the altars, they were first to appease the wrath of the demons, whom the pagans regard as capable of averting evil, and to purify themselves by the customary course of expiations. He deprived the clergy, however, of the immunities, honors, and provisions which Constantine had conferred; repealed the laws which had been enacted in their favor, and reinforced their statute liabilities. He even compelled the virgins and widows, who, on account of their poverty, were reckoned among the clergy, to refund the provision which had been assigned them from public sources. For when Constantine adjusted the temporal concerns of the Church, he devoted a sufficient portion of the taxes raised upon every city, to the support of the clergy everywhere; and to ensure the stability of ths arrangement he enacted a law which has continued in force from the death of Julian to the present day. They say these transactions were very cruel and rigorous, as appears by the receipts given by the receivers of the money to those from whom it had been extorted, and which were designed to show that the property received in accordance with the law of Constantine had been refunded.

Nothing, however, could diminish the enmity of the ruler against religion. In the intensity of his hatred against the faith, he seized every opportunity to ruin the Church. He deprived it of its property, votives, and sacred vessels, and condemned those who had demolished temples during the reign of Constantine and Constantius, to rebuild them, or to defray the expenses of their re-erection. On this ground, since they were unable to pay the sums and also on account of the inquisition for sacred money, many of the priests, clergy, and the other Christians were cruelly tortured and cast into prison.

It may be concluded from what has been said, that if Julian shed less blood than preceding persecutors of the Church, and that if he devised fewer punishments for the torture of the body, yet that he was severer in other respects; for he appears as inflicting evil upon it in every way, except that he recalled the priests who had been condemned to banishment by the Emperor Constantius; but it is said he issued this order in their behalf, not out of mercy, but that through contention among themselves, the churches might be involved in fraternal strife, and might fail of her own rights, or because he wanted to asperse Constantius; for he supposed that he could render the dead monarch odious to almost all his subjects, by favoring the pagans who were of the same sentiments as himself, and by showing compassion to those who had suffered for Christ, as having been treated unjustly. He expelled the eunuchs from the palaces, because the late emperor had been well affected towards them. He condemned Eusebius, the governor of the imperial court, to death, from a suspicion he entertained that it was at his suggestion that Gallus his brother had been slain. He recalled Aetius, the leader of the Eunomian heresy, from the region whither Constantius had banished him, who had been otherwise suspected on account of his intimacy with Gallus; and to him Julian sent letters full of benignity, and furnished him with public conveyances. For a similar reason he condemned Eleusius, bishop of Cyzicus, under the heaviest penalty, to rebuild, within two months, and at his own expense, a church belonging to the Novatians which he had destroyed under Constantius. Many other things might be found which he did from hatred to his predecessor, either himself effecting these or permitting others to accomplish them.

8. *Codex Theodosianus*, 16.1.2

Emperors Gratian, Valentinian, and Theodosius Augustuses: An Edict to the People of the City of Constantinople

It is Our will that all the peoples who are ruled by the administration of Our Clemency shall practice that religion which the divine Peter the Apostle transmitted to the Romans, as the religion which he introduced makes clear even unto this day. It is evident that this is the religion that is followed by the Pontiff Damasus and by Peter, Bishop of Alexandria, a man of apostolic sanctity; that is, according to the apostolic discipline and the evangelic doctrine, we shall believe in the single Deity of the Father, the Son, and the Holy Spirit, under the concept of equal majesty and of the Holy Trinity.

I. We command that those persons who follow this rule shall embrace the name of Catholic Christians. The rest, however, whom We adjudge demented and insane, shall sustain the infamy of heretical dogmas, their meeting places shall not receive the name of churches, and they shall be

From *The Theodosian Code and Novels and the Sirmondian Constitutions*, translated by Clyde Pharr (Princeton: Princeton University Press, 1952), p. 440. © 1952 by Clyde Pharr; © renewed 1980 by Roy Pharr. All footnotes deleted. Reprinted by permission of the publisher.

smitten first by divine vengeance and secondly by the retribution of Our own initiative, which We shall assume in accordance with the divine judgment.

Given on the third day before the kalends of March at Thessalonica in the year of the fifth consulship of Gratian Augustus and the first consulship of Theodosius Augustus. [February 28, 380.]

9. Augustine, *Letter 185: On the Correction of the Donatists*

Chaps. 5, 19

But as to the argument of those men who are unwilling that their impious deeds should be checked by the enactment of righteous laws, when they say that the apostles never sought such measures from the kings of the earth, they do not consider the different character of that age, and that everything comes in its own season. For what emperor had as yet believed in Christ, so as to serve Him in the cause of piety by enacting laws against impiety, when as yet the declaration of the prophet was only in the course of its fulfillment, "Why do the heathen rage, and the people imagine a vain thing? The kings of the earth set themselves, and their rulers take counsel together, against the Lord, and against His Anointed;" and there was as yet no sign of that which is spoken a little later in the same psalm: "Be wise now, therefore, O ye kings; be instructed, ye judges of the earth. Serve the Lord with fear, and rejoice with trembling." [1] How then are kings to serve the Lord with fear, except by preventing and chastising with religious severity all those acts which are done in opposition to the commandments of the Lord? For a man serves God in one way in that he is man, in another way in that he is also king. In that he is man, he serves Him by living faithfully; but in that he is also king, he serves Him by enforcing with suitable rigor such laws as ordain what is righteous, and punish what is the reverse. Even as Hezekiah served Him, by destroying the groves and the temples of the idols, and the high places which had been built in violation of the commandments of God; [2] or even as Josiah served Him, by doing the same things in his turn; [3] or as the king of the Ninevites served Him, by compelling all the men of his city to make satisfaction to the Lord; [4] or as Darius served Him, by giving the idol into the power of Daniel to be broken, and

---

From *On the Correction of the Donatists*, chaps. 5.19–6.24, in *Nicene and Post-Nicene Fathers*, vol. 4 (Buffalo, N. Y.: Christian Literature Co., 1887), pp. 640–42.

1. Ps. 2:1, 2, 10, 11.   3. 2 Kings 23:4, 5.
2. 2 Kings 18:4.   4. Jonah 3:6–9.

by casting his enemies into the den of lions;[5] or as Nebuchadnezzar served Him, of whom I have spoken before, by issuing a terrible law to prevent any of his subjects from blaspheming God.[6] In this way, therefore, kings can serve the Lord, even in so far as they are kings, when they do in His service what they could not do were they not kings.

20

Seeing, then, that the kings of the earth were not yet serving the Lord in the time of the apostles, but were still imagining vain things against the Lord and against His Anointed, that all might be fulfilled which was spoken by the prophets, it must be granted that at that time acts of impiety could not possibly be prevented by the laws, but were rather performed under their sanction. For the order of events was then so rolling on, that even the Jews were killing those who preached Christ, thinking that they did God service in so doing, just as Christ had foretold,[7] and the heathen were raging against the Christians, and the patience of the martyrs was overcoming them all. But so soon as the fulfillment began of what is written in a later psalm, "All kings shall fall down before Him; all nations shall serve Him,"[8] what sober-minded man could say to the kings, "Let not any thought trouble you within your kingdom as to who restrains or attacks the Church of your Lord; deem it not a matter in which you should be concerned, which of your subjects may choose to be religious or sacrilegious," seeing that you cannot say to them, "Deem it no concern of yours which of your subjects may choose to be chaste, or which unchaste"? For why, when free-will is given by God to man, should adulteries be punished by the laws, and sacrilege allowed? Is it a lighter matter that a soul should not keep faith with God, than that a woman should be faithless to her husband? Or if those faults which are committed not in contempt but in ignorance of religious truth are to be visited with lighter punishment, are they therefore to be neglected altogether?

Chaps. 6, 21

It is indeed better (as no one ever could deny) that men should be led to worship God by teaching, than that they should be driven to it by fear of punishment or pain; but it does not follow that because the former course produces the better men, therefore those who do not yield to it should be

---

5. Bel and Drag. vv. 22, 42.
6. Dan. 3:29.

7. John 16:2.
8. Ps. 72:11.

neglected. For many have found advantage (as we have proved, and are daily proving by actual experiment), in being first compelled by fear or pain, so that they might afterwards be influenced by teaching, or might follow out in act what they had already learned in word. Some, indeed, set before us the sentiments of a certain secular author, who said,

'Tis well, I ween, by shame the young to train,
And dread of meanness, rather than by pain.[9]

This is unquestionably true. But while those are better who are guided aright by love, those are certainly more numerous who are corrected by fear. For, to answer these persons out of their own author, we find him saying in another place,

Unless by pain and suffering thou art taught,
Thou canst not guide thyself aright in aught.[10]

But, moreover, holy Scripture has both said concerning the former better class, "There is no fear in love; but perfect love casteth out fear;"[11] and also concerning the latter lower class, which furnishes the majority, "A servant will not be corrected by words; for though he understand, he will not answer."[12] In saying, "He will not be corrected by words," he did not order him to be left to himself, but implied an admonition as to the means whereby he ought to be corrected; otherwise he would not have said, "He will not be corrected by words," but without any qualification, "He will not be corrected." For in another place he says that not only the servant, but also the undisciplined son, must be corrected with stripes, and that with great fruits as the result; for he says, "Thou shalt beat him with the rod, and shalt deliver his soul from hell;"[13] and elsewhere he says, "He that spareth the rod hateth his son."[14] For, give us a man who with right faith and true understanding can say with all the energy of his heart, "My soul thirsteth for God, for the living God: when shall I come and appear before God?"[15] and for such an one there is no need of the terror of hell, to say nothing of temporal punishments or imperial laws, seeing that with him it is so indispensable a blessing to cleave unto the Lord, that he not only dreads being parted from that happiness as a heavy punishment, but can scarcely even bear delay in its attainment. But yet, before the good sons can say they have "a desire to depart, and to be with Christ,"[16] many must

---

9. Ter. *Adelph.* act I. sc. 1. 32, 33.

10. This is not found in the extant plays of Terence.

11. 1 John 4:18.

12. Prov. 29:19.

13. Prov. 23:14.

14. Prov. 13:24.

15. Ps. 42:2.

16. Phil. 1:23.

first be recalled to their Lord by the stripes of temporal scourging, like evil slaves, and in some degree like good-for-nothing fugitives.

22

For who can possibly love us more than Christ, who laid down His life for His sheep?[17] And yet, after calling Peter and the other apostles by His words alone, when He came to summon Paul, who was before called Saul, subsequently the powerful builder of His Church, but originally its cruel persecutor, He not only constrained him with His voice, but even dashed him to the earth with His power; and that He might forcibly bring one who was raging amid the darkness of infidelity to desire the light of the heart, He first struck him with physical blindness of the eyes. If that punishment had not been inflicted, he would not afterwards have been healed by it; and since he had been wont to see nothing with his eyes open, if they had remained unharmed, the Scripture would not tell us that at the imposition of Ananias' hands, in order that their sight might be restored, there fell from them as it had been scales, by which the sight had been obscured.[18] Where is what the Donatists were wont to cry: Man is at liberty to believe or not believe? Towards whom did Christ use violence? Whom did He compel? Here they have the Apostle Paul. Let them recognize in his case Christ first compelling, and afterwards teaching; first striking, and afterwards consoling. For it is wonderful how he who entered the service of the gospel in the first instance under the compulsion of bodily punishment, afterwards labored more in the gospel than all they who were called by word only;[19] and he who was compelled by the greater influence of fear to love, displayed that perfect love which casts out fear.

23

Why, therefore, should not the Church use force in compelling her lost sons to return, if the lost sons compelled others to their destruction? Although even men who have not been compelled, but only led astray, are received by their loving mother with more affection if they are recalled to her bosom through the enforcement of terrible but salutary laws, and are the objects of far more deep congratulation than those whom she had never lost. Is it not a part of the care of the shepherd, when any sheep have left the flock, even though not violently forced away, but led astray by tender words and coaxing blandishments, to bring them back to the fold of his master when he has

17. John 10:15.   19. 1 Cor. 15:10.
18. Acts 9:1–18.

found them, by the fear or even the pain of the whip, if they show symptoms of resistance; especially since, if they multiply with growing abundance among the fugitive slaves and robbers, he has the more right in that the mark of the master is recognized on them, which is not outraged in those whom we receive but do not rebaptize? For the wandering of the sheep is to be corrected in such wise that the mark of the Redeemer should not be destroyed on it. For even if any one is marked with the royal stamp by a deserter who is marked with it himself, and the two receive forgiveness, and the one returns to his service, and the other begins to be in the service in which he had no part before, that mark is not effaced in either of the two, but rather it is recognized in both of them, and approved with the honor which is due to it because it is the king's. Since then they cannot show that the destination is bad to which they are compelled, they maintain that they ought to be compelled by force even to what is good. But we have shown that Paul was compelled by Christ; therefore the Church, in trying to compel the Donatists, is following the example of her Lord, though in the first instance she waited in the hopes of needing to compel no one, that the prediction of the prophet might be fulfilled concerning the faith of kings and peoples.

24

For in this sense also we may interpret without absurdity the declaration of the blessed Apostle Paul, when he says, "Having in a readiness to revenge all disobedience, when your obedience is fulfilled." [20] Whence also the Lord Himself bids the guests in the first instance to be invited to His great supper, and afterwards compelled; for on His servants making answer to Him, "Lord, it is done as Thou hast commanded, and yet there is room," He said to them, "Go out into the highways and hedges, and compel them to come in." [21] In those, therefore, who were first brought in with gentleness, the former obedience is fulfilled; but in those who were compelled, the disobedience is avenged. For what else is the meaning of "Compel them to come in," after it had previously said, "Bring in," and the answer had been made, "Lord, it is done as Thou commanded, and yet there is room"? If He had wished it to be understood that they were to be compelled by the terrifying force of miracles, many divine miracles were rather wrought in the sight of those who were first called, especially in the sight of the Jews, of whom it was said, "The Jews require a sign;" [22] and, moreover, among the Gentiles themselves the gospel was so commended

20. 2 Cor. 10:6.   22. 1 Cor. 1:22.
21. Luke 14:22, 23.

by miracles in the time of the apostles, that had these been the means by which they were ordered to be compelled, we might rather have had good grounds for supposing, as I said before, that it was the earlier guests who were compelled. Wherefore, if the power which the Church has received by divine appointment in its due season, through the religious character and the faith of kings, be the instrument by which those who are found in the highways and hedges—that is, in heresies and schisms—are compelled to come in, then let them not find fault with being compelled, but consider whether they be so compelled. The supper of the Lord is the unity of the body of Christ, not only in the sacrament of the altar, but also in the bond of peace.

3
Relations between Church Government and Imperial Administration

The mutual assimilation of Church and Empire stirred up controversies, some of which have continued unabated to the present day. One such conflict centered on what is now known as the relation between Church and State. So long as emperors were non-Christian, and, especially, so long as the Empire persecuted the Church, the right and duty of the civil ruler to intervene in Church affairs were not issues. It was enough to point out that the Empire originated in human institutions, contaminated by sin, while the Church had been established by God directly to be His "holy nation" and "royal priesthood." However, beginning with the conversion of Constantine the Great to Christianity (312/3), imperial intervention in matters previously reserved to ecclesiastical judgment became chronic. The following documents indicate the spectrum of positions taken. They culminate in what came to be the classic statement on the subject, Pope Gelasius I's highly problematic declaration that the world was governed by two offices, the episcopal and the imperial. Each, he said, was supreme in its own sphere, though the spiritual office was the higher in intangible dignity.

Eusebius of Caesarea's *Life of Constantine the Great* is a composite of texts written in the 320s and 330s. Eusebius experienced and profited from the abrupt change brought about by Constantine's conversion to Christianity. Instead of being persecuted, Christians were raised to imperial favor. They saw magnificent churches built, the clergy exalted with wealth and privilege, and, most delightful of all, their patron, Constantine, crushing his pagan rivals into the dust. Suspending his critical faculties, Eusebius portrayed Constantine as a "friend of God," recipient of divine revelations, and mediator between God and men. Laying up a dangerous precedent for the future, he justified the forceful intervention by the Emperor in matters of faith and order. (On Eusebius, see Introduction to topic 2.)

The excerpts from Athanasius's *History of the Arians*, included above as document 6 in topic 2, are also relevant here. They illustrate how powerfully Constantine the Great's son and successor, Constantius II (337–361) continued to intervene in the paramount concerns of the Church and to force bishops into compliance with his personal commitments. (See also the general comment regarding this document and its author in the Introduction to topic 2.)

Formerly an imperial governor, Bishop Ambrose of Milan (339–397) was suddenly elected by popular acclaim, and against his own will, as bishop. Though he had not even been baptized at the time of his election, he was even then living according to norms of ascetic Christianity then practiced in Egypt, and his knowledge of Alexandrine theology (both Jewish and Christian) later made him an important conveyer of eastern thought and discipline into the mainstream of Latin Christianity. As a spokesman for the Church, he had numerous occasions to rebuke emperors whom, had he remained governor, he would have served. One such occasion occurred in 390, when Theodosius I (379–395) avenged an affront to imperial order by commanding a massacre of the people of Thessaloniki. In the letter included below, as so often, Ambrose argued that the emperor was within, not above, the Church, a direct reversal of the position stated by Eusebius of Caesarea.

Codex Theodosianus, 16.2.41 is a decree issued by the son and grandson of Theodosius I, the co-emperors Honorius and Theodosius II, in 411/412. It confirms the crucial right that came to be called "privilege of clergy": namely, the right of clerics to be tried by ecclesiastical rather than by civil courts. This decree was an important step toward constructing the Church hierarchy as a "state within the state."

Like all the other Latin Fathers—Ambrose, Augustine of Hippo, and Pope Gregory I—Jerome (about 347–420) launched his ecclesiastical career after a spectacular conversion. His early training in the liberal arts and the cheerful, exuberant sins of his youth gave way to a life haunted by guilt, mortification, and sorrow. The still dominant pull of eastern Christianity drew Jerome to Syria and Palestine, where he became a relentless example and advocate of monastic discipline. Jerome made many contributions to Latin Christianity by his translation of the Scriptures into Latin, his treatises and Scriptural commentaries, his scathing controversial writings, and his letters. The letter included below, among the earliest (about 370), illustrates the nature of judicial investigation applied to Christians in the Christian Empire.

Cicero formulated a definition of community, as "commonwealth," appropriate to pagan Rome, and, indeed, to any secular state. Augustine of Hippo's (354–430) extensive critique of that definition, asserting that justice was possible only among orthodox Christians, marks an abrupt break with earlier ways of thinking about the legitimacy of government. It also implies the field of conflict between civil power and religious authority that figured prominently later in European history.

Gelasius I (492–496) was one of the greatest popes in the age of the Church Fathers. He took a forceful part in the virulent theological disputes of his time, which engrossed both the eastern and the western halves of the Empire. His place in the history of political thought was assured by the following letter to the Emperor Anastasius I (496–498), defining an ideal balance between the Church's authority and the Empire's power. The problem lay in finding an actual state of affairs that could correspond with this abstract ideal.

---

10. Eusebius of Caesarea, *Life of Constantine the Great*

Book 1

22

Nor did the imperial throne remain long unoccupied: for Constantine invested himself with his father's purple, and proceeded from his father's palace, presenting to all a renewal, as it were, in his own person, of his father's life and reign. He then conducted the funeral procession in company with his father's friends, some preceding, others following the train, and performed the last offices for the pious deceased with an extraordinary degree of magnificence, and all united in honoring this thrice blessed prince with acclamations and praises, and while with one mind and voice they glorified the rule of the son as a living again of him who was dead, they hastened at once to hail their new sovereign by the titles of Imperial and Worshipful Augustus, with joyful shouts. Thus the memory of the deceased emperor received honor from the praises bestowed upon his son, while the latter was pronounced blessed in being the successor of such a father. All the nations also under his dominion were filled with joy and inexpressible gladness at not being even for a moment deprived of the benefits of a well-ordered government.

From *Life of Constantine the Great*, bk. 1, chaps. 22–40, in *The Nicene and Post-Nicene Fathers*, 2d ser., vol. 1, edited by Philip Schaff and Henry Wale (New York: Christian Literature Co., 1890).

In the instance of the Emperor Constantius, God has made manifest to our generation what the end of those is who in their lives have honored and loved him.

23

With respect to the other princes, who made war against the churches of God, I have not thought it fit in the present work to give any account of their downfall, nor to stain the memory of the good by mentioning them in connection with those of an opposite character. The knowledge of the facts themselves will of itself suffice for the wholesome admonition of those who have witnessed or heard of the evils which severally befell them.

24

Thus then the God of all, the Supreme Governor of the whole universe, by his own will appointed Constantine, the descendant of so renowned a parent, to be prince and sovereign: so that, while others have been raised to this distinction by the election of their fellow-men, he is the only one to whose elevation no mortal may boast of having contributed.

25

As soon then as he was established on the throne, he began to care for the interests of his paternal inheritance, and visited with much considerate kindness all those provinces which had previously been under his father's government. Some tribes of the barbarians who dwelt on the banks of the Rhine, and the shores of the Western ocean, having ventured to revolt, he reduced them all to obedience, and brought them from their savage state to one of gentleness. He contented himself with checking the inroads of others, and drove from his dominions, like untamed and savage beasts, those whom he perceived to be altogether incapable of the settled order of civilized life. Having disposed of these affairs to his satisfaction, he directed his attention to other quarters of the world, and first passed over to the British nations, which lie in the very bosom of the ocean. These he reduced to submission, and then proceeded to consider the state of the remaining portions of the empire, that he might be ready to tender his aid wherever circumstances might require it.

26

While, therefore, he regarded the entire world as one immense body, and perceived that the head of it all, the royal city of the Roman empire, was bowed down by the weight of a tyrannous oppression; at first he had left the task of liberation to those who governed the other divisions of the empire, as being his superiors in point of age. But when none of these proved able to afford relief, and those who had attempted it had experienced a disastrous termination of their enterprise, he said that life was without enjoyment to him as long as he saw the imperial city thus afflicted, and prepared himself for the overthrowal of the tyranny.

27

Being convinced, however, that he needed some more powerful aid than his military forces could afford him, on account of the wicked and magical enchantments which were so diligently practiced by the tyrant, he sought Divine assistance, deeming the possession of arms and a numerous soldiery of secondary importance, but believing the co-operating power of Deity invincible and not to be shaken. He considered, therefore, on what God he might rely for protection and assistance. While engaged in this enquiry, the thought occurred to him, that, of the many emperors who had preceded him, those who had rested their hopes in a multitude of gods, and served them with sacrifices and offerings, had in the first place been deceived by flattering predictions, and oracles which promised them all prosperity, and at last had met with an unhappy end, while not one of their gods had stood by to warn them of the impending wrath of heaven; while one alone who had pursued an entirely opposite course, who had condemned their error, and honored the one Supreme God during his whole life, had found him to be the Saviour and Protector of his empire, and the Giver of every good thing. Reflecting on this, and well weighing the fact that they who had trusted in many gods had also fallen by manifold forms of death, without leaving behind them either family or offspring, stock, name, or memorial among men: while the God of his father had given to him, on the other hand, manifestations of his power and very many tokens: and considering farther that those who had already taken arms against the tyrant, and had marched to the battlefield under the protection of a multitude of gods, had met with a dishonorable end (for one of them had shamefully retreated from the contest without a blow, and the other, being slain in the midst of his own troops, became, as it were, the mere sport of death); reviewing, I say, all these considerations, he judged it to be folly indeed to join in the idle worship of those who were no gods, and after such convincing evidence, to err from the truth; and therefore felt it incumbent on him to honor his father's God alone.

28

Accordingly he called on him with earnest prayer and supplications that he would reveal to him who he was, and stretch forth his right hand to help him in his present difficulties. And while he was thus praying with fervent entreaty, a most marvelous sign appeared to him from heaven, the account of which it might have been hard to believe had it been related by any other person. But since the victorious emperor himself long afterwards declared it to the writer of this history, when he was honored with his acquaintance and society, and confirmed his statement by an oath, who could hesitate to accredit the relation, especially since the testimony of after-time has established its truth? He said that about noon, when the day was already beginning to decline, he saw with his own eyes the trophy of a cross of light in the heavens, above the sun, and bearing the inscription, CONQUER BY THIS. At this sight he himself was struck with amazement, and his whole army also, which followed him on this expedition, and witnessed the miracle.

29

He said, moreover, that he doubted within himself what the import of this apparition could be. And while he continued to ponder and reason on its meaning, night suddenly came on; then in his sleep the Christ of God appeared to him with the same sign which he had seen in the heavens, and commanded him to make a likeness of that sign which he had seen in the heavens, and to use it as a safeguard in all engagements with his enemies.

30

At dawn of day he arose, and communicated the marvel to his friends: and then, calling together the workers in gold and precious stones, he sat in the midst of them, and described to them the figure of the sign he had seen, bidding them represent it in gold and precious stones. And this representation I myself have had an opportunity of seeing.

31

Now it was made in the following manner. A long spear, overlaid with gold, formed the figure of the cross by means of a transverse bar laid over it. On the top of the whole was fixed a wreath of gold and precious stones; and within this, the symbol of the Saviour's name, two letters indicating the name of Christ by means of its initial characters, the letter P being intersected by X in its centre: and these letters the emperor was in the habit of wearing on his helmet at a later period. From the cross-bar of the spear was suspended a cloth, a royal piece, covered with a profuse embroidery of most brilliant precious stones; and which, being also richly interlaced with gold, presented an indescribable degree of beauty to the beholder. This banner was of a square form, and the upright staff, whose lower section was of great length, bore a golden half-length portrait of the pious emperor and his children on its upper part, beneath the trophy of the cross, and immediately above the embroidered banner.

The emperor constantly made use of this sign of salvation as a safeguard against every adverse and hostile power, and commanded that others similar to it should be carried at the head of all his armies.

32

These things were done shortly afterwards. But at the time above specified, being struck with amazement at the extraordinary vision, and resolving to worship no other God save Him who had appeared to him, he sent for those who were acquainted with the mysteries of His doctrines, and enquired who that God was, and what was intended by the sign of the vision he had seen.

They affirmed that He was God, the only begotten Son of the one and only God: that the sign which had appeared was the symbol of immortality, and the trophy of that victory over death which He had gained in time past when sojourning on earth. They taught him also the causes of His advent, and explained to him the true account of His incarnation. Thus he was instructed in these matters, and was impressed with wonder at the divine manifestation which had been presented to his sight. Comparing, therefore, the heavenly vision with the interpretation given, he found his judgment confirmed; and, in the persuasion that the knowledge of these things had been imparted to him by Divine teaching, he determined thenceforth to devote himself to the reading of the inspired writings.

Moreover, he made the priests of God his counselors, and deemed it incumbent on him to honor the God who had appeared to him with all devotion. And after this, being fortified by well-grounded hopes in Him, he hastened to quench the threatening fire of tyranny.

33

For he who had tyrannically possessed himself of the imperial city, had proceeded to great lengths in impiety and wickedness, so as to venture without hesitation on every vile and impure action.

For example: he would separate women from their husbands, and after a time send them back to them again, and these insults he offered not to men of mean or obscure condition, but to those who held the first places in the Roman senate. Moreover, though he shamefully dishonored almost numberless free women, he was unable to satisfy his ungoverned and intemperate desires. But when he assayed to corrupt Christian women also, he could no longer secure success to his designs, since they chose rather to submit their lives to death than yield their persons to be defiled by him.

34

Now a certain woman, wife of one of the senators who held the authority of prefect, when she understood that those who ministered to the tyrant in such matters were standing before her house (she was a Christian), and knew that her husband through fear had bidden them take her and lead her away, begged a short space of time for arraying herself in her usual dress, and entered her chamber. There being left alone, she sheathed a sword in her own breast, and immediately expired, leaving indeed her dead body to the procurers, but declaring to all mankind, both to present and future generations, by an act which spoke louder than any words, that the chastity for which Christians are famed is the only thing which is invincible and indestructible. Such was the conduct displayed by this woman.

35

All men, therefore, both people and magistrates, whether of high or low degree, trembled through fear of him whose daring wickedness was such as I have described, and were oppressed by his grievous tyranny. Nay, though they submitted quietly, and endured this bitter servitude, still there was no escape from the tyrant's sanguinary cruelty. For at one time, on some trifling pretence, he exposed the populace to be slaughtered by his own body-guard; and countless multitudes of the Roman people were slain in the very midst of the city by the lances and weapons, not of Scythians or barbarians, but of their own fellow-citizens. And besides this, it is impossible to calculate the number of senators whose blood was shed with a view to the seizure of their respective estates, for at different times and on various fictitious charges, multitudes of them suffered death.

36

But the crowning point of the tyrant's wickedness was his having recourse to sorcery: sometimes for magic purposes ripping up women with child, at other times searching into the bowels of new-born infants. He slew lions also, and practiced certain horrid arts for evoking demons, and averting the approaching war, hoping by these means to get the victory. In short, it is impossible to describe the manifold acts of oppression by which this tyrant of Rome enslaved his subjects: so that by this time they were reduced to the most extreme penury and want of necessary food, a scarcity such as our contemporaries do not remember ever before to have existed at Rome.

37

Constantine, however, filled with compassion on account of all these miseries, began to arm himself with all warlike preparation against the tyranny. Assuming therefore the Supreme God as his patron, and invoking His Christ to be his preserver and aid, and setting the victorious trophy, the salutary symbol, in front of his soldiers and body-guard, he marched with his whole forces, trying to obtain again for the Romans the freedom they had inherited from their ancestors.

And whereas, Maxentius, trusting more in his magic arts than in the affection of his subjects, dared not even advance outside the city gates, but had guarded every place and district and city subject to his tyranny, with large bodies of soldiers, the emperor, confiding in the help of God, advanced against the first and second and third divisions of the tyrant's forces, defeated them all with ease at the first assault, and made his way into the very interior of Italy.

38

And already he was approaching very near Rome itself, when, to save him from the necessity of fighting with all the Romans for the tyrant's sake, God himself drew the tyrant, as it were by secret cords, a long way outside the gates. And now those miracles recorded in Holy Writ, which God of old wrought against the ungodly (discredited by most as fables, yet believed by the faithful), did he in every deed confirm to all alike, believers and unbelievers, who were eye-witnesses of the wonders. For as once in the days of Moses and the Hebrew nation, who were worshipers of God, "Pharaoh's chariots and his host hath he cast into the sea, and his chosen chariot-captains are drowned in the Red Sea,"—so at this time Maxentius, and the soldiers and guards with him, "went down into the depths like stone," when, in his flight before the divinely-aided forces of Constantine, he essayed to cross the river which lay in his way, over which, making a strong bridge of boats, he had framed an engine of destruction, really against himself, but in the hope of ensnaring thereby him who was beloved by God. For his God stood by the one to protect him, while the other, godless, proved to be the miserable contriver of these secret devices to his own ruin. So that one might well say, "He hath made a pit, and digged it, and is fallen into the ditch which he made. His mischief shall return upon his own head, and his violence shall come down upon his own pate." Thus, in the present instance, under divine direction, the machine erected on the bridge, with the ambuscade concealed therein, giving way unexpectedly before the appointed time, the bridge began to sink, and the boats with the men in them went bodily to the bottom. And first the wretch himself, then his armed attendants and guards, even as the sacred oracles had before described, "sank as lead in the mighty waters." So that they who thus obtained victory from God might well, if not in the same words, yet in fact in the same spirit as the people of his great servant Moses, sing and speak as they did concerning the impious tyrant of old: "let us sing unto the Lord, for he hath been glorified exceedingly: the horse and his rider hath he thrown into the sea. He is become my helper and my shield unto salvation." And again, "Who is like unto thee, O Lord, among the gods? who is like thee, glorious in holiness, marvelous in praises, doing wonders?"

39

Having then at this time sung these and suchlike praises to God, the Ruler of all and the Author of victory, after the example of his great servant Moses, Constantine entered the imperial city in triumph. And here the whole body of the senate, and others of rank and distinction in the city, freed as it were from the restraint of a prison, along with the whole Roman populace, their countenances expressive of the gladness of their hearts, received him with acclamations and abounding joy; men, women, and children, with countless multitudes of servants, greeting him as deliverer, preserver, and benefactor, with incessant shouts. But he, being possessed of inward piety toward God, was neither rendered arrogant by these plaudits, nor uplifted by the praises he heard: but, being sensible that he had received help from God, he immediately rendered a thanksgiving to him as the Author of his victory.

40

Moreover, by loud proclamation and monumental inscriptions he made known to all men the salutary symbol, setting up this great trophy of victory over his enemies in the midst of the imperial city, and expressly causing it to be engraven in indelible characters, that the salutary symbol was the safeguard of the Roman government and of the entire empire. Accordingly, he immediately ordered a lofty spear in the figure of a cross to be placed beneath the hand of a statue representing himself, in the most frequented part of Rome, and the following inscription to be engraved on it in the Latin language: BY VIRTUE OF THIS SALUTARY SIGN, WHICH IS THE TRUE TEST OF VALOR, I HAVE PRESERVED AND LIBERATED YOUR CITY FROM THE YOKE OF TYRANNY. I HAVE ALSO SET AT LIBERTY THE ROMAN SENATE AND PEOPLE, AND RESTORED THEM TO THEIR ANCIENT DISTINCTION AND SPLENDOR.

11. Ambrose, *Letter 51: To Theodosius*

Ambrose, Bishop, to His Majesty the Emperor Theodosius

1. Very pleasant to me is the remembrance of your long friendship, and I also bear a grateful sense of those benefits which at my frequent entreaties you have most graciously extended to others. You may be sure then that it could not be from any ungrateful feeling that on your arrival, which I was wont to long for so ardently, I shunned your presence. The motives of my conduct I will now briefly explain.

2. I found that I alone in all your court was denied the natural right of hearing, in order to deprive me of the power of speaking too: for you were frequently displeased at decisions having reached me which were made in your Consistory. Thus I have been debarred from the common privilege of men, though the Lord Jesus says, *Nothing is secret which shall not be made manifest.* Wherefore I did my utmost to obey with reverence your royal will, and I provided both for you and for myself; for you, that you should have no cause of disturbance, to which end I endeavoured that no intelligence should be brought me of the Imperial decrees; and as to myself, I provided against my not seeming to hear, when present, from fear of others, and thus incurring the charge of connivance, and also against hearing in such manner that while my ears were open my mouth must be closed, and I must not utter what I heard, lest I should injure those who had fallen under suspicion of treachery.

3. What then was I to do? was I not to listen? But I could not close my

From *The Letters of Ambrose* (Oxford: James Parker and Co., 1881), pp. 324–29.

ears with the wax of the old tales. Must I disclose what I heard? But then I had reason to fear that the same result which I apprehended from your commands would ensue from my own words; that they might become the cause for bloodshed. Was I then to be silent? But this would be the most miserable of all, for my conscience would be bound, my liberty of speech taken away. And what then of the text, *if the priest warn not the wicked from his wicked way, the wicked man shall die in his iniquity*, but the priest shall be liable to punishment, because he did not warn him?

4. Suffer me, gracious Emperor. You have a zeal for the faith, I own it, you have the fear of God, I confess it; but you have a vehemence of temper, which if soothed may readily be changed into compassion, but if inflamed, becomes so violent that you can scarcely restrain it. If no one will allay it, let no one at least inflame it. To yourself I would willingly trust, for you are wont to exercise self-control, and by your love of mercy to conquer this violence of your nature.

5. This vehemence of yours I have preferred secretly to commend to your consideration, rather than run the risk of rousing it publicly by my acts. And so I have preferred to be lacking somewhat in duty rather than in humility, and that others should complain of my want of priestly authority, rather than that you should find any want of respect in me, who am so devoted to you; and this in order that you may restrain your emotions, and have full power of choosing what counsel to follow. I alleged as my reason bodily sickness, which was in fact severe, and not to be mitigated but by more gentle treatment; still I would rather have died than not have waited two or three days for your arrival. But I could not do so.

6. An act has been committed in the city of Thessalonica, the like of which is not recorded, the perpetration of which I could not prevent, which in my frequent petitions before the court I had declared to be most atrocious, and which by your tardy revocation you have yourself pronounced to be very heinous: such an act as this I could not extenuate. Intelligence of it was first brought to a synod held on the arrival of the Gallican bishops: all present deplored it, no one viewed it leniently; your friendship with Ambrose, so far from excusing your deed, would have even brought a heavier weight of odium on my head, had there been no one found to declare the necessity of your being reconciled to God.

7. Is your Majesty ashamed to do that which the royal Prophet David did, the forefather of Christ according to the flesh? It was told him that a rich man, who had numerous flocks, on the arrival of a guest took a poor man's lamb and killed it, and recognizing in this act his own condemnation, he said, *I have sinned against the Lord.* Let not your Majesty then be impatient at being told, as David was by the prophet, *Thou art the man.* For if you listen thereto obediently and say, *I have sinned against the Lord,* if you

will use those words of the royal Prophet, *O come let us worship and fall down, and kneel before the Lord our Maker*, to you also it shall be said, Because thou repentest, *the Lord hath put away thy sin, thou shalt not die*.

8. Another time, when David had commanded the people to be numbered, his heart smote him, and he said unto the Lord, *I have sinned greatly in that I have done, and now, I beseech thee O Lord, take away the iniquity of thy servant, for I have done very foolishly*. And Nathan the prophet was sent again to him, to offer him three things, to choose one of them, which he would; seven years famine in the land, or to flee three months before his enemies, or three days pestilence in the land. And David said, *I am in a great strait, let us now fall into the hand of the Lord, for His mercies are great, and let me not fall into the hand of man*. His fault lay in wishing to know the number of all the people which were with him, a knowledge which ought to have been reserved for God.

9. And Scripture tells us that when the people were dying, on the very first day and at dinner time, David saw the Angel that smote the people, he said, *Lo, I have sinned and done wickedly; but these sheep, what have they done? let Thine hand, I pray Thee, be against me, and against my father's house*. So the Lord repented, and commanded the Angel to spare the people, and that David should offer sacrifice: for there were then sacrifices for sin, but we have now the sacrifices of penitence. So by that humility he was made more acceptable to God, for it is not wonderful that man should sin, but it is indeed blameable if he do not acknowledge his error, and humble himself before God.

10. Holy Job, himself also powerful in this world, saith, *I covered not my sin, but declared it before all the people*. And to the cruel king Saul Jonathan his son said, *Let not the king sin against his servant, against David*; and *Wherefore then wilt thou sin against innocent blood to slay David without a cause*? For although he was a king he still would have sinned in slaying the innocent. Again when David was possessed of the kingdom, and heard that innocent Abner had been slain by Joab the Captain of his host, he said, *I and my kingdom are guiltless before the Lord for ever from the blood of Abner the son of Ner*, and he fasted for sorrow.

11. This I have written, not to confound you, but that these royal examples may induce you to put away this sin from your kingdom; for this you will do by humbling your soul before God. You are a man; temptation has fallen upon you; vanquish it. Sin is not washed away but by tears and penitence. Neither Angel nor Archangel can do it. The Lord Himself, Who alone can say *I am with you*; even He grants no remission of sin save to the penitent.

12. I advise, I entreat, I exhort, I admonish; for I am grieved that you who were an example of singular piety, who stood so high for clemency,

who would not suffer even single offenders to be put in jeopardy, should not mourn over the death of so many innocent persons. Successful as you have been in battle, and great in other respects, yet mercy was ever the crown of your actions. The devil has envied you your chief excellence: overcome him, while you still have the means. Add not sin to sin by acting in a manner which has injured so many.

13. For my part, debtor as I am to your clemency in all other things; grateful as I must ever be for this clemency, which I have found superior to that of many Emperors and equalled only by one, though I have no ground for charging you with contumacy, I have still reason for apprehension: if you purpose being present, I dare not offer the Sacrifice. That which may not be done when the blood of one innocent person has been shed, may it be done where many have been slain? I trow not.

14. Lastly, I will write with my own hand what I wish should be read by yourself only. As I hope for deliverance from all tribulation from the Lord, it has not been from man, nor by man's agency that this has been forbidden me, but by His own manifest interposition. For in the midst of my anxiety, on the very night whereon I was about to set out, I saw you in a vision coming into the Church, but I was withheld from offering Sacrifice. Other things I pass over, which I might have avoided, but I bore them for your sake, I believe. May the Lord cause all things to turn out peacefully. Our God gives us divers admonitions, by heavenly signs, by prophetic warnings; and by visions vouchsafed even to sinners, He would have us understand that we ought to beseech Him to remove from us commotions, that He would bestow peace on you, our rulers, that the Church, for whose benefit it is that we should have pious and Christian Emperors, may be kept in faith and tranquillity.

15. Doubtless you wish to be approved by God. *To every thing there is a season*, as it is written; *It is time for Thee Lord*, saith the prophet, *to lay to Thine hand*, and, It is an acceptable time to God. You shall make your oblation when you have received permission to sacrifice, when your offering will be pleasing to God. Would it not be a delight to me to enjoy your Majesty's favour, and act in accordance with your will, if the case permitted it? Prayer by itself is a sacrifice; it obtains pardon while the oblation would be rejected, for the former is evidence of humility, the latter of contempt: for God Himself tells us that He prefers the performance of His commandments to sacrifice. God proclaims this, Moses announces it to the people, Paul preaches it to them. Do that which you understand is for the time better. *I will have mercy*, it is said, *and not sacrifice*. Are not those therefore rather to be called Christians who condemn their own sin than those who think to excuse it? *The just accuses himself in the beginning of his*

words. He who, having sinned, accuses himself, not he who praises himself, is just.

16. I would that previously to this I had trusted rather to myself than to your accustomed habits. Remembering that you quickly pardon, and revoke your sentence, as you have often done, you have been anticipated, and I have not shunned that which I had no need to fear. But thanks to the Lord, Who chastises His servants, that they may not be lost. This I share with the prophets, and you shall share it with the saints.

17. Shall not I value the father of Gratian at more than my own eyes? Your other sacred pledges too claim pardon for you. On those whom I regarded with impartial affection I conferred by anticipation a name that is dear to me. You have my love, my affection, my prayers. If you believe my words, I call on you to act according to them; if, I say, you believe, acknowledge it, but if not, excuse my conduct in that I prefer God to my sovereign. May your gracious Majesty, with your holy offspring, enjoy in happiness and prosperity perpetual peace.

12. *Codex Theodosianus*, 16.2.41

The same Augustuses [Honorius and Theodosius II] to Melitius, Praetorian Prefect.

Clerics must not be accused except before bishops. Therefore, if a bishop, a priest, a deacon, or any person of inferior rank who is a minister of the Christian faith should be accused by any person whatever before the bishops, since he must not be accused elsewhere, that man, whether of lofty honor or of any other dignity, who may undertake such a laudable type of suit, shall know that he must allege only what may be demonstrated by proofs and supported by documents. If any man, therefore, should lodge unprovable complaints about such persons, he shall understand that by the authority of this sanction he will be subject to the loss of his own reputation, and thus by the loss of his honor and the forfeiture of his status he shall learn that he will not be permitted, for the future at least, to assail with impunity the respect due to another. For, just as it is equitable that bishops, priests, deacons, and all other clerics should be removed from the venerable Church as persons attainted if the allegations against them can be proved, so that they shall be despised thereafter and bowed under the contempt of wretched humiliation and shall not have an action for slander,

From *The Theodosian Code and Novels and the Sirmondian Constitutions*, translated by Clyde Pharr (Princeton: Princeton University Press, 1952), p. 447. © 1952 by Clyde Pharr; © renewed 1980 by Roy Pharr. All footnotes deleted. Reprinted by permission of the publisher.

so it must appear to be an act of similar justice that We have ordered an appropriate punishment for assailed innocence. Bishops, therefore, must hear such cases only under the attestation of many persons and in formal proceedings.

Given on the third day before the ides of December at Ravenna in the year of the ninth consulship of Honorius Augustus and the fifth consulship of Theodosius Augustus. [December 11, 412; 411.]

13. Jerome, *Letter 1: To Innocent*

1. You have frequently asked me, dearest Innocent, not to pass over in silence the marvellous event which has happened in our own day. I have declined the task from modesty and, as I now feel, with justice, believing myself to be incapable of it, at once because human language is inadequate to the divine praise, and because inactivity, acting like rust upon the intellect, has dried up any little power of expression that I have ever had. You in reply urge that in the things of God we must look not at the work which we are able to accomplish, but at the spirit in which it is undertaken, and that he can never be at a loss for words who has believed on the Word.

2. What, then, must I do? The task is beyond me, and yet I dare not decline it. I am a mere unskilled passenger, and I find myself placed in charge of a freighted ship. I have not so much as handled a rowboat on a lake, and now I have to trust myself to the noise and turmoil of the Euxine. I see the shores sinking beneath the horizon, "sky and sea on every side"; darkness lowers over the water, the clouds are black as night, the waves only are white with foam. You urge me to hoist the swelling sails, to loosen the sheets, and to take the helm. At last I obey your commands, and as charity can do all things, I will trust in the Holy Ghost to guide my course, and I shall console myself, whatever the event. For, if our ship is wafted by the surf into the wished-for haven, I shall be content to be told that the pilotage was poor. But, if through my unpolished diction we run aground amid the rough cross-currents of language, you may blame my lack of power, but you will at least recognize my good intentions.

3. To begin, then: Vercellae is a Ligurian town, situated not far from the base of the Alps, once important, but now sparsely peopled and fallen into decay. When the consular was holding his visitation there, a poor woman and her paramour were brought before him—the charge of adultery had been fastened upon them by the husband—and were both consigned to the penal horrors of a prison. Shortly after an attempt was made to elicit the

From *Nicene and Post-Nicene Fathers*, 2d ser., vol. 6 (New York: Christian Literature Co., 1893), pp. 1–4.

truth by torture, and when the blood-stained hook smote the young man's livid flesh and tore furrows in his side, the unhappy wretch sought to avoid prolonged pain by a speedy death. Falsely accusing his own passions, he involved another in the charge; and it appeared that he was of all men the most miserable, and that his execution was just inasmuch as he had left to an innocent woman no means of self-defence. But the woman, stronger in virtue if weaker in sex, though her frame was stretched upon the rack, and though her hands, stained with the filth of the prison, were tied behind her, looked up to heaven with her eyes, which alone the torturer had been unable to bind, and while the tears rolled down her face, said: "Thou art witness, Lord Jesus, to whom nothing is hid, who triest the reins and the heart.[1] Thou art witness that it is not to save my life that I deny this charge. I refuse to lie because to lie is sin. And as for you, unhappy man, if you are bent on hastening your death, why must you destroy not one innocent person, but two? I also, myself, desire to die. I desire to put off this hated body, but not as an adulteress. I offer my neck; I welcome the shining sword without fear; yet I will take my innocence with me. He does not die who is slain while purposing so to live."

4. The consular, who had been feasting his eyes upon the bloody spectacle, now, like a wild beast, which after once tasting blood always thirsts for it, ordered the torture to be doubled, and cruelly gnashing his teeth, threatened the executioner with like punishment if he failed to extort from the weaker sex a confession which a man's strength had not been able to keep back.

5. Send help, Lord Jesus. For this one creature of Thine every species of torture is devised. She is bound by the hair to a stake, her whole body is fixed more firmly than ever on the rack; fire is brought and applied to her feet; her sides quiver beneath the executioner's probe; even her breasts do not escape. Still the woman remains unshaken; and, triumphing in spirit over the pain of the body, enjoys the happiness of a good conscience, round which the tortures rage in vain. The cruel judge rises, overcome with passion. She still prays to God. Her limbs are wrenched from their sockets; she only turns her eyes to heaven. Another confesses what is thought their common guilt. She, for the confessor's sake, denies the confession, and, in peril of her own life, clears one who is in peril of his.

6. Meantime she has but one thing to say: "Beat me, burn me, tear me, if you will; I have not done it. If you will not believe my words, a day will come when this charge shall be carefully sifted. I have One who will judge me." Wearied out at last, the torturer sighed in response to her groans; nor could he find a spot on which to inflict a fresh wound. His cruelty over-

1. Ps. 7:9.

come, he shuddered to see the body he had torn. Immediately the consular cried, in a fit of passion, "Why does it surprise you, bystanders, that a woman prefers torture to death? It takes two people, most assuredly, to commit adultery; and I think it more credible that a guilty woman should deny a sin than that an innocent young man should confess one."

7. Like sentence, accordingly, was passed on both, and the condemned pair were dragged to execution. The entire people poured out to see the sight; indeed, so closely were the gates thronged by the outrushing crowd, that you might have fancied the city itself to be migrating. At the very first stroke of the sword the head of the hapless youth was cut off, and the headless trunk rolled over in its blood. Then came the woman's turn. She knelt down upon the ground, and the shining sword was lifted over her quivering neck. But though the headsman summoned all his strength into his bared arm, the moment it touched her flesh the fatal blade stopped short, and, lightly glancing over the skin, merely grazed it sufficiently to draw blood. The striker saw, with terror, his hand unnerved, and, amazed at his defeated skill and at his drooping sword, he whirled it aloft for another stroke. Again the blade fell forceless on the woman, sinking harmlessly on her neck, as though the steel feared to touch her. The enraged and panting officer, who had thrown open his cloak at the neck to give his full strength to the blow, shook to the ground the brooch which clasped the edges of his mantle, and not noticing this, began to poise his sword for a fresh stroke. "See," cried the woman, "a jewel has fallen from your shoulder. Pick up what you have earned by hard toil, that you may not lose it."

8. What, I ask, is the secret of such confidence as this? Death draws near, but it has no terrors for her. When smitten she exults, and the executioner turns pale. Her eyes see the brooch, they fail to see the sword. And, as if intrepidity in the presence of death were not enough, she confers a favor upon her cruel foe. And now the mysterious Power of the Trinity rendered even a third blow vain. The terrified soldier, no longer trusting the blade, proceeded to apply the point to her throat, in the idea that though it might not cut, the pressure of his hand might plunge it into her flesh. Marvel unheard of through all the ages! The sword bent back to the hilt, and in its defeat looked to its master, as if confessing its inability to slay.

9. Let me call to my aid the example of the three children,[2] who, amid the cool, encircling fire, sang hymns,[3] instead of weeping, and around whose turbans and holy hair the flames played harmlessly. Let me recall, too, the story of the blessed Daniel,[4] in whose presence, though he was their natural prey, the lions crouched, with fawning tails and frightened

---

2. Shadrach, Meshach and Abednego.   4. Dan. 6.
3. Song of the Three Holy Children.

mouths. Let Susannah also rise in the nobility of her faith before the thoughts of all; who, after she had been condemned by an unjust sentence, was saved through a youth inspired by the Holy Ghost.[5] In both cases the Lord's mercy was alike shewn; for while Susannah was set free by the judge, so as not to die by the sword, this woman, though condemned by the judge, was acquitted by the sword.

10. Now at length the populace rise in arms to defend the woman. Men and women of every age join in driving away the executioner, shouting round him in a surging crowd. Hardly a man dares trust his own eyes. The disquieting news reaches the city close at hand, and the entire force of constables is mustered. The officer who is responsible for the execution of criminals bursts from among his men, and

"Staining his hoary hair with soiling dust,"

exclaims: "What! citizens, do you mean to seek my life? Do you intend to make me a substitute for her? However much your minds are set on mercy, and however much you wish to save a condemned woman, yet assuredly I—I who am innocent—ought not to perish." His tearful appeal tells upon the crowd, they are all benumbed by the influence of sorrow, and an extraordinary change of feeling is manifested. Before it had seemed a duty to plead for the woman's life, now it seemed a duty to allow her to be executed.

11. Accordingly a new sword is fetched, a new headsman appointed. The victim takes her place, once more strengthened only with the favor of Christ. The first blow makes her quiver, beneath the second she sways to and fro, by the third she falls wounded to the ground. Oh, majesty of the divine power highly to be extolled! She who previously had received four strokes without injury, now, a few moments later, seems to die that an innocent man may not perish in her stead.

12. Those of the clergy whose duty it is to wrap the blood-stained corpse in a winding-sheet, dig out the earth and, heaping together stones, form the customary tomb. The sunset comes on quickly, and by God's mercy the night of nature arrives more swiftly than is its wont. Suddenly the woman's bosom heaves, her eyes seek the light, her body is quickened into new life. A moment after she sighs, she looks round, she gets up and speaks. At last she is able to cry: "The Lord is on my side; I will not fear. What can man do unto me?"[6]

13. Meantime an aged woman, supported out of the funds of the church, gave back her spirit to heaven from which it came. It seemed as if

5. Susannah 45; the youth spoken of is   6. Ps. 118:6.
Daniel.

the course of events had been thus purposely ordered, for her body took the place of the other beneath the mound. In the gray dawn the devil comes on the scene in the form of a constable, asks for the corpse of her who had been slain, and desires to have her grave pointed out to him. Surprised that she could have died, he fancies her to be still alive. The clergy show him the fresh turf, and meet his demands by pointing to the earth lately heaped up, taunting him with such words as these: "Yes, of course, tear up the bones which have been buried! Declare war anew against the tomb, and if even that does not satisfy you, pluck her limb from limb for birds and beasts to mangle! Mere dying is too good for one whom it took seven strokes to kill."

14. Before such opprobrious words the executioner retires in confusion, while the woman is secretly revived at home. Then, lest the frequency of the doctor's visits to the church might give occasion for suspicion, they cut her hair short and send her in the company of some virgins to a sequestered country house. There she changes her dress for that of a man, and scars form over her wounds. Yet even after the great miracles worked on her behalf, the laws still rage against her. So true is it that, where there is most law, there, there is also most injustice.

15. But now see whither the progress of my story has brought me; we come upon the name of our friend Evagrius. So great have his exertions been in the cause of Christ that, were I to suppose it possible adequately to describe them, I should only show my own folly; and were I minded deliberately to pass them by, I still could not prevent my voice from breaking out into cries of joy. Who can fittingly praise the vigilance which enabled him to bury, if I may so say, before his death Auxentius of Milan, that curse brooding over the church? Or who can sufficiently extol the discretion with which he rescued the Roman bishop from the toils of the net in which he was fairly entangled, and showed him the means at once of overcoming his opponents and of sparing them in their discomfiture? But

Such topics I must leave to other bards,
Shut out by envious straits of time and space.[7]

I am satisfied now to record the conclusion of my tale. Evagrius seeks a special audience of the Emperor; importunes him with his entreaties, wins his favor by his services, and finally gains his cause through his earnestness. The Emperor restored to liberty the woman whom God had restored to life.

7. Virg. G. 4. 147, 148.

14. Augustine, *The City of God*, Book 19

4. What the Christians Believe Regarding the Supreme Good and Evil, in Opposition to the Philosophers, Who Have Maintained That the Supreme Good Is in Themselves

If, then, we be asked what the city of God has to say upon these points, and, in the first place, what its opinion regarding the supreme good and evil is, it will reply that life eternal is the supreme good, death eternal the supreme evil, and that to obtain the one and escape the other we must live rightly. And thus it is written, "The just lives by faith,"[1] for we do not as yet see our good, and must therefore live by faith; neither have we in ourselves power to live rightly, but can do so only if He who has given us faith to believe in His help do help us when we believe and pray. As for those who have supposed that the sovereign good and evil are to be found in this life, and have placed it either in the soul or the body, or in both, or, to speak more explicitly, either in pleasure or in virtue, or in both; in repose or in virtue, or in both; in pleasure and repose, or in virtue, or in all combined; in the primary objects of nature, or in virtue, or in both—all these have, with a marvellous shallowness, sought to find their blessedness in this life and in themselves. Contempt has been poured upon such ideas by the Truth, saying by the prophet, "The Lord knoweth the thoughts of men" (or, as the Apostle Paul cites the passage, "The Lord knoweth the thoughts of the *wise*") "that they are vain."[2]

For what flood of eloquence can suffice to detail the miseries of this life? Cicero, in the *Consolation* on the death of his daughter, has spent all his ability in lamentation; but how inadequate was even his ability here? For when, where, how, in this life can these primary objects of nature be possessed so that they may not be assailed by unforeseen accident? Is the body of the wise man exempt from any pain which may dispel pleasure, from any disquietude which may banish repose? The amputation or decay of the members of the body puts an end to its integrity, deformity blights its beauty, weakness its health, lassitude its vigour, sleepiness or sluggishness its activity—and which of these is it that may not assail the flesh of the wise man? Comely and fitting attitudes and movements of the body are numbered among the prime natural blessings; but what if some sickness makes the members tremble? what if a man suffers from curvature of the

From Saint Augustine, *The City of God*, translated by Marcus Dods (Edinburgh: T. & T. Clark, 1871; reprint ed., New York: Random House, Modern Library, 1950), 19.4, 6–7, 10–11, 16–17, 21, 23–26.

1. Hab. 2:4.   2. Ps. 94:11, and 1 Cor. 3:20.

spine to such an extent that his hands reach the ground, and he goes upon all fours like a quadruped? Does not this destroy all beauty and grace in the body, whether at rest or in motion? What shall I say of the fundamental blessings of the soul, sense and intellect, of which the one is given for the perception, and the other for the comprehension of truth? But what kind of sense is it that remains when a man becomes deaf and blind? where are reason and intellect when disease makes a man delirious? We can scarcely, or not at all, refrain from tears, when we think of or see the actions and words of such frantic persons, and consider how different from and even opposed to their own sober judgment and ordinary conduct their present demeanour is. And what shall I say of those who suffer from demoniacal possession? Where is their own intelligence hidden and buried while the malignant spirit is using their body and soul according to his own will? And who is quite sure that no such thing can happen to the wise man in this life? Then, as to the perception of truth, what can we hope for even in this way while in the body, as we read in the true book of Wisdom, "The corruptible body weigheth down the soul, and the earthly tabernacle presseth down the mind that museth upon many things?"[3] And eagerness, or desire of action, if this is the right meaning to put upon the Greek "*hormé*," is also reckoned among the primary advantages of nature; and yet is it not this which produces those pitiable movements of the insane, and those actions which we shudder to see, when sense is deceived and reason deranged?

In fine, virtue itself, which is not among the primary objects of nature, but succeeds to them as the result of learning, though it holds the highest place among human good things, what is its occupation save to wage perpetual war with vices—not those that are outside of us, but within; not other men's, but our own—a war which is waged especially by that virtue which the Greeks call "*sophrosyne*," and we temperance,[4] and which bridles carnal lusts, and prevents them from winning the consent of the spirit to wicked deeds? For we must not fancy that there is no vice in us, when, as the apostle says, "The flesh lusteth against the spirit";[5] for to this vice there is a contrary virtue, when, as the same writer says, "The spirit lusteth against the flesh." "For these two," he says, "are contrary one to the other, so that you cannot do the things which you would." But what is it we wish to do when we seek to attain the supreme good, unless that the flesh should cease to lust against the spirit, and that there be no vice in us against which the spirit may lust? And as we cannot attain to this in the present life, however ardently we desire it, let us by God's help accomplish at least this, to preserve the soul from succumbing and yielding to the flesh

3. Wisdom 9:15.   5. Gal. 5:17.
4. Cicero, *Tusc. Quaest.* 3:8.

that lusts against it, and to refuse our consent to the perpetration of sin. Far be it from us, then, to fancy that while we are still engaged in this intestine war, we have already found the happiness which we seek to reach by victory. And who is there so wise that he has no conflict at all to maintain against his vices?

What shall I say of that virtue which is called prudence? Is not all its vigilance spent in the discernment of good from evil things, so that no mistake may be admitted about what we should desire and what avoid? And thus it is itself a proof that we are in the midst of evils, or that evils are in us; for it teaches us that it is an evil to consent to sin, and a good to refuse this consent. And yet this evil, to which prudence teaches and temperance enables us not to consent, is removed from this life neither by prudence nor by temperance. And justice, whose office it is to render to every man his due, whereby there is in man himself a certain just order of nature, so that the soul is subjected to God, and the flesh to the soul, and consequently both soul and flesh to God—does not this virtue demonstrate that it is as yet rather labouring towards its end than resting in its finished work? For the soul is so much the less subjected to God as it is less occupied with the thought of God; and the flesh is so much the less subjected to the spirit as it lusts more vehemently against the spirit. So long, therefore, as we are beset by this weakness, this plague, this disease, how shall we dare to say that we are safe? and if not safe, then how can we be already enjoying our final beatitude? Then that virtue which goes by the name of fortitude is the plainest proof of the ills of life, for it is these ills which it is compelled to bear patiently. And this holds good, no matter though the ripest wisdom co-exists with it. And I am at a loss to understand how the Stoic philosophers can presume to say that these are no ills, though at the same time they allow the wise man to commit suicide and pass out of this life if they become so grievous that he cannot or ought not to endure them. But such is the stupid pride of these men who fancy that the supreme good can be found in this life, and that they can become happy by their own resources, that their wise man, or at least the man whom they fancifully depict as such, is always happy, even though he become blind, deaf, dumb, mutilated, racked with pains, or suffer any conceivable calamity such as may compel him to make away with himself; and they are not shamed to call the life that is beset with these evils happy. O happy life, which seeks the aid of death to end it! If it is happy, let the wise man remain in it; but if these ills drive him out of it, in what sense is it happy? Or how can they say that these are not evils which conquer the virtue of fortitude, and force it not only to yield, but so to rave that it in one breath calls life happy and recommends it to be given up? For who is so blind as not to see that if it were happy it would not be fled from? And if they say we should flee from it on account of the infirmities that beset it, why then do they not lower their pride and acknowledge that it is miserable? Was it, I would ask, fortitude or weakness which prompted Cato to kill himself? for he would not have done so had he not been too weak to endure Caesar's victory. Where, then, is his fortitude? It has yielded, it has succumbed, it has been so thoroughly overcome as to abandon, forsake, flee this happy life. Or was it no longer happy? Then it was miserable. How, then, were these not evils which made life miserable, and a thing to be escaped from?

And therefore those who admit that these are evils, as the Peripatetics do, and the Old Academy, the sect which Varro advocates, express a more intelligible doctrine; but theirs also is a surprising mistake, for they contend that this is a happy life which is beset by these evils, even though they be so great that he who endures them should commit suicide to escape them. "Pains and anguish of body," says Varro, "are evils, and so much the worse in proportion to their severity; and to escape them you must quit this life." What life, I pray? This life, he says, which is oppressed by such evils. Then it is happy in the midst of these very evils on account of which you say we must quit it? Or do you call it happy because you are at liberty to escape these evils by death? What, then, if by some secret judgment of God you were held fast and not permitted to die, nor suffered to live without these evils? In that case, at least, you would say that such a life was miserable. It is soon relinquished, no doubt, but this does not make it not miserable; for were it eternal, you yourself would pronounce it miserable. Its brevity, therefore, does not clear it of misery; neither ought it to be called happiness because it is a brief misery. Certainly there is a mighty force in these evils which compel a man—according to them, even a wise man—to cease to be a man that he may escape them, though they say, and say truly, that it is as it were the first and strongest demand of nature that a man cherish himself, and naturally therefore avoid death, and should so stand his own friend as to wish and vehemently aim at continuing to exist as a living creature, and subsisting in this union of soul and body. There is a mighty force in these evils to overcome this natural instinct by which death is by every means and with all a man's efforts avoided, and to overcome it so completely that what was avoided is desired, sought after, and if it cannot in any other way be obtained, is inflicted by the man on himself. There is a mighty force in these evils which make fortitude a homicide—if, indeed, that is to be called fortitude which is so thoroughly overcome by these evils, that it not only cannot preserve by patience the man whom it undertook to govern and defend, but is itself obliged to kill him. The wise man, I admit, ought to bear death with patience, but when it is inflicted by another. If, then, as these men maintain, he is obliged to inflict it on himself, certainly it must be owned that the ills which compel him to this are not only evils, but intolerable evils. The life, then, which is either subject to accidents, or environed with evils so considerable and grievous, could never have been called happy, if the men who give it this name had condescended to yield to the truth, and to be conquered by valid arguments, when they inquired after the happy life, as they yield to unhappiness, and are overcome by overwhelming evils, when they put themselves to death, and if they had not fancied that the supreme good was to be found in this mortal life; for the very virtues of this life, which are certainly its best and most useful possessions, are all the more telling proofs of its miseries in proportion as they are helpful against the violence of its dangers, toils, and woes. For if these are true virtues—and such cannot exist save in those who have true piety—they do not profess to be able to deliver the men who possess them from all miseries; for true virtues tell no such lies, but they profess that by the hope of the future world this life, which is miserably involved in the many and great evils of this world, is happy as it is also safe. For if not yet safe, how could it be happy? And therefore the Apostle Paul, speaking not of men without prudence, temperance, fortitude, and justice, but of those whose lives were regulated by true piety, and whose virtues were therefore true, says, "For we are saved by hope: now hope which is seen is not hope; for what a man seeth, why doth he yet hope for? But if we hope for that we see not, then do we with patience wait for it." [6] As, therefore, we are saved, so we are made happy by hope. And as we do not as yet possess a present, but look for a future salvation, so is it with our happiness, and this "with patience"; for we are encompassed with evils, which we ought patiently to endure, until we come to the ineffable enjoyment of unmixed good; for there shall be no longer anything to endure. Salvation, such as it shall be in the world to come, shall itself be our final happiness. And this happiness these philosophers refuse to believe in, because they do not see it, and attempt to fabricate for themselves a happiness in this life, based upon a virtue which is as deceitful as it is proud.

6. Of the Error of Human Judgments When the Truth Is Hidden

What shall I say of these judgments which men pronounce on men, and which are necessary in communities, whatever outward peace they enjoy? Melancholy and lamentable judgments they are, since the judges are men who cannot discern the consciences of those at their bar, and are therefore frequently compelled to put innocent witnesses to the torture to ascertain

6. Rom. 8:24.

the truth regarding the crimes of other men. What shall I say of torture applied to the accused himself? He is tortured to discover whether he is guilty, so that, though innocent, he suffers most undoubted punishment for crime that is still doubtful, not because it is proved that he committed it, but because it is not ascertained that he did not commit it. Thus the ignorance of the judge frequently involves an innocent person in suffering. And what is still more unendurable—a thing, indeed, to be bewailed, and, if that were possible, watered with fountains of tears—is this, that when the judge puts the accused to the question, that he may not unwittingly put an innocent man to death, the result of this lamentable ignorance is that this very person, whom he tortured that he might not condemn him if innocent, is condemned to death both tortured and innocent. For if he has chosen, in obedience to the philosophical instructions to the wise man, to quit this life rather than endure any longer such tortures, he declares that he has committed the crime which in fact he has not committed. And when he has been condemned and put to death, the judge is still in ignorance whether he has put to death an innocent or a guilty person, though he put the accused to the torture for the very purpose of saving himself from condemning the innocent; and consequently he has both tortured an innocent man to discover his innocence, and has put him to death without discovering it. If such darkness shrouds social life, will a wise judge take his seat on the bench or no? Beyond question he will. For human society, which he thinks it a wickedness to abandon, constrains him and compels him to this duty. And he thinks it no wickedness that innocent witnesses are tortured regarding the crimes of which other men are accused; or that the accused are put to the torture, so that they are often overcome with anguish, and, though innocent, make false confessions regarding themselves, and are punished; or that, though they be not condemned to die, they often die during, or in consequence of, the torture; or that sometimes the accusers, who perhaps have been prompted by a desire to benefit society by bringing criminals to justice, are themselves condemned through the ignorance of the judge, because they are unable to prove the truth of their accusations though they are true, and because the witnesses lie, and the accused endures the torture without being moved to confession. These numerous and important evils he does not consider sins; for the wise judge does these things, not with any intention of doing harm, but because his ignorance compels him, and because human society claims him as a judge. But though we therefore acquit the judge of malice, we must none the less condemn human life as miserable. And if he is compelled to torture and punish the innocent because his office and his ignorance constrain him, is he a happy as well as a guiltless man? Surely it were proof of more profound considerateness and finer feeling were he to recognise the misery of these necessities, and shrink from his own implication in that misery; and had he any piety about him, he would cry to God, "From my necessities deliver Thou me." [7]

7. Of the Diversity of Languages, by Which the Intercourse of Men Is Prevented; and of the Misery of Wars, Even of Those Called Just

After the state or city comes the world, the third circle of human society—the first being the house, and the second the city. And the world, as it is larger, so it is fuller of dangers, as the greater sea is the more dangerous. And here, in the first place, man is separated from man by the difference of languages. For if two men, each ignorant of the other's language, meet, and are not compelled to pass, but, on the contrary, to remain in company, dumb animals, though of different species, would more easily hold intercourse than they, human beings though they be. For their common nature is no help to friendliness when they are prevented by diversity of language from conveying their sentiments to one another; so that a man would more readily hold intercourse with his dog than with a foreigner. But the imperial city has endeavoured to impose on subject nations not only her yoke, but her language, as a bond of peace, so that interpreters, far from being scarce, are numberless. This is true; but how many great wars, how much slaughter and bloodshed, have provided this unity! And though these are past, the end of these miseries has not yet come. For though there have never been wanting, nor are yet wanting, hostile nations beyond the empire, against whom wars have been and are waged, yet, supposing there were no such nations, the very extent of the empire itself has produced wars of a more obnoxious description—social and civil wars—and with these the whole race has been agitated, either by the actual conflict or the fear of a renewed outbreak. If I attempted to give an adequate description of these manifold disasters, these stern and lasting necessities, though I am quite unequal to the task, what limit could I set? But, say they, the wise man will wage just wars. As if he would not all the rather lament the necessity of just wars, if he remembers that he is a man; for if they were not just he would not wage them, and would therefore be delivered from all wars. For it is the wrong-doing of the opposing party which compels the wise man to wage just wars; and this wrong-doing, even though it gave rise to no war, would still be matter of grief to man because it is man's wrong-doing. Let every one, then, who thinks with pain on all these great evils, so horrible, so ruthless, acknowledge that this is misery. And if any one either endures or thinks of them without mental pain, this is a more miserable plight still, for he thinks himself happy because he has lost human feeling.

7. Ps. 25:17.

10. The Reward Prepared for the Saints after They Have Endured the Trial of This Life

But not even the saints and faithful worshippers of the one true and most high God are safe from the manifold temptations and deceits of the demons. For in this abode of weakness, and in these wicked days, this state of anxiety has also its use, stimulating us to seek with keener longing for that security where peace is complete and unassailable. There we shall enjoy the gifts of nature, that is to say, all that God the Creator of all natures has bestowed upon ours—gifts not only good, but eternal—not only of the spirit, healed now by wisdom, but also of the body renewed by the resurrection. There the virtues shall no longer be struggling against any vice or evil, but shall enjoy the reward of victory, the eternal peace which no adversary shall disturb. This is the final blessedness, this the ultimate consummation, the unending end. Here, indeed, we are said to be blessed when we have such peace as can be enjoyed in a good life; but such blessedness is mere misery compared to that final felicity. When we mortals possess such peace as this mortal life can afford, virtue, if we are living rightly, makes a right use of the advantages of this peaceful condition; and when we have it not, virtue makes a good use even of the evils a man suffers. But this is true virtue, when it refers all the advantages it makes a good use of, and all that it does in making good use of good and evil things, and itself also, to that end in which we shall enjoy the best and greatest peace possible.

11. Of the Happiness of the Eternal Peace, Which Constitutes the End or True Perfection of the Saints

And thus we may say of peace, as we have said of eternal life, that it is the end of our good; and the rather because the Psalmist says of the city of God, the subject of this laborious work, "Praise the Lord, O Jerusalem; praise thy God, O Zion: for He hath strengthened the bars of thy gates; He hath blessed thy children within thee; who hath made thy borders peace." [8] For when the bars of her gates shall be strengthened, none shall go in or come out from her; consequently we ought to understand the peace of her borders as that final peace we are wishing to declare. For even the mystical name of the city itself, that is, *Jerusalem*, means, as I have already said, "Vision of Peace." But as the word peace is employed in connection with things in this world in which certainly life eternal has no place, we have preferred to call the end or supreme good of this city life eternal rather than

8. Ps. 147:12–14.

peace. Of this end the apostle says, "But now, being freed from sin, and become servants to God, ye have your fruit unto holiness, and the end life eternal."[9] But, on the other hand, as those who are not familiar with Scripture may suppose that the life of the wicked is eternal life, either because of the immortality of the soul, which some of the philosophers even have recognised, or because of the endless punishment of the wicked, which forms a part of our faith, and which seems impossible unless the wicked live for ever, it may therefore be advisable, in order that every one may readily understand what we mean, to say that the end or supreme good of this city is either peace in eternal life, or eternal life in peace. For peace is a good so great, that even in this earthly and mortal life there is no word we hear with such pleasure, nothing we desire with such zest, or find to be more thoroughly gratifying. So that if we dwell for a little longer on this subject, we shall not, in my opinion, be wearisome to our readers, who will attend both for the sake of understanding what is the end of this city of which we speak, and for the sake of the sweetness of peace which is dear to all.

16. Of Equitable Rule

And therefore, although our righteous fathers[10] had slaves, and administered their domestic affairs so as to distinguish between the condition of slaves and the heirship of sons in regard to the blessings of this life, yet in regard to the worship of God, in whom we hope for eternal blessings, they took an equally loving oversight of all the members of their household. And this is so much in accordance with the natural order, that the head of the household was called *paterfamilias*; and this name has been so generally accepted, that even those whose rule is unrighteous are glad to apply it to themselves. But those who are true fathers of their households desire and endeavour that all the members of their household, equally with their own children, should worship and win God, and should come to that heavenly home in which the duty of ruling men is no longer necessary, because the duty of caring for their everlasting happiness has also ceased; but, until they reach that home, masters ought to feel their position of authority a greater burden than servants their service. And if any member of the family interrupts the domestic peace by disobedience, he is corrected either by word or blow, or some kind of just and legitimate punishment, such as society permits, that he may himself be the better for it, and be readjusted to the family harmony from which he had dislocated himself. For as it is not benevolent to give a man help at the expense of some greater benefit he

9. Rom. 6:22.   10. The patriarchs.

might receive, so it is not innocent to spare a man at the risk of his falling into graver sin. To be innocent, we must not only do harm to no man, but also restrain him from sin or punish his sin, so that either the man himself who is punished may profit by his experience, or others be warned by his example. Since, then, the house ought to be the beginning or element of the city, and every beginning bears reference to some end of its own kind, and every element to the integrity of the whole of which it is an element, it follows plainly enough that domestic peace has a relation to civic peace—in other words, that the well-ordered concord of domestic obedience and domestic rule has a relation to the well-ordered concord of civic obedience and civic rule. And therefore it follows, further, that the father of the family ought to frame his domestic rule in accordance with the law of the city, so that the household may be in harmony with the civic order.

17. What Produces Peace, and What Discord, between the Heavenly and Earthly Cities

But the families which do not live by faith seek their peace in the earthly advantages of this life; while the families which live by faith look for those eternal blessings which are promised, and use as pilgrims such advantages of time and of earth as do not fascinate and divert them from God, but rather aid them to endure with greater ease, and to keep down the number of those burdens of the corruptible body which weigh upon the soul. Thus the things necessary for this mortal life are used by both kinds of men and families alike, but each has its own peculiar and widely different aim in using them. The earthly city, which does not live by faith, seeks an earthly peace, and the end it proposes, in the well-ordered concord of civic obedience and rule, is the combination of men's wills to attain the things which are helpful to this life. The heavenly city, or rather the part of it which sojourns on earth and lives by faith, makes use of this peace only because it must, until this mortal condition which necessitates it shall pass away. Consequently, so long as it lives like a captive and a stranger in the earthly city, though it has already received the promise of redemption, and the gift of the Spirit as the earnest of it, it makes no scruple to obey the laws of the earthly city, whereby the things necessary for the maintenance of this mortal life are administered; and thus, as this life is common to both cities, so there is a harmony between them in regard to what belongs to it. But, as the earthly city has had some philosophers whose doctrine is condemned by the divine teaching, and who, being deceived either by their own conjectures or by demons, supposed that many gods must be invited to take an interest in human affairs, and assigned to each a separate function and a separate department—to one the body, to another the soul; and in the body itself, to one the head, to another the neck, and each of the other members to one of the gods; and in like manner, in the soul, to one god the natural capacity was assigned, to another education, to another anger, to another lust; and so the various affairs of life were assigned—cattle to one, corn to another, wine to another, oil to another, the woods to another, money to another, navigation to another, wars and victories to another, marriages to another, births and fecundity to another, and other things to other gods: and as the celestial city, on the other hand, knew that one God only was to be worshipped, and that to Him alone was due that service which the Greeks call "*latreia*," and which can be given only to a god, it has come to pass that the two cities could not have common laws of religion, and that the heavenly city has been compelled in this matter to dissent, and to become obnoxious to those who think differently, and to stand the brunt of their anger and hatred and persecutions, except in so far as the minds of their enemies have been alarmed by the multitude of the Christians and quelled by the manifest protection of God accorded to them. This heavenly city, then, while it sojourns on earth, calls citizens out of all nations, and gathers together a society of pilgrims of all languages, not scrupling about diversities in the manners, laws, and institutions whereby earthly peace is secured and maintained, but recognising that, however various these are, they all tend to one and the same end of earthly peace. It therefore is so far from rescinding and abolishing these diversities, that it even preserves and adapts them, so long only as no hindrance to the worship of the one supreme and true God is thus introduced. Even the heavenly city, therefore, while in its state of pilgrimage, avails itself of the peace of earth, and, so far as it can without injuring faith and godliness, desires and maintains a common agreement among men regarding the acquisition of the necessaries of life, and makes this earthly peace bear upon the peace of heaven; for this alone can be truly called and esteemed the peace of the reasonable creatures, consisting as it does in the perfectly ordered and harmonious enjoyment of God and of one another in God. When we shall have reached that peace, this mortal life shall give place to one that is eternal, and our body shall be no more this animal body which by its corruption weighs down the soul, but a spiritual body feeling no want, and in all its members subjected to the will. In its pilgrim state the heavenly city possesses this peace by faith; and by this faith it lives righteously when it refers to the attainment of that peace every good action towards God and man; for the life of the city is a social life.

21. Whether There Ever Was a Roman Republic Answering to the Definitions of Scipio in Cicero's Dialogue

This, then, is the place where I should fulfil the promise I gave in the second book of this work,[11] and explain, as briefly and clearly as possible, that if we are to accept the definitions laid down by Scipio in Cicero's *De Republica*, there never was a Roman republic; for he briefly defines a republic as the weal of the people. And if this definition be true, there never was a Roman republic, for the people's weal was never attained among the Romans. For the people, according to his definition, is an assemblage associated by a common acknowledgment of right and by a community of interests. And what he means by a common acknowledgment of right he explains at large, showing that a republic cannot be administered without justice. Where, therefore, there is no true justice there can be no right. For that which is done by right is justly done, and what is unjustly done cannot be done by right. For the unjust inventions of men are neither to be considered nor spoken of as rights; for even they themselves say that right is that which flows from the fountain of justice, and deny the definition which is commonly given by those who misconceive the matter, that right is that which is useful to the stronger party. Thus, where there is not true justice there can be no assemblage of men associated by a common acknowledgment of right, and therefore there can be no people, as defined by Scipio or Cicero; and if no people, then no weal of the people, but only of some promiscuous multitude unworthy of the name of people. Consequently, if the republic is the weal of the people, and there is no people if it be not associated by a common acknowledgment of right, and if there is no right where there is no justice, then most certainly it follows that there is no republic where there is no justice. Further, justice is that virtue which gives every one his due. Where, then, is the justice of man, when he deserts the true God and yields himself to impure demons? Is this to give every one his due? Or is he who keeps back a piece of ground from the purchaser, and gives it to a man who has no right to it, unjust, while he who keeps back himself from the God who made him, and serves wicked spirits, is just?

This same book, *De Republica*, advocates the cause of justice against injustice with great force and keenness. The pleading for injustice against justice was first heard, and it was asserted that without injustice a republic could neither increase nor even subsist, for it was laid down as an absolutely unassailable position that it is unjust for some men to rule and some to serve; and yet the imperial city to which the republic belongs cannot rule

11. Ch. 21.

her provinces without having recourse to this injustice. It was replied in behalf of justice, that this ruling of the provinces is just, because servitude may be advantageous to the provincials, and is so when rightly administered—that is to say, when lawless men are prevented from doing harm. And further, as they became worse and worse so long as they were free, they will improve by subjection. To confirm this reasoning, there is added an eminent example drawn from nature: for "why," it is asked, "does God rule man, the soul the body, the reason the passions and other vicious parts of the soul?" This example leaves no doubt that, to some, servitude is useful; and, indeed, to serve God is useful to all. And it is when the soul serves God that it exercises a right control over the body; and in the soul itself the reason must be subject to God if it is to govern as it ought the passions and other vices. Hence, when a man does not serve God, what justice can we ascribe to him, since in this case his soul cannot exercise a just control over the body, nor his reason over his vices? And if there is no justice in such an individual, certainly there can be none in a community composed of such persons. Here, therefore, there is not that common acknowledgment of right which makes an assemblage of men a people whose affairs we call a republic. And why need I speak of the advantageousness, the common participation in which, according to the definition, makes a people? For although, if you choose to regard the matter attentively, you will see that there is nothing advantageous to those who live godlessly, as every one lives who does not serve God but demons, whose wickedness you may measure by their desire to receive the worship of men though they are most impure spirits, yet what I have said of the common acknowledgment of right is enough to demonstrate that, according to the above definition, there can be no people, and therefore no republic, where there is no justice. For if they assert that in their republic the Romans did not serve unclean spirits, but good and holy gods, must we therefore again reply to this evasion, though already we have said enough, and more than enough, to expose it? He must be an uncommonly stupid, or a shamelessly contentious person, who has read through the foregoing books to this point, and can yet question whether the Romans served wicked and impure demons. But, not to speak of their character, it is written in the law of the true God, "He that sacrificeth unto any god save unto the Lord only, he shall be utterly destroyed." [12] He, therefore, who uttered so menacing a commandment decreed that no worship should be given either to good or bad gods.

12. Ex. 22:20.

23. Porphyry's Account of the Responses Given by the Oracles of the Gods concerning Christ

. . . And therefore, where there is not this righteousness whereby the one supreme God rules the obedient city according to His grace, so that it sacrifices to none but Him, and whereby, in all the citizens of this obedient city, the soul consequently rules the body and reason the vices in the rightful order, so that, as the individual just man, so also the community and people of the just, live by faith, which works by love, that love whereby man loves God as He ought to be loved, and his neighbour as himself—there, I say, there is not an assemblage associated by a common acknowledgment of right, and by a community of interests. But if there is not this, there is not a people, if our definition be true, and therefore there is no republic; for where there is no people there can be no republic.

24. The Definition Which Must Be Given of a People and a Republic, in Order to Vindicate the Assumption of These Titles by the Romans and by Other Kingdoms

But if we discard this definition of a people, and, assuming another, say that a people is an assemblage of reasonable beings bound together by a common agreement as to the objects of their love, then, in order to discover the character of any people, we have only to observe what they love. Yet whatever it loves, if only it is an assemblage of reasonable beings and not of beasts, and is bound together by an agreement as to the objects of love, it is reasonably called a people; and it will be a superior people in proportion as it is bound together by higher interests, inferior in proportion as it is bound together by lower. According to this definition of ours, the Roman people is a people, and its weal is without doubt a commonwealth or republic. But what its tastes were in its early and subsequent days, and how it declined into sanguinary seditions and then to social and civil wars, and so burst asunder or rotted off the bond of concord in which the health of a people consists, history shows, and in the preceding books I have related at large. And yet I would not on this account say either that it was not a people, or that its administration was not a republic, so long as there remains an assemblage of reasonable beings bound together by a common agreement as to the objects of love. But what I say of this people and of this republic I must be understood to think and say of the Athenians or any Greek state, of the Egyptians, of the early Assyrian Babylon, and of every other nation, great or small, which had a public government. For, in general, the city of the ungodly, which did not obey the command of God that it should offer no sacrifice save to Him alone, and which, therefore, could not give to the soul its proper command over the body, nor to the reason its just authority over the vices, is void of true justice.

25. That Where There Is No True Religion There Are No True Virtues

For though the soul may seem to rule the body admirably, and the reason the vices, if the soul and reason do not themselves obey God, as God has commanded them to serve Him, they have no proper authority over the body and the vices. For what kind of mistress of the body and the vices can that mind be which is ignorant of the true God, and which, instead of being subject to His authority, is prostituted to the corrupting influences of the most vicious demons? It is for this reason that the virtues which it seems to itself to possess, and by which it restrains the body and the vices that it may obtain and keep what it desires, are rather vices than virtues so long as there is no reference to God in the matter. For although some suppose that virtues which have a reference only to themseves, and are desired only on their own account, are yet true and genuine virtues, the fact is that even then they are inflated with pride, and are therefore to be reckoned vices rather than virtues. For as that which gives life to the flesh is not derived from flesh, but is above it, so that which gives blessed life to man is not derived from man, but is something above him; and what I say of man is true of every celestial power and virtue whatsoever.

26. Of the Peace Which Is Enjoyed by the People That Are Alienated from God, and the Use Made of It by the People of God in the Time of Its Pilgrimage

Wherefore, as the life of the flesh is the soul, so the blessed life of man is God, of whom the sacred writings of the Hebrews say, "Blessed is the people whose God is the Lord."[13] Miserable, therefore, is the people which is alienated from God. Yet even this people has a peace of its own which is not to be lightly esteemed, though, indeed, it shall not in the end enjoy it, because it makes no good use of it before the end. But it is our interest that it enjoy this peace meanwhile in this life; for as long as the two cities are commingled, we also enjoy the peace of Babylon. For from Babylon the people of God is so freed that it meanwhile sojourns in its company. And therefore the apostle also admonished the Church to pray for kings and those in authority, assigning as the reason, "that we may live a quiet and tranquil life in all godliness and love."[14] And the prophet

---

13. Ps. 144:15.   14. 1 Tim. 2:2; var. reading, "purity."

Jeremiah, when predicting the captivity that was to befall the ancient people of God, and giving them the divine command to go obediently to Babylonia, and thus serve their God, counselled them also to pray for Babylonia, saying, "In the peace thereof shall ye have peace" [15]—the temporal peace which the good and the wicked together enjoy.

15. Jer. 29:7.

15. Pope Gelasius I, *Letter to the Emperor Anastasius*

Two [elements] there are indeed, Imperator Augustus, by which this world is principally ruled: the consecrated authority of the priests and the royal power. Of these, the burden of the priests is much the weightier, because they will have to answer for even the kings of men on the day of divine judgment. For you know, most clement son, that although it is your right to take precedence over the human race in dignity, you bow your head obediently to those in charge of divine affairs, and look to them for the means of your salvation; and in partaking of the heavenly sacraments, when they are properly dispensed, you recognize that you rather must subject yourself in the realm of religion than rule in it, and, in these matters, rely on the judgment of the priests and not wish that they be bent to your will. For if, in matters pertaining to the realm of public discipline, the religious dignitaries, recognizing that royal power was given to you by divine disposition, for their part obey your laws, lest they seem to neglect and reject your decree in worldly affairs; then with what fervor, I pray you, ought one to obey those who have been charged with celebrating the holy mysteries? Just as no light judgment falls on bishops for having kept silent where they should have acted for the honor of God, so, the danger is not small for those who are contemptuous—which God forbid—when they ought to be obedient. And if it is proper for the hearts of the faithful to be submitted to all priests in general who correctly administer divine matters, how much the more ought one to respect the opinion of the bishop of that seat which the Most High chose to place over all priests, and which, therefore, the piety of the Church has honored without cease?

Translated by Emile Karafiol for an earlier volume of *Select Readings* in the Western Civilization course at Chicago.

4
Christianity and Paganism

The personal conversion of the Emperor Constantine I to Christianity by no means entailed the conversion of the Empire. As the following texts indicate, paganism persisted in many areas and social classes well over two centuries later, and the reconversion from Christianity to paganism was widespread enough to elicit imperial legislation. Immersed as they were in non-Christian society, many Christians observed public ceremonies of pagan cults, including the religious veneration of emperors and their families. The burning of the imperial palace, which precipitated the ferocious persecution under the Emperor Diocletian, was alleged to have been an act of divine vengeance upon Christians who, witnessing pagan rituals at court, made religious gestures to ward off the demonic presence. Just as the echelons of imperial government were replicated in the Church hierarchy, so too were many pagan rituals assimilated into Christian worship. Yet, as in so many other regards, judgments in the Church varied concerning the assimilation of the hostile world's customs. Many Christian writers condemned pagan beliefs and practices as empty, or dangerous, parodies of the truth that God had entrusted to His chosen people.

The following documents fall into three clusters. The first cluster emphasizes the compelling attraction that pagan cults continued to exert, even on Christians. Bishop Augustine of Hippo (354–430) wrote *The City of God* as a massive rebuttal to pagan charges that the Empire's acceptance of Christianity had led to famine, plague, and the decay of public order as the offended pagan gods withdrew their favor. Unfolding a vast historical panorama, Augustine recalled many experiences in his own tangled religious pilgrimage. He witnessed to the fascination and delight that he had found in what he later condemned as the obscenities of the theater and the demonic illusions of pagan cults. (For more on Augustine, see Introductions to topics 2 and 3 above.)

Augustine converted to Christianity in 386. The two imperial decrees, included below, were issued about the same time (in 381 and 391). By imposing disgrace and civil disabilities on persons who reconverted from Christianity to paganism, they underscore the widespread emotional force that spectacles, such as those remembered by Augustine, continued to exert.

The second cluster of documents illustrates the assimilation of pagan usages into Christian cults. Jerome's (about 347–420) tract *Against Vigilantius*, written against a former friend (as were many of the Father's sharpest invectives) dealt with the growing cult of martyrs, in which Christian critics detected elements of the pagan cult of the dead. (For more on Jerome, see Introduction to topic 2.)

The veneration of imperial images provided another point at which old ways found new life, despite Christian repugnance for idolatry. Christian martyrs went cheerfully to their deaths for refusing to offer incense in veneration before statues of emperors. Yet, in view of his opposition to prevailing imperial policies, it is curious that Bishop Athanasius of Alexandria (295–373) provided one of the most striking justifications for the veneration of imperial images. (On Athanasius, see Introduction to topic 2.)

Fuller evidence for the role of that practice in civil life occurs in the sermons of John Chrysostom (344/354–407). One of the Greek Fathers of the Church, John Chrysostom was born in Antioch. Like Augustine, he was spiritually formed in childhood by his mother. Splendidly educated in pagan philosophy and rhetoric, he early embraced the monastic life. As preacher in the church at Antioch, he laid the basis for his tragic rise in the Church hierarchy. His greatest achievement as preacher in Antioch was the series of twenty-one sermons delivered in 387, after urban riots against tax increases. Holding firmly to the pagan idea that statues were surrogates for the emperors they represented, the court equated the Antiochenes' desecration of imperial statues with an attack on the persons of the Emperor Theodosius I and his family, and prepared to avenge the crime by laying Antioch waste. John Chrysostom and his bishop, Flavian, gained clemency. Later (397), Chrysostom was elected bishop of Constantinople, only to be deposed and exiled until he died in great affliction, a victim of ecclesiastical politics.

As the following excerpt from the historian Sozomen recalls, Chrysostom's downfall was accelerated because he himself expressed ire at the cult surrounding a statue of the Empress Eudoxia. (On Sozomen, see document 7 above.)

Codex Theodosianus, 15.4.1, an imperial decree of 425, indicates the legal sanctions enforcing veneration of imperial images, and the hauntingly elusive distinction between veneration and idolatry. This decree is ironic in view of the persecution that early Christians embraced by refusing to venerate the images of pagan emperors.

The third cluster of texts concerns moments at which Christians unequivocally opposed pagan practices:

1. Bishop Ambrose of Milan's (about 340–397) opposition (391) to the restoration of the Altar of Victory, installed in the Senate House at Rome after Augustus's victory at Actium (27 B.C.), and thereafter a talisman of imperial greatness;

2. Augustine of Hippo's (354–430) denunciations of practices taken over from the cult of the dead;

3. Pope Gregory I's (590–604) description of Saint Benedict's destruction of a pagan shrine on the site where he intended to build Monte Cassino (about 526), perhaps the greatest center of western monasticism; and

4. the Emperor Justinian's (527–565) prohibition of various pagan practices. (On Ambrose and Augustine, see documents 9 and 11 above.)

It is important to notice the extent of these protests, over the space of two centuries, the lingering penetration of paganism into many aspects of public and private life, and, above all, the range of social classes and the geographical diffusion in which these confrontations arose.

---

16. Augustine, *The City of God*, Book 2

4. That the Worshippers of the Gods Never Received from Them Any Healthy Moral Precepts, and That in Celebrating Their Worship All Sorts of Impurities Were Practised

First of all, we would ask why their gods took no steps to improve the morals of their worshippers. That the true God should neglect those who did not seek His help, that was but justice; but why did those gods, from whose worship ungrateful men are now complaining that they are prohibited, issue no laws which might have guided their devotees to a virtuous life? Surely it was but just, that such care as men showed to the worship of the gods, the gods on their part should have to the conduct of men. But, it is replied, it is by his own will a man goes astray. Who denies it? But none the less was it incumbent on these gods, who were men's guardians, to publish

From Saint Augustine, *The City of God*, translated by Marcus Dods (Edinburgh: T. & T. Clark, 1871; reprint ed., New York: Random House, Modern Library, 1950), 2.4–5, 26–27.

in plain terms the laws of a good life, and not to conceal them from their worshippers. It was their part to send prophets to reach and convict such as broke these laws, and publicly to proclaim the punishments which await evildoers, and the rewards which may be looked for by those that do well. Did ever the walls of any of their temples echo to any such warning voice? I myself, when I was a young man, used sometimes to go to the sacrilegious entertainments and spectacles; I saw the priests raving in religious excitement, and heard the choristers; I took pleasure in the shameful games which were celebrated in honour of gods and goddesses, of the virgin Coelestis, and Berecynthia, the mother of all the gods. And on the holy day consecrated to her purification, there were sung before her couch productions so obscene and filthy for the ear—I do not say of the mother of the gods, but of the mother of any senator or honest man—nay, so impure, that not even the mother of the foul-mouthed players themselves could have formed one of the audience. For natural reverence for parents is a bond which the most abandoned cannot ignore. And, accordingly, the lewd actions and filthy words with which these players honoured the mother of the gods, in presence of a vast assemblage and audience of both sexes, they could not for very shame have rehearsed at home in presence of their own mothers. And the crowds that were gathered from all quarters by curiosity, offended modesty must, I should suppose, have scattered in the confusion of shame. If these are sacred rites, what is sacrilege? If this is purification, what is pollution? This festivity was called the Tables, as if a banquet were being given at which unclean devils might find suitable refreshment. For it is not difficult to see what kind of spirits they must be who are delighted with such obscenities, unless, indeed, a man be blinded by these evil spirits passing themselves off under the name of gods, and either disbelieves in their existence, or leads such a life as prompts him rather to propitiate and fear them than the true God.

5. Of the Obscenities Practised in Honour of the Mother of the Gods

In this matter I would prefer to have as my assessors in judgment, not those men who rather take pleasure in these infamous customs than take pains to put an end to them, but that same Scipio Nasica who was chosen by the senate as the citizen most worthy to receive in his hands the image of that demon Cybele, and convey it into the city. He would tell us whether he would be proud to see his own mother so highly esteemed by the state as to have divine honours adjudged to her; as the Greeks and Romans and other nations have decreed divine honours to men who had been of material service to them, and have believed that their mortal benefactors were thus made immortal and enrolled among the gods. Surely he would desire that his mother should enjoy such felicity were it possible. But if we proceeded to ask him whether, among the honours paid to her, he would wish such shameful rites as these to be celebrated, would he not at once exclaim that he would rather his mother lay stone-dead, than survive as a goddess to lend her ear to these obscenities? Is it possible that he who was of so severe a morality, that he used his influence as a Roman senator to prevent the building of a theatre in that city dedicated to the manly virtues, would wish his mother to be propitiated as a goddess with words which would have brought the blush to her cheek when a Roman matron? Could he possibly believe that the modesty of an estimable woman would be so transformed by her promotion to divinity, that she would suffer herself to be invoked and celebrated in terms so gross and immodest, that if she had heard the like while alive upon earth, and had listened without stopping her ears and hurrying from the spot, her relatives, her husband, and her children would have blushed for her? Therefore, the mother of the gods being such a character as the most profligate man would be ashamed to have for his mother, and meaning to enthrall the minds of the Romans, demanded for her service their best citizen, not to ripen him still more in virtue by her helpful counsel, but to entangle him by her deceit, like her of whom it is written, "The adultress will hunt for the precious soul."[1] Her intent was to puff up this high-souled man by an apparently divine testimony to his excellence, in order that he might rely upon his own eminence in virtue, and make no further efforts after true piety and religion, without which natural genius, however brilliant, vapours into pride and comes to nothing. For what but a guileful purpose could that goddess demand the best man, seeing that in her own sacred festivals she requires such obscenities as the best men would be covered with shame to hear at their own tables?

26. That the Demons Gave in Secret Certain Obscure Instructions in Morals, While in Public Their Own Solemnities Inculcated All Wickedness

Seeing that this is so—seeing that the filthy and cruel deeds, the disgraceful and criminal actions of the gods, whether real or feigned, were at their own request published, and were consecrated, and dedicated in their honour as sacred and stated solemnities; seeing they vowed vengeance on those who refused to exhibit them to the eyes of all, that they might be proposed as deeds worthy of imitation, why is it that these same demons, who, by taking pleasure in such obscenities, acknowledge themselves to be unclean spirits, and by delighting in their own villanies and iniquities, real

1. Prov. 6:26.

or imaginary, and by requesting from the immodest, and extorting from the modest, the celebration of these licentious acts, proclaim themselves instigators to a criminal and lewd life;—why, I ask, are they represented as giving some good moral precepts to a few of their own elect, initiated in the secrecy of their shrines? If it be so, this very thing only serves further to demonstrate the malicious craft of these pestilent spirits. For so great is the influence of probity and chastity, that all men, or almost all men, are moved by the praise of these virtues; nor is any man so depraved by vice, but he hath some feeling of honour left in him. So that, unless the devil sometimes transformed himself, as Scripture says, into an angel of light,[2] he could not compass his deceitful purpose. Accordingly, in public, a bold impurity fills the ear of the people with noisy clamour; in private, a feigned chastity speaks in scarce audible whispers to a few: an open stage is provided for shameful things, but on the praiseworthy the curtain falls: grace hides, disgrace flaunts: a wicked deed draws an overflowing house, a virtuous speech finds scarce a hearer, as though purity were to be blushed at, impurity boasted of. Where else can such confusion reign, but in devils' temples? Where, but in the haunts of deceit? For the secret precepts are given as a sop to the virtuous, who are few in number; the wicked examples are exhibited to encourage the vicious, who are countless.

Where and when those initiated in the mysteries of Coelestis received any good instructions, we know not. What we do know is, that before her shrine, in which her image is set, and amidst a vast crowd gathering from all quarters, and standing closely packed together, we were intensely interested spectators of the games which were going on, and saw, as we pleased to turn the eye, on this side a grand display of harlots, on the other the virgin goddess: we saw this virgin worshipped with prayer and with obscene rites. There we saw no shamefaced mimes, no actress overburdened with modesty: all that the obscene rites demanded was fully complied with. We were plainly shown what was pleasing to the virgin deity, and the matron who witnessed the spectacle returned home from the temple a wiser woman. Some, indeed, of the more prudent women turned their faces from the immodest movements of the players, and learned the art of wickedness by a furtive regard. For they were restrained, by the modest demeanour due to men, from looking boldly at the immodest gestures; but much more were they restrained from condemning with chaste heart the sacred rites of her whom they adored. And yet this licentiousness—which if practised in one's home, could only be done there in secret—was practised as a public lesson in the temple; and if any modesty remained in men, it was occupied in marvelling that wickedness which men could not unrestrainedly commit

2. 2 Cor. 11:14.

should be part of the religious teaching of the gods, and that to omit its exhibition should incur the anger of the gods. What spirit can that be, which by a hidden inspiration stirs men's corruption, and goads them to adultery, and feeds on the full-fledged iniquity, unless it be the same that finds pleasure in such religious ceremonies, sets in the temples images of devils, and loves to see in play the images of vices; that whispers in secret some righteous sayings to deceive the few who are good, and scatters in public invitations to profligacy, to gain possession of the millions who are wicked?

27. That the Obscenities of Those Plays Which the Romans Consecrated in Order to Propitiate Their Gods, Contributed Largely to the Overthrow of Public Order

Cicero, a weighty man, and a philosopher in his way, when about to be made edile, wished the citizens to understand that, among the other duties of his magistracy, he must propitiate Flora by the celebration of games. And these games are reckoned devout in proportion to their lewdness. In another place, and when he was now consul, and the state in great peril, he says that games had been celebrated for ten days together, and that nothing had been omitted which could pacify the gods: as if it had not been more satisfactory to irritate the gods by temperance, than to pacify them by debauchery; and to provoke their hate by honest living, than soothe it by such unseemly grossness. For no matter how cruel was the ferocity of those men who were threatening the state, and on whose account the gods were being propitiated: it could not have been more hurtful than the alliance of gods who were won with the foulest vices. To avert the danger which threatened men's bodies, the gods were conciliated in a fashion that drove virtue from their spirits; and the gods did not enrol themselves as defenders of the battlements against the besiegers, until they had first stormed and sacked the morality of the citizens. This propitiation of such divinities—a propitiation so wanton, so impure, so immodest, so wicked, so filthy, whose actors the innate and praiseworthy virtue of the Romans disabled from civic honours, erased from their tribe, recognised as polluted and made infamous;—this propitiation, I say, so foul, so detestable, and alien from every religious feeling, these fabulous and ensnaring accounts of the criminal actions of the gods, these scandalous actions which they either shamefully and wickedly committed, or more shamefully and wickedly feigned, all this the whole city learned in public both by the words and gestures of the actors. They saw that the gods delighted in the commission of these things, and therefore believed that they wished them not only to be exhibited to them, but to be imitated by themselves. But as for that good and honest instruction which they speak of, it was given in such secrecy, and to so few (if indeed given at all), that they seemed rather to fear it might be divulged, than that it might not be practised.

17. *Codex Theodosianus*, 16.7.1,5

1. Emperors Gratian, Valentinian, and Theodosius Augustuses to Eutropius, Praetorian Prefect.

Those Christians who have become pagans shall be deprived of the power and right to make testaments, and every testament of such decedent, if there is a testament, shall be rescinded by the annulment of its foundation.

Given on the sixth day before the nones of May at Constantinople in the year of the consulship of Syagrius and Eucherius. [May 2, 381.]

5. The same Augustuses to Flavianus, Praetorian Prefect.

If any splendor of rank has been conferred upon or is inborn in those persons who have departed from the faith and are blinded in mind, who have deserted the cult and worship of the sacrosanct religion and have given themselves over to sacrifices, they shall forfeit such rank, so that, removed from their position and status, they shall be branded with perpetual infamy and shall not be numbered even among the lowest dregs of the ignoble crowd. For what can they have in common with men if with nefarious and feral minds they scorn the grace of communion and withdraw from mankind?

Given on the fifth day before the ides of May at Concordia in the year of the consulship of Tatianus and Symmachus. [May 11 (June 9), 391.]

From *The Theodosian Code and Novels and the Sirmondian Constitutions*, translated by Clyde Pharr (Princeton: Princeton University Press, 1952), pp. 465, 466. © 1952 by Clyde Pharr; © renewed 1980 by Roy Pharr. All footnotes deleted. Reprinted by permission of the publisher.

18. Jerome, *Against Vigilantius*

3. . . . . This little treatise, which I now dictate, is due to the reverend presbyters Riparius and Desiderius, who write that their parishes have been defiled by being in his neighbourhood, and have sent me, by our brother Sisinnius, the books which he vomited forth in a drunken fit. They also declare that some persons are found who, from their inclination to his vices, assent to his blasphemies. He is a barbarian both in speech and knowledge. His style is rude. He cannot defend even the truth; but, for the

From *Against Vigilantius*, chaps. 3–5, 7–8, in *Nicene and Post-Nicene Fathers*, 2d ser., vol. 6 (New York: Christian Literature Co., 1893), pp. 418–19, 420.

sake of laymen, and poor women, laden with sins, ever learning and never coming to a knowledge of the truth, I will spend upon his melancholy trifles a single night's labour, otherwise I shall seem to have treated with contempt the letters of the reverend persons who have entreated me to undertake the task.

4. He certainly well represents his race. Sprung from a set of brigands and persons collected together from all quarters (I mean those whom Cnaeus Pompey, after the conquest of Spain, when he was hastening to return for his triumph, brought down from the Pyrenees and gathered together into one town, whence the name of the city Convenae), he has carried on their brigand practices by his attack upon the Church of God. Like his ancestors the Vectones, the Arrabaci, and the Celtiberians, he makes his raids upon the churches of Gaul, not carrying the standard of the cross, but, on the contrary, the ensign of the devil. Pompey did just the same in the East. After overcoming the Cilician and Isaurian pirates and brigands, he founded a city, bearing his own name, between Cilicia and Isauria. That city, however, to this day, observes the ordinances of its ancestors, and no Dormitantius has arisen in it; but Gaul supports a native foe, and sees seated in the Church a man who has lost his head and who ought to be put in the strait-jacket which Hippocrates recommended. Among other blasphemies, he may be heard to say, "What need is there for you not only to pay such honour, not to say adoration, to the thing, whatever it may be, which you carry about in a little vessel and worship?" And again, in the same book, "Why do you kiss and adore a bit of powder wrapped up in a cloth?" And again, in the same book, "Under the cloak of religion we see what is all but a heathen ceremony introduced into the churches: while the sun is still shining, heaps of tapers are lighted, and everywhere a paltry bit of powder, wrapped up in a costly cloth, is kissed and worshipped. Great honour do men of this sort pay to the blessed martyrs, who, they think, are to be made glorious by trumpery tapers, when the Lamb who is in the midst of the throne, with all the brightness of His majesty, gives them light?"

5. Madman, who in the world ever adored the martyrs? who ever thought man was God? Did not Paul and Barnabas, when the people of Lycaonia thought them to be Jupiter and Mercury, and would have offered sacrifices to them, rend their clothes and declare they were men?[1] Not that they were not better than Jupiter and Mercury, who were but men long ago dead, but because, under the mistaken ideas of the Gentiles, the honour due to God was being paid to them. And we read the same respecting Peter, who, when Cornelius wished to adore him, raised him by the hand, and

1. Acts 14:11.

said, "Stand up, for I also am a man." [2] And have you the audacity to speak of "the mysterious something or other which you carry about in a little vessel and worship?" I want to know what it is that you call "something or other." Tell us more clearly (that there may be no restraint on your blasphemy) what you mean by the phrase "a bit of powder wrapped up in a costly cloth in a tiny vessel." It is nothing less than the relics of the martyrs which he is vexed to see covered with a costly veil, and not bound up with rags or hair-cloth, or thrown on the midden, so that Vigilantius alone in his drunken slumber may be worshipped. Are we, therefore, guilty of sacrilege when we enter the basilicas of the Apostles? Was the Emperor Constantius I guilty of sacrilege when he transferred the sacred relics of Andrew, Luke, and Timothy to Constantinople? In their presence the demons cry out, and the devils who dwell in Vigilantius confess that they feel the influence of the saints. And at the present day is the Emperor Arcadius guilty of sacrilege, who after so long a time has conveyed the bones of the blessed Samuel from Judea to Thrace? Are all the bishops to be considered not only sacrilegious, but silly into the bargain, because they carried that most worthless thing, dust and ashes, wrapped in silk in a golden vessel? Are the people of all the Churches fools, because they went to meet the sacred relics, and welcomed them with as much joy as if they beheld a living prophet in the midst of them, so that there was one great swarm of people from Palestine to Chalcedon with one voice re-echoing the praises of Christ? They were, forsooth, adoring Samuel and not Christ, whose Levite and prophet Samuel was. You show mistrust because you think only of the dead body, and therefore blaspheme. Read the Gospel—"The God of Abraham, the God of Isaac, the God of Jacob: He is not the God of the dead, but of the living." [3] If then they are alive, they are not, to use your expression, kept in honourable confinement.

7. As to the question of tapers, however, we do not, as you in vain misrepresent us, light them in the daytime, but by their solace we would cheer the darkness of the night, and watch for the dawn, lest we should be blind like you and sleep in darkness. And if some persons, being ignorant and simple minded laymen, or, at all events, religious women—of whom we can truly say, "I allow that they have a zeal for God, but not according to knowledge" [4]—adopt the practice in honour of the martyrs, what harm is thereby done to you? Once upon a time even the Apostles pleaded that the ointment was wasted, but they were rebuked by the voice of the Lord. [5] Christ did not need the ointment, nor do martyrs need the light of tapers; and yet that woman poured out the ointment in honour of Christ, and her

2. Acts 10:26.   4. Rom. 10:2.
3. Matt. 22:32.   5. Matt. 26:8; Mark 14:4.

heart's devotion was accepted. All those who light these tapers have their reward according to their faith, as the Apostle says: "Let every one abound in his own meaning."[6] Do you call men of this sort idolaters? I do not deny that all of us who believe in Christ have passed from the error of idolatry. For we are not born Christians, but become Christians by being born again. And because we formerly worshipped idols, does it follow that we ought not now to worship God lest we seem to pay like honour to Him and to idols? In the one case respect was paid to idols, and therefore the ceremony is to be abhorred; in the other the martyrs are venerated, and the same ceremony is therefore to be allowed. Throughout the whole Eastern Church, even when there are no relics of the martyrs, whenever the Gospel is to be read the candles are lighted, although the dawn may be reddening the sky, not of course to scatter the darkness, but by way of evidencing our joy. And accordingly the virgins in the Gospel always have their lamps lighted.[7] And the Apostles are told to have their loins girded, and their lamps burning in their hands.[8] And of John Baptist we read, "He was the lamp that burneth and shineth;"[9] so that, under the figure of corporeal light, that light is represented of which we read in the Psalter, "Thy word is a lamp unto my feet, O Lord, and a light unto my paths."[10]

8. Does the bishop of Rome do wrong when he offers sacrifices to the Lord over the venerable bones of the dead men Peter and Paul, as we should say, but according to you, over a worthless bit of dust, and judges their tombs worthy to be Christ's altars? And not only is the bishop of one city in error, but the bishops of the whole world, who, despite the tavern-keeper Vigilantius, enter the basilicas of the dead, in which "a worthless bit of dust and ashes lies wrapped up in a cloth," defiled and defiling all else. Thus, according to you, the sacred buildings are like the sepulchres of the Pharisees, whitened without, while within they have filthy remains, and are full of foul smells and uncleanliness.

6. Rom. 14:5. Let each man be fully assured in his own mind. R. V.
7. Matt. 25:1.

8. Luke 12:35.
9. John 5:35.
10. Ps. 119:105.

19. Athanasius, *Discourse 3 against the Arians*

3. . . . For the Father is in the Son, since the Son is what is from the Father and proper to Him, as in the radiance the sun, and in the word the thought, and in the stream the fountain: for whoso thus contemplates the Son, contemplates what is proper to the Father's Essence, and knows that the Father

From *Discourse 3 against the Arians*, chaps. 3–5, in *Nicene and Post-Nicene Fathers*, 2d ser., vol. 4 (New York: Christian Literature Co., 1892), pp. 395–96.

is in the Son. For whereas the Form and Godhead of the Father is the Being of the Son, it follows that the Son is in the Father and the Father in the Son.

4. . . . . For "all things," says the Son Himself, "whatsoever the Father hath, are Mine;"[1] and again, "And Mine are Thine."

5. And on hearing the attributes of the Father spoken of a Son, we shall thereby see the Father in the Son; and we shall contemplate the Son in the Father, when what is said of the Son is said of the Father also. And why are the attributes of the Father ascribed to the Son, except that the Son is an Offspring from Him? and why are the Son's attributes proper to the Father, except again because the Son is the proper Offspring of His Essence? And the Son, being the proper Offspring of the Father's Essence, reasonably says that the Father's attributes are His own also; whence suitably and consistently with saying, "I and the Father are One," He adds, "that ye may know that I am in the Father and the Father in Me."[2] Moreover, He has added this again, "He that hath seen Me, hath seen the Father;"[3] and there is one and the same sense in these three passages. For he who in this sense understands that the Son and the Father are one, knows that He is in the Father and the Father in the Son; for the Godhead of the Son is the Father's, and it is in the Son; and whoso enters into this, is convinced that "He that hath seen the Son, hath seen the Father;" for in the Son is contemplated the Father's Godhead. And we may perceive this at once from the illustration of the Emperor's image. For in the image is the shape and form of the Emperor, and in the Emperor is that shape which is in the image. For the likeness of the Emperor in the image is exact; so that a person who looks at the image, sees in it the Emperor; and he again who sees the Emperor, recognises that it is he who is in the image. And from the likeness not differing, to one who after the image wished to view the Emperor, the image might say, "I and the Emperor are one; for I am in him, and he in me; and what thou seest in me, that thou beholdest in him, and what thou hast seen in him, that thou beholdest in me." Accordingly he who worships the image, in it worships the Emperor also; for the image is his form and appearance. Since then the Son too is the Father's Image it must necessarily be understood that the Godhead and propriety of the Father is the Being of the Son.

1. John 16:15; 17:10.   3. Ib. 14:9.
2. John 10:30, 38; 14:10.

20. John Chrysostom, *Homilies Concerning the Statues*

Homily 3

2. . . . God will not disdain to look upon such earnestness and zeal, nor will He suffer his servant [Bishop Flavian of Antioch] to return without success. I know that when he has barely seen our pious Emperor, and been seen by him, he will be able at once by his very countenance to allay his wrath. For not only the words of the saints, but their very countenances are full of grace. . . . He will also make the special season his advocate and shelter himself behind the sacred festival of the Passover; and will remind the Emperor of the season when Christ remitted the sins of the whole world. He will exhort him to imitate his Lord. He will also remind him of that parable of the ten thousand talents, and the hundred pence. I know the boldness of our father, that he will not hesitate to alarm him from the parable, and to say, "Take heed lest thou also hear it said in that day, 'O thou wicked servant, I forgave thee all that debt, because thou desirest me; you ought also to forgive thy fellow-servants!'[1] Thou dost to thyself a greater benefit than them, since by pardoning these few offences thou gainest an amnesty for greater." To this address he will add that prayer, which those who initiated him into the sacred mystery taught him to offer up, and say, "Forgive us our debts, as we forgive our debtors."[2]

3. He will moreover inform him, that the offence was not common to the whole city, but the deed of certain strangers and adventurers, men that act upon no deliberate plan, but with every sort of audacity and lawlessness; and that it would not be just for the disorderly conduct of a few to extirpate so great a city, and to punish those who had done no wrong; and that even though all had been transgressors, they had paid a sufficient punishment, being consumed by fear so many days, and expecting every day to be put to death, and being exiles and fugitives; thus living more wretchedly than condemned criminals, carrying their life in their hands, and having no confidence of escape! "Let this punishment (he will say) suffice. Carry not thy resentment further! Make the Judge above merciful to thyself, by humanity towards thy fellow-servants! Think of the greatness of the city, and that the question now is not concerning one, or two, or three, or ten souls, but of a vast multitude too numerous to be reckoned up! It is a question

From *Homily 3*, chaps. 2–6, 16–20; *Homily 21*, chaps. 6–11, 13, 16–18, in *Nicene and Post-Nicene Fathers*, vol. 9 (New York: Christian Literature Co., 1889), pp. 355–57, 361–63, 484–87.

1. Matt. 18:32, 33.   2. Matt. 6:12.

which affects the capital of the whole world. This is the city in which Christians were first called by that name.[3] Honor Christ. Reverence the city which first proclaimed that name, so lovely and sweet to all! This city hath been the tabernacle of Apostles; the dwelling place of the just! And now this is the first and only instance of insurrection against its rulers; and all past time will bear favourable witness to the manners of the city. For had the people been continually given to sedition, it might have been necessary to make an example of such iniquity; but if this hath happened only once in all time, it is plain that the offence has not arisen from the habit of the city, but that it was the transgression of those who had in an evil hour by mere random chance arrived there.

4. These things and more than these the priest will say with still greater boldness; and the Emperor will listen to them; and one is humane, and the other is faithful; so that on both sides we entertain favourable hopes. But much more do we rely upon the mercy of God, than upon the fidelity of our Teacher and the humanity of the Emperor. For whilst the Emperor is supplicated, and the priest is supplicating, He Himself will interpose, softening the heart of the Emperor, and exciting the tongue of the priest; facilitating his utterance;—preparing the mind of the other to receive what is said and with much indulgence, to accede to the petitions. For our city is dearer to Christ than all others both because of the virtue of our ancestors, and of your own. And as Peter was the first among the apostles to preach Christ, so as I said before, this city was the first of cities that adorned itself by assuming the Christian appellation, as a sort of admirable diadem. But if where only ten just men were found, God promised to save all who dwelt therein, why should we not expect a favourable issue, and become assured of all our lives, when there are not only ten, twenty, or twice so many only, but far more; who are serving God with all strictness.

5. I have heard many saying, "The threats of a king are like the wrath of a lion;"[4] being full of dejection and lamentation. What then should we say to such? That He who said, "The wolves and the lambs shall feed together; and the leopard shall lie down with the kid, and the lion shall eat straw like the ox,"[5] will be able to convert the lion into a mild lamb. Let us therefore supplicate Him; let us send an embassy to Him; and He will doubtless allay the Emperor's wrath, and deliver us from the impending distress. Our Father hath gone thither on this embassy. Let us go on embassy from hence to the Majesty of Heaven! Let us assist him by prayers! The community of the Church can do much, if with a sorrowful soul, and with a contrite spirit,

3. Acts 11:26, probably in derision; the people of Antioch being notorious for the invention of scurrilous nicknames.

4. Prov. 19:12.
5. Isa. 11:6, 7.

we offer up our prayers! It is unnecessary to cross the ocean, or to undertake a long journey. Let every man and woman among us, whether meeting together at church, or remaining at home, call upon God with much earnestness, and He will doubtless accede to these petitions.

6. . . . Let this be the prayer which we offer to God for our Teacher. For if a woman, supplicating on behalf of the Jews, prevailed to allay the wrath of a barbarian, much rather will our Teacher, entreating on behalf of so great a city, and in conjunction with so great a Church, be able to persuade this most mild and merciful Emperor. For if he hath received authority to loose sins committed against God, much more will he be able to take away and blot out those which have been committed against a man. He is also himself a ruler and a ruler of more dignity than the other. For the sacred laws take and place under his hands even the royal head. And when there is need of any good thing from above, the Emperor is accustomed to fly to the priest: but not the priest to the Emperor. He too hath his breast-plate, that of righteousness. He too hath his girdle, that of truth, and sandals of much greater dignity, those of the Gospel of peace. He too hath a sword, not of iron, but of the Spirit; he too hath a crown resting on his head. This panoply is the more splendid. The weapons are grander, the license of speech greater, and mightier the strength. So that from the weight of his authority, and from his own greatness of soul; and more than all the rest, from the hope which he has in God, he will address the Emperor with much freedom and much discretion.

16. . . . Let us then expel from our mouth all slander, knowing that if we do not abstain from it, though we might feed upon ashes, this austerity would avail us nothing. "For not that which entereth into, but that which cometh out of the mouth defileth the man." If any one were to stir up a cesspool, when you were passing, say, would you not reproach and rate the man who did it? This then also do with respect to the slanderer. For the stirred cesspool does not so grossly offend the sense of those who smell that ill savour, as the stirring up other men's sins, and the exposure of an impure life, offends and disturbs the soul of those who hear of it. Therefore let us abstain from evil speaking, from foul language, from blasphemy; and let us not speak ill of our neighbor, nor of God!

17. For many of our evil speakers have run into such madness, as to lift up their own tongue from their fellow servants against their Master. But how great an evil this is, you may learn from the affairs in which we are now involved. A man is insulted, and, lo! we are all fearing and trembling, both those who were guilty of the insult, and those who are conscious of nothing of the kind! But God is insulted every day! Why do I say every day?—every hour rather, by the rich, by the poor, by those who are at

ease, by the afflicted, by those who calumniate, and those who are calum-
niated, and yet no one ever hears a word of this! Therefore He has permitted our fellow servant to be insulted, in order that from the danger which
has happened through this insult, thou mayest learn the benignity of the
Lord! And notwithstanding that this is our first and only offence, we do not
on that account expect to gain an excuse, or pardon. But we provoke God
every day, and we show no signs of returning to Him, and yet He endures it
with all long-suffering! Seest thou then how great the benignity of the Lord
is? Yet, in this present outrage, those who had done amiss were taken and
thrust into prison, and paid the penalty; nevertheless we are still in fear, for
he who has been insulted has not as yet heard what has taken place, nor
pronounced sentence, and we are all trembling. But God every day hears of
the insults offered Him, and no one heeds it, although God is thus merciful
and loving toward man. With Him it suffices only to acknowledge the sin,
and so to cancel the accusation. But with man it is altogether the reverse.
When those who have sinned confess, then they are punished the more;
which indeed has happened in the present instance. And some have perished by the sword, some by fire; some given to wild beasts, and not men
only, but children. And neither this immaturity of age, nor the tumult of the
people, nor the circumstance that they were infuriated by demons when
they perpetrated these deeds; nor that the exaction was thought to be intolerable; nor poverty, nor having offended in company with all; nor promising that they would never hereafter dare to repeat such deeds; nor anything
else, could at all rescue them; but they were led away to the pit, without
reprieve; armed soldiers conducting and guarding them on either side, lest
any one should carry off the criminals; whilst mothers also followed afar
off, seeing their children beheaded, but not daring to bewail their calamity;
for terror conquered grief, and fear overcame nature! And just as when
men beholding from the land those who are shipwrecked, are deeply dis-
tressed, but are not able to approach and to rescue the drowning, so too
here, the mothers restrained through fear of the soldiers, as it were by so
many waves, not only dared not go near to their children, and rescue them
from condemnation, but were afraid even to shed tears?

18. Assuredly ye gather from thence the mercy of God, how unspeakable, how boundless, how transcending all description! Here indeed the
person who has been insulted is of the same nature; and only once in all his
lifetime has experienced this; and then it was not done to his face; nor
while he was present to see or hear it; and nevertheless, none of those who
perpetrated these deeds obtained pardon. But with regard to God nothing
of the kind can be said; for the interval between man and God, is so great,
as no language can at all express; and throughout every day He is insulted,
although present, and seeing and hearing it: and yet He sends not forth the

lightning, nor commands the sea to overflow the land, and submerge all men; nor does He bid the earth to cleave asunder and swallow up all the contumelious; but He forbears, and suffers long, and still offers to pardon those who have insulted Him, if they only repent and promise to do these things no more! Truly now is the season to proclaim, "Who can utter the mighty acts of the Lord? who can show forth all His praise?" [6] How many men have not only cast down, but also trodden under foot the images of God! For when thou throttlest a debtor, when thou strippest him, when thou draggest him away, thou tramplest under foot God's image. Hear for a certainty Paul saying, that "a man ought not to cover his head, forasmuch as he is the image and glory of God." [7] And again, hear God Himself saying, "Let us make man in Our Image, after Our likeness." [8] But if thou sayest that man is not of the same substance as God,—what matters that? For neither was the brazen statue of the same substance as the Emperor; yet nevertheless, they who defied it paid the penalty. Thus also with regard to mankind, if men are not of the same substance as God, (as indeed they are not), still they have been called His image; and it were fitting they should receive honour on account of the appellation. But thou for the sake of a little gold dost trample them under foot, dost throttle them, and drag them away; and hast not to this day in any wise paid the penalty!

19. . . . Surely it is not sufficient by way of apology that we supplicate two or three days, but it is necessary that we should make a change in our whole life, and that whilst abstaining from wickedness we should persevere continually in virtue. . . . For many times, when we have been surprised by earthquakes, as well as famine and drought, after becoming more sober and gentle for three or four days, we did but return again to the former course. For this cause our present troubles have happened. But if we have not done so before; yet, now at least let us all persevere in the same piety; let us preserve the same meekness, that we may not again need another stroke. Was not God able to have prevented what has taken place? He did, however, permit it, that He might make those who despised Him more sober-minded, through dread of a fellow-servant!

20. But let not any one say, that many of the guilty escaped, and that many of the innocent incurred punishment. For I hear of numerous persons who frequently say this; not only in the case of the present sedition, but also in many other circumstances of this nature. What then should I reply to those who make such observations? Why, that if he who was captured was innocent of the present sedition, he had wrought some other transgression before this still more grievous, for which, not having afterwards re-

---

6. Ps. 106:2.   8. Gen. 1:26.
7. 1 Cor. 11:7.

pented, he has paid the penalty at the present time. For thus is the custom of God to deal with us. When we sin, He does not straightway visit the transgression, but lets it pass, giving us space for repentance, in order that we may be amended and converted. But if, because we have not paid the penalty, we suppose that the offence too is blotted out, and make light of it; then somewhere, where we think not of it, we are sure afterwards to be punished. And this takes place in order that, when we sin and are not punished, we may not be free from fear, unless we amend, knowing that we shall certainly fall into punishment where we do not expect it. So that if thou sinnest, beloved, and art not punished, do not grow presumptuous, but for this very cause be the more alarmed, knowing that it is an easy matter with God to recompense again when he pleases. . . . Nothing is so apt to bring sin to remembrance as punishment and chastisement.

Homily 21

6. . . . he [Bishop Flavian of Antioch] stood before the Emperor at a distance,—speechless,—weeping—with downcast eyes,—covering his face as if he himself had been the doer of all the mischief; and this he did, wishing first to incline him to mercy by his posture, and aspect, and tears; and then to begin an apology on our behalf; since there is but one hope of pardon for those who have offended, which is to be silent, and to utter nothing in defence of what has been done. For he was desirous that one feeling should be got rid of, and that another should take its place; that anger should be expelled, and sadness introduced, in order that he might thus prepare the way for the words of his apology; which indeed actually took place. And just as Moses going up to the mount, when the people had offended, stood speechless himself, until God called him, saying, "Let me alone, and I will blot out this people;"[9] so also did he now act. The Emperor therefore, when he saw him shedding tears, and bending toward the ground, himself drew near; and what he really felt on seeing the tears of the priest, he made evident by the words he addressed to him; for they were not those of a person provoked or inflamed, but of one in sorrow; not of one enraged, but rather dejected, and under constraint of extreme pain.

7. And that this is true, ye will understand when ye hear what were his words. For he did not say, "What does this mean? Hast thou come heading an embassy on behalf of impious and abominable men, such as ought not even to live; on behalf of rebels, of revolutionists, who deserve the utmost punishment?" But dismissing all words of that sort, he composed a defence of himself full of respectfulness and dignity; and he enumerated the bene-

9. Exod. 32:10.

fits, which during the whole time of his reign he had conferred upon the city; and at each of these he said, "Was it thus I should have been treated in return for these things? What injuries had I done, that they should take such revenge? What complaint had they, great or small, that they must not insult me only, but the deceased also? Was it not sufficient to wreak their resentment against the living? Yet they thought they were doing nothing grand, unless they insulted those now in their graves. Granting that I had injured them, as they suppose; surely it would have been becoming to spare the dead, who had done them no wrong; for they could not have the same complaint against them. Did I not ever esteem this city above every thing, and account it as dearer than my native place? And was it not a matter of my continual prayers to visit this city; and did I not make this my oath to all men?"

8. Upon this, the priest sobbing bitterly, and shedding warmer tears, no longer kept silence: for he saw that the defence of the Emperor was raising our crime to a still higher amount; but heaving from the bottom of his heart a deep and bitter sigh, he said, "We must confess, O Emperor, this love which you have shewn towards our country! We cannot deny it! On this account, especially, we mourn, that a city thus beloved has been bewitched by demons; and that we should have appeared ungrateful towards her bene- factor, and have provoked her ardent lover. And although you were to over- throw; although you were to burn; although you were to put to death; or whatever else you might do, you would never yet have taken on us the re- venge we deserve. We ourselves have, by anticipation, inflicted on our- selves what is worse than a thousand deaths! For what can be more bitter, than when we are found to have unjustly provoked our benefactor, and one who loved us so much, and the whole world knows it, and condemns us for the most monstrous ingratitude! If Barbarians had made an incursion on our city, and razed its walls, and burnt its houses, and had taken and car- ried us away captive, the evil had been less.

9. . . . Though it is a strange thing, [O Emperor,] I must say, display towards us now still greater kindness than ever; and again write this city's name among the foremost in your love;—if you are indeed desirous of being revenged upon the demons who were the instigators of these crimes! For if you pull down, and overturn, and raze the city, you will be doing those very things which they have long been desiring. But if you dismiss your anger, and again avow that you love it even as you did before, you have given them a deadly blow. You have taken the most perfect revenge upon them by shewing, not only that nothing whatever has come for them of their evil designs; but that all hath proved the very opposite of what they wished. . . .

10. You say now, that you have been insulted, and sustained wrongs such

as no Emperor ever yet did. But if you will, O most gracious, most wise, and most religious Sovereign, this contempt will procure you a crown, more honourable and splendid than the diadem you wear! For this diadem is a display of your princely virtue, but it is also a token of the munificence of him who gave it; but the crown woven from this your humanity will be entirely your own good work, and all men will admire you less for the sake of these precious stones, than they will applaud you for your superiority over this wrath. Were your Statues thrown down? You have it in your power again to set up others yet more splendid. For if you remit the offences of those who have done you injury, and take no revenge upon them, they will erect a statue to you, not one in the forum of brass, nor of gold, nor inlaid with gems; but one arrayed in that robe which is more precious than any material, that of humanity and tender mercy! Every man will thus set you up in his own soul; and you will have as many statues, as there are men who now inhabit, or shall hereafter inhabit, the whole world! For not only we, but all those who come after us, and their successors, will hear of these things, and will admire and love you, just as if they themselves had experienced this kindness!

11. And to shew that I do not speak this in a way of flattery, but that it will certainly be so, I will relate to you an ancient piece of history, that you may understand that no armies, nor warlike weapons, nor money, nor multitude of subjects, nor any other such things are wont to make sovereigns so illustrious, as wisdom of soul and gentleness. It is related of the blessed Constantine, that on one occasion, when a statue of himself had been pelted with stones, and many were instigating him to proceed against the perpetrators of the outrage; saying, that they had disfigured his whole face by battering it with stones, he stroked his face with his hand, and smiling gently, said, "I am quite unable to perceive any wound inflicted upon my face. The head appears sound, and the face also quite sound." Thus these persons, overwhelmed with shame, desisted from their unrighteous counsel.

This saying, even to the present day, all repeat; and length of time hath neither weakened nor extinguished the memory of such exalted wisdom. How much more illustrious is such an action, than any number of warlike trophies! Many and great cities did he build, and many barbarous tribes did he conquer; not one of which we now remember; but this saying is repeated over and over again, to the present day; and those who follow us, as well as those who come after them, will all hear of it. Nor indeed is this the only admirable thing; that they will hear of it; but that when men speak of it, they do so with approbation and applause; and those who hear of it, receive it with the like; and there is no one who, when he has heard it, is able to remain silent, but each at once cries out, and applauds the man who uttered it, and prays that innumerable blessings may be his lot even now deceased. But if amongst men, this saying has gained him so much honour, how many crowns will he obtain with the merciful God! . . .

13. Reflect, that the matter now for your consideration is not respecting this city only, but is one that concerns your own glory; or rather, one that affects the cause of Christianity in general. . . .

16. For consider, what it is for all posterity to hear it reported, that when so great a city had become obnoxious to punishment and vengeance, that when all were terrified, when its generals, its magistrates and judges, were all in horror and alarm, and did not dare to utter a word on behalf of the wretched people; a single old man, invested with the priesthood of God, came and moved the heart of the Monarch by his mere aspect and intercourse; and that the favour which he bestowed upon no other of his subjects, he granted to this one old man, being actuated by a reverence for God's laws! For in this very thing, O Emperor, that I have been sent hither on this embassy, the city hath done you no small honour; for they have thus pronounced the best and most honourable judgment on you, which is, that you respect the priests of God, however insignificant they may be, more than any office placed under your authority!

17. But at the present time I have come not from these only, but rather from One who is the common Lord of angels and men, to address these words to your most merciful and most gentle soul, "If ye forgive men their debts, your heavenly Father will forgive you your trespasses." [10] Remember then that Day when we shall all give an account of our actions! Consider that if you have sinned in any respect, you will be able to wipe away all offences by this sentence and by this determination, and that without difficulty and without toil. Some when they go on an embassy, bring gold, and silver, and other gifts of that kind. But I am come into your royal presence with the sacred laws; and instead of all other gifts, I present these; and I exhort you to imitate your Lord, who whilst He is daily insulted by us, unceasingly ministers His blessings to all! And do not confound our hopes, nor defeat our promises. For I wish you withal to understand, that if it be your resolution to be reconciled, and to restore your former kindness to the city, and to remit this just displeasure, I shall go back with great confidence. But if you determine to cast off the city, I shall not only never return to it, nor see its soil again, but I shall in future utterly disown it, and enroll myself a member of some other city; for God forbid that I should ever belong to that country, which you, the most mild and merciful of all men, refuse to admit to peace and reconciliation!

18. Having said this, and much more to the same effect, he so overcame

10. Matt. 6:12.

the Emperor, that the same thing occurred which once happened to Joseph. For just as he, when he beheld his brethren, longed to shed tears, but restrained his feeling, in order that he might not spoil the part which he was playing; even so did the Emperor mentally weep, but did not let it be seen, for the sake of those who were present. He was not, however, able to conceal the feeling at the close of the conference; but betrayed himself, though against his will. For after this speech was finished, no further words were necessary, but he gave utterance to one only sentiment, which did him much more honour than the diadem. And what was that? "How," said he, "can it be any thing wonderful or great, that we should remit our anger against those who have treated us with indignity; we, who ourselves are but men; when the Lord of the universe, having come as He did on earth, and having been made a servant for us, and crucified by those who had experienced His kindness, besought the Father on behalf of His crucifiers, saying, 'Forgive them, for they know not what they do?' [11] What marvel, then, if we also should forgive our fellow servants!" . . .

11. Luke 23:34.

21. Sozomen, *Ecclesiastical History*, Book 8

16. The Dispute between the Empress and John. Arrival of Theophilus from Egypt. Cyrinus, Bishop of Chalcedon.

After the departure of Epiphanius, John, when preaching in the church as usual, chanced to inveigh against the vices to which females are peculiarly prone. The people imagined that his strictures were enigmatically directed against the wife of the emperor. The enemies of the bishop did not fail to report his discourse in this sense to the empress; and she, conceiving herself to have been insulted, complained to the emperor, and urged the necessity for the speedy presence of Theophilus and the convocation of a council. Severian, bishop of Gabala, who had not yet changed his former resentment against John, cooperated in the promotion of these measures. I am not in possession of sufficient data to determine whether there was any truth in the current report that John delivered the discourse above mentioned with express allusion to the empress, because he suspected her of having excited Epiphanius against him. Theophilus arrived soon after at Chalcedon in Bithynia, and was followed thither by many bishops. Some of the bishops joined him in obedience to the commands of the emperor. The bishops whom John had deposed in Asia repaired to Chalcedon with

From *Ecclesiastical History*, bk. 8, chaps. 16, 20–21, in *Nicene and Post-Nicene Fathers*, 2d ser., vol. 2 (New York: Christian Literature Co., 1890), pp. 409–12.

the utmost alacrity, as likewise all those who cherished any feeling of hostility against him. The ships which Theophilus expected from Egypt had already come to Chalcedon. When they had convened again in the same place, and when they had deliberated how the attempt against John might be judiciously forwarded by them, Cyrinus, leader of the church of Chalcedon, who was an Egyptian and a relative of Theophilus, and who had besides some other difficulties with John, spoke very abusively of him. Justice, however, seemed to follow him speedily; for Maruthas, a native of Mesopotamia, who had accompanied the bishops, happened to tread on his foot; and Cyrinus suffered so severely from this accident that he was unable to repair with the other bishops to Constantinople, although his aid was necessary to the execution of the designs that had been formed against John. The wound assumed so alarming an appearance, that the surgeons were obliged to perform several operations on the leg; and at length mortification took place, and spread over the whole body, and even extended to the other foot. He expired soon afterwards in great agony.

20. The Statue of the Empress; What Happened There; The Teaching of John; Convocation of Another Synod Against John; His Deposition.

Not long after these occurrences the silver statue of the empress, which is still to be seen to the south of the church opposite the grand council-chamber, was placed upon a column of porphyry on a high platform, and the event was celebrated there with applause and popular spectacles of dances and mimes, as was then customary on the erection of the statues of the emperors. In a public discourse to the people John charged that these proceedings reflected dishonor on the Church. This remark recalled former grievances to the recollection of the empress, and irritated her so exceedingly at the insult that she determined to convene another council. He did not yield, but added fuel to her indignation by still more openly declaiming against her in the church; and it was at this period that he pronounced the memorable discourse commencing with the words, "Herodias is again enraged; again she dances; again she seeks to have the head of John in a basin."

Several bishops arrived soon after at Constantinople, and amongst them were Leontius, bishop of Ancyra, and Acacius, bishop of Berea. The festival of our Lord's Nativity was then at hand, and the emperor, instead of repairing to the church as usual, sent to acquaint John that he could not hold communion with him until he had cleared himself of the charges. John spiritedly replied that he was ready to prove his innocence; and this so intimidated his accusers that they did not dare to follow up the charges. The judges decided that, having been once deposed, he ought not to be admitted to a second trial. But they called on John to defend himself on this point only, that after he had been deposed, he had sat on the episcopal throne before a synod had reinstated him. In his defense he appealed to the decision of the bishops who had, subsequently to the council of "The Oak," held communion with him. The judges waived this argument, under the plea that those who had held communion with John were inferior in point of number to those who had deposed him, and that a canon was in force by which he stood condemned. Under this pretext they therefore deposed him, although the law in question had been enacted by heretics; for the Arians, after having taken advantage of various calumnies to expel Athanasius from the church of Alexandria, enacted this law from the apprehension of a change in public affairs, for they struggled to have the decisions against him remain uninvestigated.

21. Calamities Suffered by the People After the Expulsion of John. The Plots Against Him of Assassination.

After his deposition, John held no more assemblies in the church, but quietly remained in the episcopal dwelling-house. At the termination of the season of Quadragesima, on the same holy night in which the yearly festival in commemoration of the resurrection of Christ is celebrated, the followers of John were expelled from the church by the soldiers and his enemies, who attacked the people while still celebrating the mysteries. Since this occurrence was unforeseen, a great disturbance arose in the baptistery. The women wept and lamented, and the children screamed; the priests and the deacons were beaten, and were forcibly ejected from the church, in the priestly garments in which they had been officiating. They were charged with the commission of such disorderly acts as can be readily conceived by those who have been admitted to the mysteries, but which I consider it requisite to pass over in silence, lest my work should fall into the hands of the uninitiated. . . .

22. *Codex Theodosianus*, 15.4.1

Emperor Theodosius Augustus and Valentinian Caesar to Aetius, Praetorian Prefect.

   If at any time, whether on festal days, as is usual, or on ordinary days, statues or images of Us are erected, the judge shall be present without em-

From *The Theodosian Code and Novels and the Sirmondian Constitutions*, translated by Clyde Pharr (Princeton: Princeton University Press, 1952), p. 432. © 1952 by Clyde Pharr; © renewed 1980 by Roy Pharr. All footnotes deleted. Reprinted by permission of the publisher.

ploying the vainglorious heights of adoration, but so that he may show that his presence has graced the day, the place, and Our memory. Likewise if Our images are shown at plays or games, they shall demonstrate that Our divinity and glory live only in the hearts and the secret places of the minds of those who attend. A worship in excess of human dignity shall be reserved for the Supernal Divinity.

Given on the third day before the nones of May in the year of the eleventh consulship of Theodosius Augustus and the consulship of Valentinian Caesar. [May 5, 425.]

23. Ambrose, *Letters 17 and 18*

Letter 17

Ambrose, Bishop, to the most blessed Prince and most Christian Emperor Valentinian [II].

1. As all men who live under the Roman sway engage in military service under you, the Emperors and Princes of the world, so too do you yourselves owe service to Almighty God and our holy faith. For salvation is not sure unless everyone worship in truth the true God, that is the God of the Christians, under Whose sway are all things; for He alone is the true God, Who is to be worshipped from the bottom of the heart; for "the gods of the heathen," as Scripture says, "are devils." [1]

2. Now everyone is a soldier of this true God, and he who receives and worships Him in his inmost spirit, does not bring to His service dissimulation, or pretence, but earnest faith and devotion. And if, in fine, he does not attain to this, at least he ought not to give any countenance to the worship of idols and to profane ceremonies. For no one deceives God, to whom all things, even the hidden things of the heart, are manifest.

3. Since, then, most Christian Emperor, there is due from you to the true God both faith and zeal, care and devotion for the faith, I wonder how the hope has risen up to some, that you would feel it a duty to restore by your command altars to the gods of the heathen, and furnish the funds requisite for profane sacrifices; for whatsoever has long been claimed by either the imperial or the city treasury you will seem to give rather from your own funds, than to be restoring what is theirs.

4. And they are complaining of their losses, who never spared our blood, who destroyed the very buildings of the churches. And they petition

From *Nicene and Post-Nicene Fathers*, 2d ser., vol. 10 (New York: Christian Literature Co., 1896), pp. 411–22.

1. Ps. 96 [95]:5.

you to grant them privileges, who by the last Julian law denied us the common right of speaking and teaching, and those privileges whereby Christians also have often been deceived; for by those privileges they endeavoured to ensnare some, partly through inadvertance, partly in order to escape the burden of public requirements; and, because all are not found to be brave, even under Christian princes, many have lapsed.

5. Had these things not been abolished I could prove that they ought to be done away by your authority; but since they have been forbidden and prohibited by many princes throughout nearly the whole world, and were abolished at Rome by Gratian of august memory, the brother of your Clemency, in consideration of the true faith, and rendered void by a rescript; do not, I pray you, either pluck up what has been established in accordance with the faith, nor rescind your brother's precepts. In civil matters if he established anything, no one thinks that it ought to be treated lightly, while a precept about religion is trodden under foot.

6. Let no one take advantage of your youth; if he be a heathen who demands this, it is not right that he should bind your mind with the bonds of his own superstition; but by his zeal he ought to teach and admonish you how to be zealous for the true faith, since he defends vain things with all the passion of truth. I myself advise you to defer to the merits of illustrious men, but undoubtedly God must be preferred to all.

7. If we have to consult concerning military affairs, the opinion of a man experienced in warfare should be waited for, and his counsel be followed; when the question concerns religion, think upon God. No one is injured because God is set before him. He keeps his own opinion. You do not compel a man against his will to worship what he dislikes. Let the same liberty be given to you, O Emperor, and let every one bear it with patience, if he cannot extort from the Emperor what he would take it ill if the Emperor desired to extort from him. A shuffling spirit is displeasing to the heathen themselves, for everyone ought freely to defend and maintain the faith and purpose of his own mind.

8. But if any, Christians in name, think that any such decree should be made, let not bare words mislead your mind, let not empty words deceive you. Whoever advises this, and whoever decrees it, sacrifices. But that one should sacrifice is more tolerable than that all should fall. Here the whole Senate of Christians is in danger.

9. If to-day any heathen Emperor should build an altar, which God forbid, to idols, and should compel Christians to come together thither, in order to be amongst those who were sacrificing, so that the smoke and ashes from the altar, the sparks from the sacrilege, the smoke from the burning might choke the breath and throats of the faithful, and should give judgment in that court where members were compelled to vote after swear-

ing at the altar of an idol (for they explain that an altar is so placed for this purpose, that every assembly should deliberate under its sanction, as they suppose, though the Senate is now made up with a majority of Christians), a Christian who was compelled with a choice such as this to come to the Senate, would consider it to be persecution, which often happens, for they are compelled to come together even by violence. Are these Christians, when you are Emperor, compelled to swear at a heathen altar? What is an oath, but a confession of the divine power of Him Whom you invoke as watcher over your good faith? When you are Emperor, this is sought and demanded, that you should command an altar to be built, and the cost of profane sacrifices to be granted.

10. But this cannot be decreed without sacrilege, wherefore I implore you not to decree or order it, nor to subscribe to any decrees of that sort. I, as a priest of Christ, call upon your faith, all of us bishops would have joined in calling upon you, were not the report so sudden and incredible, that any such thing had been either suggested in your council, or petitioned for by the Senate. But far be it from the Senate to have petitioned this, a few heathen are making use of the common name. For, nearly two years ago, when the same attempt was being made, holy Damasus, Bishop of the Roman Church, elected by the judgment of God, sent to me a memorial, which the Christian senators in great numbers put forth, protesting that they had given no such authority, that they did not agree with such requests of the heathen, nor give consent to them, and they declared publicly and privately that they would not come to the Senate, if any such thing were decreed. Is it agreeable to the dignity of your, that is Christian, times, that Christian senators should be deprived of their dignity, in order that effect should be given to the profane will of the heathen? This memorial I sent to your Clemency's brother, and from it it was plain that the Senate had made no order about the expenses of superstition.

11. But perhaps it may be said, why were they not before present in the Senate when those petitions were made? By not being present they sufficiently say what they wish, they said enough in what they said to the Emperor. And do we wonder if those persons deprive private persons at Rome of the liberty of resisting, who are unwilling that you should be free not to command what you do not approve, or to maintain your own opinion?

12. And so, remembering the legation lately entrusted to me, I call again upon your faith. I call upon your own feelings not to determine to answer according to this petition of the heathen, nor to attach to an answer of such a sort the sacrilege of your subscription. Refer to the father of your Piety, the Emperor Theodosius, whom you have been wont to consult in almost all matters of greater importance. Nothing is greater than religion, nothing more exalted than faith.

13. If it were a civil cause the right of reply would be reserved for the opposing party; it is a religious cause, and I the bishop make a claim. Let a copy of the memorial which has been sent be given me, that I may answer more fully, and then let your Clemency's father be consulted on the whole subject, and vouchsafe an answer. Certainly if anything else is decreed, we bishops cannot contentedly suffer it and take no notice; you indeed may come to the church, but will find either no priest there, or one who will resist you.

14. What will you answer a priest who says to you, "The church does not seek your gifts, because you have adorned the heathen temples with gifts. The altar of Christ rejects your gifts, because you have made an altar for idols, for the voice is yours, the hand is yours, the subscription is yours, the deed is yours. The Lord Jesus refuses and rejects your service, because you have served idols, for He said to you: 'Ye cannot serve two masters.' The Virgins consecrated to God have no privileges from you, and do the Vestal Virgins claim them? Why do you ask for the priests of God, to whom you have preferred the profane petitions of the heathen? We cannot take up a share of the errors of others."

15. What will you answer to these words? That you who have fallen are but a boy? Every age is perfect in Christ, every age is full of God. No childhood is allowed in faith, for even children have confessed Christ against their persecutors with fearless mouth.

16. What will you answer your brother? Will he not say to you, "I did not feel that I was overcome, because I left you as Emperor; I did not grieve at dying, because I had you as my heir; I did not mourn at leaving my imperial command, because I believed that my commands, especially those concerning divine religion, would endure through all ages. I had set up these memorials of piety and virtue, I offered up these spoils gained from the world, these trophies of victory over the devil, these I offered up as gained from the enemy of all, and in them is eternal victory. What more could my enemy take away from me? You have abrogated my decrees, which so far he who took up arms against me did not do. Now do I receive a more terrible wound in that my decrees are condemned by my brother. My better part is endangered by you, that was but the death of my body, this of my reputation. Now is my power annulled, and what is harder, annulled by my own family, and that is annulled, which even my enemies spoke well of in me. If you consented of your own free will, you have condemned the faith which was mine; if you yielded unwillingly, you have betrayed your own. So, too, which is more serious, I am in danger in your person."

16. What will you answer your father also? who with greater grief will address you, saying, "You judged very ill of me, my son, when you sup-

posed that I could have connived at the heathen. No one ever told me that there was an altar in the Roman Senate House, I never believed such wickedness as that the heathen sacrificed in the common assembly of Christians and heathen, that is to say that the Gentiles should insult the Christians who were present, and that Christians should be compelled against their will to be present at the sacrifices. Many and various crimes were committed whilst I was Emperor. I punished such as were detected; if any one then escaped notice, ought one to say that I approved of that of which no one informed me? You have judged very ill of me, if a foreign superstition and not my own faith preserved the empire."

17. Wherefore, O Emperor, since you see that if you decree anything of that kind, injury will be done, first to God, and then to your father and brother, I implore you to do that which you know will be profitable to your salvation before God.

The Memorial of Symmachus, Prefect of the City

[Symmachus addresses his memorial in the name of the Senate, nominally to the three Emperors, Valentinian, Theodosius, and Arcadius, though really to the first of these alone, who was sole Emperor of the West. The memorial sets forth a request that the old religion should be restored, and the Altar of Victory again erected in the Senate House, that the ancient customs might be observed. The example of the late emperors should be followed in what they maintained, not in what they did away with. The treasury would suffer no loss, whilst it is unjust that the Vestal Virgins and priests should be deprived of ancient legacies, a sacrilege which the gods punished by a famine. The memorial is drawn up with consummate skill, both in what is brought forward and in what is left unsaid.]

1. As soon as the most honourable Senate, always devoted to you, knew that crimes were made amenable to law, and that the reputation of late times was being purified by pious princes, it, following the example of a more favourable time, gave utterance to its long suppressed grief, and bade me be once again the delegate to utter its complaints. But through wicked men audience was refused me by the divine Emperor, otherwise justice would not have been wanting, my lords and emperors, of great renown, Valentinian, Theodosius, and Arcadius, victorious and triumphant, ever august.

2. In the exercise, therefore, of a twofold office, as your Prefect I attend to public business, and as delegate I recommend to your notice the charge laid on me by the citizens. Here is no disagreement of wills, for men have now ceased to believe that they excel in courtly zeal, if they disagree. To be loved, to be reverenced, to be esteemed is more than imperial sway. Who

could endure that private disagreement should injure the state? Rightly does the Senate censure those who have preferred their own power to the reputation of the prince.

3. But it is our task to watch on behalf of your Graces. For to what is it more suitable that we defend the institutions of our ancestors, and the rights and destiny of our country, than to the glory of these times, which is all the greater when you understand that you may not do anything contrary to the custom of your ancestors? We demand then the restoration of that condition of religious affairs which was so long advantageous to the state. Let the rulers of each sect and of each opinion be counted up; a late one practised the ceremonies of his ancestors, a later did not put them away. If the religion of old times does not make a precedent, let the connivance of the last do so.

4. Who is so friendly with the barbarians as not to require an Altar of Victory? We will be careful henceforth, and avoid a show of such things. But at least let that honour be paid to the name which is refused to the goddess—your fame, which will last for ever, owes much and will owe still more to victory. Let those be averse to this power, whom it has never benefited. Do you refuse to desert a patronage which is friendly to your triumphs? That power is wished for by all, let no one deny that what he acknowledges is to be desired should also be venerated.

5. But even if the avoidance of such an omen were not sufficient, it would at least have been seemly to abstain from injuring the ornaments of the Senate House. Allow us, we beseech you, as old men to leave to posterity what we received as boys. The love of custom is great. Justly did the act of the divine Constantius last but for a short time. All precedents ought to be avoided by you, which you know were soon abolished. We are anxious for the permanence of your glory and your name, that the time to come may find nothing which needs correction.

6. Where shall we swear to obey your laws and commands? by what religious sanction shall the false mind be terrified, so as not to lie in bearing witness? All things are indeed filled with God, and no place is safe for the perjured, but to be urged in the very presence of religious forms has great power in producing a fear of sinning. That altar preserves the concord of all, that altar appeals to the good faith of each, and nothing gives more authority to our decrees than that the whole of our order issues every decree as it were under the sanction of an oath. So that a place will be opened to perjury, and this will be determined by my illustrious Princes, whose honour is defended by a public oath.

7. But the divine Constantius is said to have done the same. Let us rather imitate the other actions of that Prince, who would have undertaken nothing of the kind, if any one else had committed such an error before

him. For the fall of the earlier sets his successor right, and amendment results from the censure of a previous example. It was pardonable for your Grace's ancestor in so novel a matter to fail in guarding against blame. Can the same excuse avail us if we imitate what we know to have been disapproved?

8. Will your Majesties listen to other actions of this same Prince, which you may more worthily imitate? He diminished none of the privileges of the sacred virgins, he filled the priestly offices with nobles, he did not refuse the cost of the Roman ceremonies, and following the rejoicing Senate through all the streets of the eternal city, he contentedly beheld the shrines with unmoved countenance, he read the names of the gods inscribed on the pediments, he enquired about the origin of the temples, and expressed admiration for their builders. Although he himself followed another religion, he maintained its own for the empire, for everyone has his own customs, everyone his own rites. The divine Mind has distributed different guardians and different cults to different cities. As souls are separately given to infants as they are born, so to peoples the genius of their destiny. Here comes in the proof from advantage, which most of all vouches to man for the gods. For, since our reason is wholly clouded, whence does the knowledge of the gods more rightly come to us, than from the memory and evidence of prosperity? Now if a long period gives authority to religious customs, we ought to keep faith with so many centuries, and to follow our ancestors, as they happily followed theirs.

9. Let us now suppose that Rome is present and addresses you in these words: "Excellent princes, fathers of your country, respect my years to which pious rites have brought me. Let me use the ancestral ceremonies, for I do not repent of them. Let me live after my own fashion, for I am free. This worship subdued the world to my laws, these sacred rites repelled Hannibal from the walls, and the Senones from the capitol. Have I been reserved for this, that in my old age I should be blamed? I will consider what it is thought should be set in order, but tardy and discreditable is the reformation of old age."

10. We ask, then, for peace for the gods of our fathers and of our country. It is just that all worship should be considered as one. We look on the same stars, the sky is common, the same world surrounds us. What difference does it make by what pains each seeks the truth? We cannot attain to so great a secret by one road; but this discussion is rather for persons at ease, we offer now prayers, not conflict.

11. With what advantage to your treasury are the prerogatives of the Vestal Virgins diminished? Is that refused under the most bountiful emperors which the most parsimonious have granted? Their sole honour consists in that, so to call it, wage of chastity. As fillets are the ornament of

their heads, so is their distinction drawn from their leisure to attend to the offices of sacrifice. They seek for in a measure the empty name of immunity, since by their poverty they are exempt from payment. And so they who diminish anything of their substance increase their praise, inasmuch as virginity dedicated to the public good increases in merit when it is without reward.

12. Let such gains as these be far from the purity of your treasury. Let the revenue of good princes be increased not by the losses of priests, but by the spoils of enemies. Does any gain compensate for the odium? And because no charge of avarice falls upon your characters, they are the more wretched whose ancient revenues are diminished. For under emperors who abstain from what belongs to others, and resist avarice, that which does not move the desire of him who takes it, is taken solely to injure the loser.

13. The treasury also retains lands bequeathed to virgins and ministers by the will of dying persons. I entreat you, priests of justice, let the lost right of succession be restored to the sacred persons and places of your city. Let men dictate their wills without anxiety, and know that what has been written will be undisturbed under princes who are not avaricious. Let the happiness in this point of all men give pleasure to you, for precedents in this matter have begun to trouble the dying. Does not then the religion of Rome appertain to Roman law? What name shall be given to the taking away of property which no law nor accident has made to fail? Freedmen take legacies, slaves are not denied the just privilege of making wills; only noble virgins and the ministers of sacred rites are excluded from property sought by inheritance. What does it profit the public safety to dedicate the body to chastity, and to support the duration of the empire with heavenly guardianship, to attach the friendly powers to your arms and to your eagles, to take upon oneself vows efficacious for all, and not to have common rights with all? So, then, slavery is a better condition, which is a service rendered to men. We injure the State, whose interest it never is to be ungrateful.

14. And let no one think that I am defending the cause of religion only, for from deeds of this kind have arisen all the misfortunes of the Roman race. The law of our ancestors honoured the Vestal Virgins and the ministers of the gods with a moderate maintenance and just privileges. This grant remained unassailed till the time of the degenerate money-changers, who turned the fund for the support of sacred chastity into hire for common porters. A general famine followed upon this, and a poor harvest disappointed the hopes of all the provinces. This was not the fault of the earth, we impute no evil influence to the stars. Mildew did not injure the crops, nor wild oats destroy the corn; the year failed through the sacrilege, for it was necessary that what was refused to religion should be denied to all.

15. Certainly, if there be any instance of this evil, let us impute such a famine to the power of the season. A deadly wind has been the cause of this barrenness, life is sustained by trees and shrubs, and the need of the country folk has betaken itself once more to the oaks of Dodona. What similar evil did the provinces suffer, so long as the public charge sustained the ministers of religion? When were the oaks shaken for the use of men, when were the roots of plants torn up, when did fertility on all sides forsake the various lands, when supplies were in common for the people and for the sacred virgins? For the support of the priests was a blessing to the produce of the earth, and was rather an insurance than a bounty. Is there any doubt that what was given was for the benefit of all, seeing that the want of all has made this plain?

16. But some one will say that public support is only refused to the cost of foreign religions. Far be it from good princes to suppose that what has been given to certain persons from the common property can be in the power of the treasury. For as the State consists of individuals, that which goes out from it becomes again the property of individuals. You rule over all; but you preserve his own for each individual; and justice has more weight with you than arbitrary will. Take counsel with your own liberality whether that which you have conferred on others ought to be considered public property. Sums once given to the honour of the city cease to be the property of those who have given them, and that which at the commencement was a gift, by custom and time becomes a debt. Any one is therefore endeavouring to impress upon your minds a vain fear, who asserts that you share the responsibility of the givers unless you incur the odium of withdrawing the gifts.

17. May the unseen guardians of all sects be favourable to your Graces, and may they especially, who in old time assisted your ancestors, defend you and be worshipped by us. We ask for that state of religious matters which preserved the empire for the divine parent of your Highnesses, and furnished that blessed prince with lawful heirs. That venerable father beholds from the starry height the tears of the priests, and considers himself censured by the violation of that custom which he willingly observed.

18. Amend also for your divine brother that which he did by the counsel of others, cover over the deed which he knew not to be displeasing to the Senate. For it is allowed that that legation was denied access to him, lest public opinion should reach him. It is for the credit of former times, that you should not hesitate to abolish that which is proved not to have been the doing of the prince.

Letter 18

[Ambrose's reply to Symmachus.]

Ambrose, Bishop, to the most blessed prince and most gracious Emperor Valentianus, the august.

1. Since the illustrious Symmachus, Prefect of the city, has sent petition to your Grace that the altar, which was taken away from the Senate House of the city of Rome, should be restored to its place; and you, O Emperor, although still young in years and experience, yet a veteran in the power of faith, did not approve the prayer of the heathen, I presented a request the moment I heard of it, in which, though I stated such things as it seemed necessary to suggest, I requested that a copy of the Memorial might be given to me.

2. So, then, not being in doubt as to your faith, but anxiously considering the risk, and sure of a kindly consideration, I am replying in this document to the assertions of the Memorial, making this sole request, that you will not expect elegance of language but the force of facts. For, as the divine Scripture teaches, the tongue of wise and studious men is golden, which, gifted with glittering words and shining with the brilliancy of splendid utterance as if of some rich colour, captivates the eyes of the mind with the appearance of beauty and dazzles with the sight. But this gold, if you consider it carefully, is of value outwardly but within is base metal. Ponder well, I pray you, and examine the sect of the heathen, their utterances, sound, weighty, and grand, but defend what is without capacity for truth. They speak of God and worship idols.

3. The illustrious Prefect of the city has in his Memorial set forth three propositions which he considers of force: that Rome, as he says, asks for her rites again, that pay be given to her priests and Vestal Virgins, and that a general famine followed upon the refusal of the priests' stipends.

4. In his first proposition Rome complains with sad and tearful words, asking, as he says, for the restoration of the rites of her ancient ceremonies. These sacred rites, he says, repulsed Hannibal from the walls, and the Senones from the Capitol. And so at the same time that the power of the sacred rites is proclaimed, their weakness is betrayed. So that Hannibal long insulted the Roman rites, and while the gods were fighting against him, arrived a conqueror at the very walls of the city. Why did they suffer themselves to be besieged, for whom their gods were fighting in arms?

5. And why should I say anything of the Senones, whose entrance into the inmost Capitol the remnant of the Romans could not have prevented, had not a goose by its frightened cackling betrayed them? See what sort of protectors the Roman temples have. Where was Jupiter at that time? Was he speaking in the goose?

6. But why should I deny that their sacred rites fought for the Romans?

For Hannibal also worshipped the same gods. Let them choose then which they will. If these sacred rites conquered in the Romans, then they were overcome in the Carthaginians; if they triumphed in the Carthaginians, they certainly did not benefit the Romans.

7. Let, then, that invidious complaint of the Roman people come to an end. Rome has given no such charge. She speaks with other words. "Why do you daily stain me with the useless blood of the harmless herd? Trophies of victory depend not on the entrails of the flocks, but on the strength of those who fight. I subdued the world by a different discipline. Camillus was my soldier, who slew those who had taken the Tarpeian rock, and brought back the standards taken from the Capitol; valour laid those low whom religion had not driven off. What shall I say of Attilius [Regulus], who gave the service of his death? Africanus found his triumphs not amongst the altars of the Capitol, but amongst the lines of Hannibal. Why do you bring forward the rites of our ancestors? I hate the rites of Neros. Why should I speak of the Emperors of two months, and the ends of rulers closely joined to their commencements? Or is it perchance a new thing for the barbarians to cross their boundaries? Were they, too, Christians in whose wretched and unprecedented cases, the one, a captive Emperor, and, under the other, the captive world made manifest that their rites which promised victory were false? Was there then no Altar of Victory? I mourn over my downfall, my old age is tinged with that shameful bloodshed. I do not blush to be converted with the whole world in my old age. It is undoubtedly true that no age is too late to learn. Let that old age blush which cannot amend itself. Not the old age of years is worthy of praise but that of character. There is no shame in passing to better things. This alone was common to me with the barbarians, that of old I knew not God. Your sacrifice is a rite of being sprinkled with the blood of beasts. Why do you seek the voice of God in dead animals? Come and learn on earth the heavenly warfare; we live here, but our warfare is there. Let God Himself, Who made me, teach me the mystery of heaven, not man, who knew not himself. Whom rather than God should I believe concerning God? How can I believe you, who confess that you know not what you worship?"

8. By one road, says he, one cannot attain to so great a secret. What you know not, that we know by the voice of God. And what you seek by fancies, we have found out from the very Wisdom and Truth of God. Your ways, therefore, do not agree with ours. You implore peace for your gods from the Emperors, we ask for peace for the Emperors themselves from Christ. You worship the works of our own hands, we think it an offence that anything which can be made should be esteemed God. God wills not that He should be worshipped in stones. And, in fine, your philosophers themselves have ridiculed these things.

9. But if you deny Christ to be God, because you believe not that He

died (for you are ignorant that that death was of the body not of the God-head, which has brought it to pass that now no one of those who believe dies), what is more thoughtless than you who honour with insult, and disparage with honour, for you consider a piece of wood to be your god. O worship full of insult! You believe not that Christ could die, O perversity founded on respect!

10. But, says he, let the altars be restored to the images, and their ornaments to the shrines. Let this demand be made of one who shares in their superstitions; a Christian Emperor has learnt to honour the altar of Christ alone. Why do they exact of pious hands and faithful lips the ministry to their sacrilege? Let the voice of our Emperor utter the name of Christ alone, and speak of Him only, Whom he is conscious of, for, "the King's heart is in the hand of the Lord." [2] Has any heathen Emperor raised an altar to Christ? While they demand the restoration of things which have been, by their own example they show us how great reverence Christian Emperors ought to pay to the religion which they follow, since heathen ones offered all to their superstitions.

11a. We began long since, and now they follow those whom they excluded. We glory in yielding our blood, an expense moves them. We consider these things in the place of victories, they think them loss. Never did they confer on us a greater benefit than when they ordered Christians to be beaten and proscribed and slain. Religion made a reward of that which unbelief thought to be a punishment. See their greatness of soul! We have increased through loss, through want, through punishment; they do not believe that their rites can continue without contributions.

11. Let the Vestal Virgins, he says, retain their privileges. Let those speak thus, who are unable to believe that virginity can exist without reward, let those who do not trust virtue, encourage by gain. But how many virgins have the promised rewards gained for them? Hardly are seven Vestal Virgins received. See the whole number whom the fillets and chaplets for the head, the dye of the purple robes, the pomp of the litter surrounded by a company of attendants, the greatest privileges, immense profits, and a prescribed time of virginity have gathered together.

12. Let them lift up the eyes of soul and body, let them look upon a people of modesty, a people of purity, an assembly of virginity. Not fillets are the ornament of their heads, but a veil common in use but ennobled by chastity, the enticement of beauty not sought out but laid aside, none of those purple insignia, no delicious luxuries, but the practice of fasts, no privileges, no gains; all things, in fine, of such a kind that one would think them restrained from enjoyment whilst practising their duties. But whilst

2. Prov. 21:1.

the duty is being practised the enjoyment of it is aroused. Chastity is increased by its own sacrifices. That is not virginity which is bought with a price, and not kept through a love of virtue; that is not purity which is bought by auction for money, which is bid for for a time. The first victory of chastity is to conquer the desire of wealth, for the pursuit of gain is a temptation to modesty. Let us, however, lay down that bountiful provision should be granted to virgins. What an amount will overflow upon Christians! What treasury will supply such riches? Or if they think that gifts should be conferred on the Vestals alone, are they not ashamed that they who claimed the whole for themselves under heathen Emperors should think that we ought to have no common share under Christian Princes?

13. They complain, also, that public support is not considered due to their priests and ministers. What a storm of words has resounded on this point! But on the other hand even the inheritance of private property is denied us by recent laws, and no one complains; for we do not consider it an injury, because we grieve not at the loss. If a priest seeks the privilege of declining the municipal burdens, he has to give up his ancestral and all other property. If the heathen suffered this how would they urge their complaint, that a priest must purchase the free time necessary for his ministry by the loss of all his patrimony, and buy the power to exercise his public ministry at the expense of all his private means; and, alleging his vigils for the public safety, must console himself with the reward of domestic want, because he has not sold a service but obtained a favour.

14. Compare the cases. You wish to excuse a decurion, when it is not allowed the Church to excuse a priest. Wills are written on behalf of ministers of the temples, no profane person is excepted, no one of the lowest condition, no one shamelessly immodest, the clergy alone are excluded from the common right, by whom alone common prayer is offered for all, and common service rendered, no legacies even of grave widows, no gifts are permitted. And where no fault can be found in the character, a penalty is notwithstanding imposed on the office. That which a Christian widow has bequeathed to the priests of a temple is valid, her legacy to the ministers of God is invalid. And I have related this not in order to complain, but that they may know what I do not complain of; for I prefer that we should be poorer in money than in grace.

15. But they say that what has been given or left to the Church has not been touched. Let them also state who has taken away gifts from the temples, which has been done to Christians. If these things had been done to the heathen the wrong would have been rather a requital than an injury. Is it now only at last that justice is alleged as a pretext, and a claim made for equity? Where was this feeling when, after plundering the goods of all Christians, they grudged them the very breath of life, and forbade them the

use of that last burial nowhere denied to any dead? The sea restored those whom the heathen had thrown into it. This is the victory of faith, that they themselves now blame the acts of their ancestors whose deeds they condemn. But what reason is there in seeking benefits from those whose deeds they condemn?

16. No one, however, has denied gifts to the shrines, and legacies to the soothsayers, their land alone has been taken away, because they did not use religiously that which they claimed in right of religion. Why did they not practise what we did if they allege our example? The Church has no possessions of her own except the Faith. Hence are her returns, her increase. The possessions of the Church are the maintenance of the poor. Let them count up how many captives the temples have ransomed, what food they have contributed for the poor, to what exiles they have supplied the means of living. Their lands then have been taken away, not their rights.

17. See what was done, and a public famine avenged, as they say, the sad impiety that what was before profitable only for the comfort of the priests began to be profitable to the use of all. For this reason then, as they say, was the bark shipped from the copses, and fainting men's mouths supped up the unsavoury sap. For this reason changing corn for the Chaonian acorn, going back once more to the food of cattle and the nourishment of wretched provisions, they shook the oaks and solaced their dire hunger in the woods. These, forsooth, were new prodigies on earth, which had never happened before, while heathen superstition was fervent throughout the world! When in truth before did the crop mock the prayers of the grasping husbandman with empty straw, and the blade of corn sought in the furrows fail the hope of the rustic crew?

18. And from what did the Greeks derive the oracles of their oaks except from their thinking that the support of their sylvan food was the gift of heavenly religion? For such do they believe to be the gifts of their gods. Who but heathen people worshipped the trees of Dodona, when they gave honour to the sorry food of the woodland? It is not likely that their gods in anger inflicted on them as a punishment that which they used when appeased to confer as a gift. And what justice would there be if, being grieved that support was refused to a few priests, they denied it to all, since the vengeance would be more unbearable than the fault? The cause, then, is not adequate to bring such suffering on a failing world, as that the full-grown hope of the year should perish suddenly while the crops were green.

19. And, certainly, many years ago the lights of the temples were taken away throughout the world; has it only now at length come into the mind of the gods of the heathen to avenge the injury? And did the Nile fail to overflow in its accustomed course, in order to avenge the losses of the priests of the city, whilst it did not avenge its own?

20. But let it be that they suppose that the injuries done to their gods were avenged in the past year. Why have they been unnoticed in the present year? For now neither do the country people feed upon torn up roots, nor seek refreshment from the berries of the wood, nor pluck its food from thorns, but joyful in their prosperous labours, while wondering at their harvest, made up for their fasting by the full accomplishment of their wishes; for the earth rendered her produce with interest.

21. Who, then, is so unused to human matters as to be astonished at the difference of years? And yet even last year we know that many provinces abounded with produce. What shall I say of the Gauls which were more productive than usual? The Pannonias sold corn which they had not sown, and Phaetia Secunda experienced harm of her own fertility, for she who was wont to be safe in her scarcity, stirred up an enemy against herself by her fertility. The fruits of the autumn fed Liguria and the Venetias. So, then, the former year did not wither because of sacrilege, and the latter flourished with the fruits of faith. Let them too deny if they can that the vineyards abounded with an immense produce. And so we have both received a harvest with interest and possess the benefit of a more abundant vintage.

22. The last and most important point remains, whether, O Emperors, you ought to restore those helps which have profited you; for he says: "Let them defend you, and be worshipped by us." This it is, most faithful princes, which we cannot endure, that they should taunt us that they supplicate their gods in your names, and without your commands, commit an immense sacrilege, interpreting your shutting your eyes as consent. Let them have their guardians to themselves, let these, if they can, protect their worshippers. For, if they are not able to help those by whom they are worshipped, how can they protect you by whom they are not worshipped?

23. But, he says, the rites of our ancestors ought to be retained. But what, seeing that all things have made progress towards what is better? The world itself, which at first was compacted of the germs of the elements throughout the void, in a yielding sphere, or was dark with the shapeless confusion of the work as yet without order, did it not afterwards receive (the distinction between sky, sea, and earth being established), the forms of things whereby it appears beautiful? The lands freed from the misty darkness wondered at the new sun. The day does not shine in the beginning, but as time proceeds, it is bright with increase of light, and grows warm with increase of heat.

24. The moon herself, by which in the prophetic oracles the Church is represented, when first rising again, she waxes to her monthly age, is hidden from us in darkness, and filling up her horns little by little, so completing them opposite to the sun, glows with the brightness of clear shining.

25. The earth in former times was without experience of being worked for fruits; afterwards when the careful husbandman began to lord it over the fields, and to clothe the shapeless soil with vines, it put off its wild disposition, being softened by domestic cultivation.

26. The first age of the year itself, which has tinged us with a likeness to itself as things begin to grow, as it goes on becomes springlike with flowers soon about to fall, and grows up to full age in fruits at the end.

27. We too, inexperienced in age, have an infancy of our senses, but changing as years go on, lay aside the rudiments of our faculties.

28. Let them say, then, that all things ought to have remained in their first beginnings, that the world covered with darkness is now displeasing, because it has brightened with the shining of the sun. And how much more pleasant is it to have dispelled the darkness of the mind than that of the body, and that the ray of faith should have shone than that of the sun. So, then, the primeval state of the world as of all things has passed away, that the venerable old age of hoary faith might follow. Let those whom this touches find fault with the harvest, because its abundance comes late; let them find fault with the vintage, because it is at the close of the year; let them find fault with the olive, because it is the latest of fruits.

29. So, then, our harvest is the faith of souls; the grace of the Church is the vintage of merits, which from the beginning of the world flourished in the Saints, but in the last age has spread itself over the people, that all might notice that the faith of Christ has entered minds which were not rude (for there is no crown of victory without an adversary), but the opinion being exploded which before prevailed, that which was true is rightly preferred.

30. If the old rites pleased, why did Rome also take up foreign ones? I pass over the ground hidden by costly building, and shepherds' cottages glittering with degenerate gold. Why, that I may reply to the very matter which they complain of, have they eagerly received the images of captured cities, and conquered gods, and the foreign rites of alien superstition? Whence is the pattern for Cybele washing her chariots in a stream counterfeiting the Almo? Whence were the Phrygian bards, and the deities of unjust Carthage always hateful to the Romans? And her whom the Africans worship as Celestis, the Persians as Nitra, and the greater number as Venus, according to a difference of name, not a variety of deities. So they believed that Victory was a goddess, which is certainly a gift, not a power; is granted and does not rule, results from the aid of legions not the power of religions. Is that goddess then great whom the number of soldiers claims, or the event of battle gives?

31. They ask to have her altar erected in the Senate House of the city of Rome, that is where the majority who meet together are Christians! There

are altars in all the temples, and an altar also in the temple of Victories. Since they take pleasure in numbers they celebrate their sacrifices everywhere. To claim a sacrifice on this one altar, what is it but to insult the Faith? Is it to be borne that a heathen should sacrifice and a Christian be present? Let them imbibe, he says, let them imbibe, even against their will, the smoke with their eyes, the music with their ears, the ashes with their throats, the incense with their nostrils, and let the dust stirred up from our hearths cover their faces though they detest it. Are not the baths, the colonnades, the streets filled with images sufficient for them? Shall there not be a common lot in that common assembly? The faithful portion of the senate will be bound by the voices of those that call upon the gods, by the oaths of those that swear by them. If they oppose they will seem to exhibit their falsehood, if they acquiesce, to acknowledge what is sacrilege.

32. Where, says he, shall we swear obedience to your Grace's laws and decrees? Does then your mind, which is contained in the laws, gain assent and bind to faithfulness by heathen ceremonies? The faith is attacked, not only of those who are present but also of those who are absent, and what is more, O Emperors, your faith, too, is attacked, for you compel if you command. Constantius of august memory, though not yet initiated in the sacred Mysteries, thought that he would be polluted if he saw that altar. He commanded it to be removed, he did not command it to be replaced. The removal has the authority of an act, the restoration has not that of a command.

33. Let no one flatter himself because he is absent. He who joins himself to others in mind is more present than he whose assent is given by bodily presence. For it is more to be united in mind than to be joined in body. The Senate has you as the presidents who convene the assembly, it comes together for you; it gives its conscience to you, not to the gods of the heathen; it prefers you to its children, but not to its faith. This is a love to be desired, this is a love greater than any dominion, if faith which preserves dominion be secure.

34. But perhaps it may move some that if this be so, a most faithful Emperor has been forsaken, as if forsooth the reward of merits were to be estimated by the transitory measure of things present. For what wise man is ignorant that human affairs are ordered in a kind of round and cycle, for they have not always the same success, but their state varies and they suffer vicissitudes.

35. Whom have the Roman temples sent out more prosperous than Cneius Pompeius? Yet, when he had encompassed the earth with three triumphs, defeated in battle, a fugitive from war, and an exile beyond the bounds of his own empire, he fell by the hand of an eunuch of Canopus.

36. Whom has the whole land of the East given to the world more noble

than Cyrus, king of the Persians? He too, after conquering the most powerful princes who opposed him, and retaining them, when conquered, as
prisoners, perished, overthrown by the arms of a woman. And that king
who was acknowledged to have treated even the vanquished with honour,
had his head cut off, placed in a vessel full of blood, and was bidden to be
satiated, being thus subject to the mocking of a woman's power. So in the
course of that life of his like is not repaid by like, but far otherwise.

37. And whom do we find more devoted to sacrificing than Hamilcar,
leader of the Carthaginians? Who, having offered sacrifice between the
ranks during the whole time of the battle, when he saw that his side was
conquered, threw himself into the fire which he was feeding, that he might
extinguish even with his own body those fires which he had found to profit
him nothing.

38. What, then, shall I say of Julian? Who, having credulously trusted
the answers of the soothsayers, destroyed his own means of retreat. Therefore even in like cases there is not a like offence, for our promises have
deceived no one.

39. I have answered those who provoked me as though I had not been
provoked, for my object was to refute the Memorial, not to expose superstition. But let their very memorial make you, O Emperor, more careful.
For after narrating of former princes, that the earlier of them practised the
ceremonies of their fathers, and the later did not abolish them; and saying
in addition that, if the religious practice of the older did not make a precedent, the connivance of the later ones did; it plainly showed what you owe,
both to your faith, viz., that you should not follow the example of heathen
rites, and to your affection, that you should not abolish the decrees of your
brother. For if for their own side alone they have praised the connivance of
those princes, who, though Christians, yet in no way abolished the heathen
decrees, how much more ought you to defer to brotherly love, so that you,
who ought to overlook some things even if you did not approve them in
order not to detract from your brother's statutes, should now maintain what
you judge to be in agreement both with your own faith, and the bond of
brotherhood.

24. Augustine, *Letter 29*

8. When the day dawned on which they were accustomed to prepare themselves for excess in eating and drinking, I received notice that some, even

From Augustine, Letter 29, chaps. 8–9, in Joseph Cullen Ayer, *A Source Book for Ancient Church History* (New York: Charles Scribner's Sons, 1913), pp. 400–401. © 1913 by
Charles Scribner's Sons; © renewed 1941 by Joseph Cullen Ayer, Jr. Reprinted by permission
of the publisher.

of those who were present at my sermon, had not yet ceased complaining, and that so great was the power of detestable custom among them that, using no other argument, they asked: "Wherefore is this now prohibited? Were they not Christians who in former times did not interfere with this practice?" . . .

9. Lest, however, any slight should seem to be put by us upon those who before our time either tolerated or dared not put down such manifest wrong-doings of an undisciplined multitude, I explained to them the necessity by which this custom seems to have arisen in the Church; namely, that when, in the peace which came after such numerous and violent persecutions, crowds of heathen who wished to assume the Christian religion were kept back because, having been accustomed to celebrate the feasts connected with idols in revelling and drunkenness, they could not easily refrain from these pleasures so hurtful and so habitual; and it seemed good to our ancestors that for a time a concession should be made to this infirmity, that after they had renounced the former festivals they might celebrate other feasts, in honor of the holy martyrs, which were observed, not with the same profane design, although with similar indulgence. Now upon them as persons bound together in the name of Christ, and submissive to the yoke of His august authority, the wholesome restraints of sobriety were laid; and these restraints, on account of the honor and fear of Him who appointed them they might not resist; and that therefore it was now time that those who did not dare to deny that they were Christians should begin to live according to Christ's will; being now Christians they should reject those things conceded that they might become Christians.

25. Gregory I, *Dialogues*

Gregory. Yes, Peter, that godly man, Benedict, possessed the spirit of the One Who suffused the hearts of all the elect with the gracious gift of redemption. John says about him, "The true light that enlightens every man was coming into the world."[1] In another passage, John says, "And from His fullness have we all received."[2] For the holy men of God were able to acquire miraculous powers from the Lord, but not to transmit them to others as well. But Jesus conferred the power of producing miraculous signs upon His subordinates, and He also promised His enemies that He

---

From *Dialogues*, bk. 2, chap. 8, in *Dialogues of Gregory the Great*, bk. 2, *Saint Benedict*, translated by Myra L. Uhlfelder (Indianapolis: Bobbs-Merrill, 1967), book 2, chap. 8, pp. 17–18. © 1967 by Bobbs-Merrill, Inc., a subsidiary of ITT. Reprinted by permission of the publisher.

1. John 1:9.   2. John 1:16.

would produce the sign of Jonah by His willingness to die before the proud as an object of scorn, and to rise again before the humble as the worthy object of their reverent love.[3] Through this mystery it happened that, while the proud were noting the disgrace of His death, the humble realized the glory of His power against death.

Peter. Please tell me now where that holy man went and whether he exercised his miraculous powers there.

Gregory. The saint did not change his enemy by moving to another place. In fact, his later combats were even fiercer since he found the Master of Evil himself openly fighting against him. Now there is a citadel named Cassino on the slope of a high mountain. This mountain enfolds the citadel and then rises three miles above it as though stretching its peak to the upper air. There was a very ancient shrine here where Apollo was worshipped in the old pagan manner by an ignorant crowd of peasants. In all directions, groves had sprung up, dedicated to the worship of demons. Even at that time, the foolish pagan rabble would offer their unholy sacrifices in those groves. And so the man of God arrived there, destroyed the idol, overturned the altar, cut down the groves, and, in the very temple of Apollo, built a chapel in honor of the blessed Martin. Where the altar of Apollo had been, he built a chapel in honor of St. John. Also, by continuous preaching he converted many people who lived in that region. But the Devil did not submit silently. He forced himself on the abbot's sight by an open vision, not secretly or in a dream. When the Devil complained that he was suffering violence, he shouted so loudly that even the brothers heard the sounds although they could not make out his form. As the venerable abbot used to say to his disciples, the Devil appeared to him as a foul and fiery creature who seemed to rage against him with flaming mouth and eyes. Everyone could now hear what the Devil was saying as he first addressed Benedict by name. Then, since the man of God did not answer him, he soon hurled insults at him. For when he shouted, "Benedict, Benedict!" and saw that Benedict did not answer, he presently added, "Maledict, not Benedict. What do you have against me? Why are you persecuting me?" Now we must anticipate new contests of the Devil against God's servant. By choosing to wage war against Benedict, however, the Devil unwittingly provided him with opportunities for victory.

---

3. Matt. 12:39–40.

26. Justinian, *Codex*, 1.2.9, 10

Chapter 9

We command that our magistrates in this royal city and in the provinces take care with the greatest zeal that, having been informed by themselves or the most religious bishops of this matter, they make inquiry according to law into all impurities of pagan superstitions, that they be not committed, and if committed that they be punished; but if their repression exceed provincial power, these things are to be referred to us, that the responsibility for, and incitement of, these crimes may not rest upon them.

(1) It is permitted no one, either in testament or by gift, to leave or give anything to persons or places for the maintenance of pagan impiety, even if it is not expressly contained in the words of the will, testament, or donation, but can be truly perceived in some other way by the judges. (2) But those things which are so left or given shall be taken from the persons and places to whom they have been given or left, and shall belong to the cities in which such persons dwell or in which such places are situated, so that they may be paid as a form of revenue. (3) All penalties which have been introduced by previous emperors against the errors of pagans or in favor of the orthodox faith are to remain in force and effect forever and guarded by this present pious legislation.

Chapter 10

Because some are found who are imbued with the error of the impious and detestable pagans, and do those things which move a merciful God to just wrath, and that we may not suffer ourselves to leave uncorrected matters which concern these things, but, knowing that they have abandoned the worship of the true and only God, and have in insane error offered sacrifices, and, filled with all impiety, have celebrated solemnities, we subject those who have committed these things, after they have been held worthy of holy baptism, to the punishment appropriate to the crimes of which they have been convicted; but for the future we decree to all by this present law that they who have been made Christians and at any time have been deemed worthy of the holy and saving baptism, if it appear that they have remained still in the error of the pagans, shall suffer capital punishment.

From Joseph Cullen Ayer, *A Source Book for Ancient Church History* (New York: Charles Scribner's Sons, 1913), pp. 558–60. All footnotes deleted. © 1913 by Charles Scribner's Sons; © renewed 1941 by Joseph Cullen Ayer, Jr. Reprinted by permission of the publisher.

1. Those who have not yet been worthy of the venerable rite of baptism shall report themselves, if they dwell in this royal city or in the provinces, and go to the holy churches with their wives and children and all the household subject to them, and be taught the true faith of Christians, so that having been taught their former error henceforth to be rejected, they may receive saving baptism, or know, if they regard these things of small value, that they are to have no part in all those things which belong to our commonwealth, neither is it permitted them to become owners of anything movable or immovable, but, deprived of everything, they are to be left in poverty, and besides are subject to appropriate penalties.

2. We forbid also that any branch of learning be taught by those who labor under the insanity of the impious pagans, so that they may not for this reason pretend that they instruct those who unfortunately resort to them, but in reality corrupt the minds of their pupils; and let them not receive any support from the public treasury, since they are not permitted by the Holy Scriptures or by pragmatic forms [public decrees] to claim anything of the sort for themselves.

3. For if any one here or in the provinces shall have been convicted of not having hastened to the holy churches with his wife and children, as said, he shall suffer the aforesaid penalties, and the fisc shall claim his property, and they shall be sent into exile.

4. If any one in our commonwealth, hiding himself, shall be discovered to have celebrated sacrifices or the worship of idols, let him suffer the same capital punishment as the Manichaeans and, what is the same, the Borborani [a sect of Ophitic Gnostics], for we judge them to be similar to these.

5. Also we decree that their children of tender years shall at once and without delay receive saving baptism; but they who have passed beyond their earliest age shall attend the holy churches and be instructed in the Holy Scriptures, and so give themselves to sincere penitence that, having rejected their early error, they may receive the venerable rite of baptism, for in this way let them steadfastly receive the true faith of the orthodox and not again fall back into their former error.

6. But those who, for the sake of retaining their military rank or their dignity or their goods, shall in pretence accept saving baptism, but have left their wives and children and others who are in their households in the error of pagans, we command that they be deprived of their goods and have no part in our commonwealth, since it is manifest that they have not received holy baptism in good faith.

7. These things, therefore, we decree against the abominable pagans and the Manichaeans, of which Manichaeans the Borborani are a part.

5
Asceticism

Monasticism was among the most powerful institutions in the early Church. During the age of the Church Fathers, monks were rarely priests. An intense and regular oscillation brought monasticism and lay devotion into the same rhythm of social change. A common and widespread discipline of physical mortification and spiritual contrition was formed, responding to the evangelical call to overcome the world by denying it.

The following texts illustrate some motives that impelled men and women to embrace lives of suffering and self-denial. The *Rule* attributed to Saint Benedict, which is readily available elsewhere, provides a detailed rationale and plan of discipline for the monk's victory over the world, the flesh, and the devil through denial so complete that the monk abdicated control over his own will to his spiritual superiors. There were two chief branches of monasticism. Saint Benedict's *Rule* was written for the cenobitic branch, which gathered monks into communities. Thus, it emphasizes the virtue of obedience far more than does the *Life of Saint Anthony*, excerpted below; the *Life* portrays the second branch, the discipline of hermits (eremeticism), which dispersed its followers in solitary lives of penance.

As in several other topics, these documents emphasize the normative influence of Christianity in the Greek-speaking parts of the Empire, and in the peripheral area of North Africa, on the formation of Latin Christianity.

The *Life of Saint Anthony* dates from the same period in the career of Bishop Athanasius of Alexandria (295–373) as the *History of the Arians*, from which excerpts appear in topic 2 (document 6). Driven into hiding by the Emperor Constantius II, Athanasius took refuge for six years (356–362) with monks in the Egyptian desert. There, he wrote both the *History* and the *Life*. He had been a disciple of Anthony, and he intended the *Life* both as a reproach to the worldly powers that persecuted him and as an apology for the monastic life, to which he was devoted even as bishop. Both the Greek original and the Latin translation fulfilled Athanasius' hope that his work would serve as a compelling instrument of conversion.

Bishop Augustine of Hippo's (354–430) account of his own conversion (386) is a testimony both to the urgent appeal of world-denying asceticism and to the profound impact of Anthony's example on the life of one of the chief authors of Latin Christianity. Augustine's account is also important because it attests the diffusion of the story of Anthony as far as Trier, where Athanasius had been exiled fifty years earlier (335).

A lawyer and rhetorician in Carthage, Tertullian (about 160–ca. 220) belongs to the age of the apologists, though he is also known as the first of the Latin Church Fathers. His great achievement was to develop a vocabulary adequate to express in Latin the theological ideas already formed and debated in Greek. His personal asceticism eventually led him to doctrinal extremes (ca. 207). Before his departure from the orthodox fold, he wrote his tract *On the Apparel of Women* (ca. 197–201), a statement of the self-denial expected, not of professed monks, but of ordinary believers. It is valuable evidence of how pervasive ascetic ideals were in the general fabric of Christianity, a common thread that made possible the sort of interplay between monastic and lay vocations witnessed to by Augustine's conversion.

27. Athanasius, *Life of Saint Anthony*

The life and conversation of our holy Father, Antony: written and sent to the monks in foreign parts by our Father among the Saints, Athanasius, Bishop of Alexandria.

Athanasius the bishop to the brethren in foreign parts.

You have entered upon a noble rivalry with the monks of Egypt by your determination either to equal or surpass them in your training in the way of virtue. For by this time there are monasteries among you, and the name of monk receives public recognition. With reason, therefore, all men will approve this determination, and in answer to your prayers God will give its fulfilment. Now since you asked me to give you an account of the blessed Antony's way of life, and are wishful to learn how he began the discipline, who and what manner of man he was previous to this, how he closed his

From *Life of Saint Anthony*, Preface, chaps. 1–12, 44–47, 49–51, 54–55, 67, 69, 72–74, 77–79, 86, 89–94, in *Nicene and Post-Nicene Fathers*, 2d ser., vol. 4 (New York: Christian Literature Co., 1892), pp. 195–99, 208–10, 214–16, 219–21.

life, and whether the things told of him are true, that you also may bring yourselves to imitate him, I very readily accepted your behest, for to me also the bare recollection of Antony is a great accession of help. And I know that you, when you have heard, apart from your admiration of the man, will be wishful to emulate his determination; seeing that for monks the life of Antony is a sufficient pattern of discipline. Wherefore do not refuse credence to what you have heard from those who brought tidings of him; but think rather that they have told you only a few things, for at all events they scarcely can have given circumstances of so great import in any detail. And because I at your request have called to mind a few circumstances about him, and shall send as much as I can tell in a letter, do not neglect to question those who sail from here: for possibly when all have told their tale, the account will hardly be in proportion to his merits. On account of this I was desirous, when I received your letter, to send for certain of the monks, those especially who were wont to be more frequently with him, that if I could learn any fresh details I might send them to you. But since the season for sailing was coming to an end and the letter-carrier urgent, I hastened to write to your piety what I myself know, having seen him many times, and what I was able to learn from him, for I was his attendant for a long time, and poured water on his hands; in all points being mindful of the truth, that no one should disbelieve through hearing too much, nor on the other hand by hearing too little should despise the man.

1. Antony you must know was by descent an Egyptian: his parents were of good family and possessed considerable wealth, and as they were Christians he also was reared in the same Faith. In infancy he was brought up with his parents, knowing nought else but them and his home. But when he was grown and arrived at boyhood, and was advancing in years, he could not endure to learn letters, not caring to associate with other boys; but all his desire was, as it is written of Jacob, to live a plain man at home. With his parents he used to attend the Lord's House, and neither as a child was he idle nor when older did he despise them; but was both obedient to his father and mother and attentive to what was read, keeping in his heart what was profitable in what he heard. And though as a child brought up in moderate affluence, he did not trouble his parents for varied or luxurious fare, nor was this a source of pleasure to him; but was content simply with what he found nor sought anything further.

2. After the death of his father and mother he was left alone with one little sister: his age was about eighteen or twenty, and on him the care both of home and sister rested. Now it was not six months after the death of his parents, and going according to custom into the Lord's House, he communed with himself and reflected as he walked how the Apostles left all and followed the Saviour; and how they in the Acts sold their possessions

and brought and laid them at the Apostles' feet for distribution to the needy, and what and how great a hope was laid up for them in heaven. Pondering over these things he entered the church, and it happened the Gospel was being read, and he heard the Lord saying to the rich man, "If thou wouldest be perfect, go and sell that thou hast and give to the poor; and come follow Me and thou shalt have treasure in heaven."[1] Antony, as though God had put him in mind of the Saints, and the passage had been read on his account, went out immediately from the church, and gave the possessions of his forefathers to the villagers—they were three hundred acres, productive and very fair—that they should be no more a clog upon himself and his sister. And all the rest that was movable he sold, and having got together much money he gave it to the poor, reserving a little however for his sister's sake.

3. And again as he went into the church, hearing the Lord say in the Gospel, "be not anxious for the morrow,"[2] he could stay no longer, but went out and gave those things also to the poor. Having committed his sister to known and faithful virgins, and put her into a convent to be brought up, he henceforth devoted himself outside his house to discipline, taking heed to himself and training himself with patience. For there were not yet so many monasteries in Egypt, and no monk at all knew of the distant desert; but all who wished to give heed to themselves practised the discipline in solitude near their own village. Now there was then in the next village an old man who had lived the life of a hermit from his youth up. Antony, after he had seen this man, imitated him in piety. And at first he began to abide in places outside the village: then if he heard of a good man anywhere, like the prudent bee, he went forth and sought him, nor turned back to his own place until he had seen him; and he returned, having got from the good man as it were supplies for his journey in the way of virtue. So dwelling there at first, he confirmed his purpose not to return to the abode of his fathers nor to the remembrance of his kinsfolk; but to keep all his desire and energy for perfecting his discipline. He worked, however, with his hands, having heard, "he who is idle let him not eat,"[3] and part he spent on bread and part he gave to the needy. And he was constant in prayer, knowing that a man ought to pray in secret unceasingly.[4] For he had given such heed to what was read that none of the things that were written fell from him to the ground, but he remembered all, and afterwards his memory served him for books.

4. Thus conducting himself, Antony was beloved by all. He subjected himself in sincerity to the good men whom he visited, and learned thor-

---

1. Matt. 19:21.
2. Matt. 6:34.
3. 2 Thess. 3:10.
4. Matt. 6:7; 1 Thess. 5:17.

oughly where each surpassed him in zeal and discipline. He observed the graciousness of one; the unceasing prayer of another; he took knowledge of another's freedom from anger and another's loving-kindness; he gave heed to one as he watched, to another as he studied; one he admired for his endurance, another for his fasting and sleeping on the ground; the meekness of one and the long-suffering of another he watched with care, while he took note of the piety towards Christ and the mutual love which animated all. Thus filled, he returned to his own place of discipline, and henceforth would strive to unite the qualities of each, and was eager to show in himself the virtues of all. With others of the same age he had no rivalry; save this only, that he should not be second to them in higher things. And this he did so as to hurt the feelings of nobody, but made them rejoice over him. So all they of that village and the good men in whose intimacy he was, when they saw that he was a man of this sort, used to call him God-beloved. And some welcomed him as a son, others as a brother.

5. But the devil, who hates and envies what is good, could not endure to see such a resolution in a youth, but endeavoured to carry out against him what he had been wont to effect against others. First of all he tried to lead him away from the discipline, whispering to him the remembrance of his wealth, care for his sister, claims of kindred, love of money, love of glory, the various pleasures of the table and the other relaxations of life, and at last the difficulty of virtue and the labour of it; he suggested also the infirmity of the body and the length of the time. In a word he raised in his mind a great dust of debate, wishing to debar him from his settled purpose. But when the enemy saw himself to be too weak for Antony's determination, and that he rather was conquered by the other's firmness, overthrown by his great faith and falling through his constant prayers, then at length putting his trust in the weapons which are "in the navel of his belly"[5] and boasting in them—for they are his first snare for the young—he attacked the young man, disturbing him by night and harassing him by day, so that even the onlookers saw the struggle which was going on between them. The one would suggest foul thoughts and the other counter them with prayers: the one fire him with lust, the other, as one who seemed to blush, fortify his body with faith, prayers, and fasting. And the devil, unhappy wight, one night even took upon him the shape of a woman and imitated all her acts simply to beguile Antony. But he, his mind filled with Christ and the nobility inspired by Him, and considering the spirituality of the soul, quenched the coal of the other's deceit. Again the enemy suggested the ease of pleasure. But he like a man filled with rage and grief turned his thoughts to the threatened fire and the gnawing worm, and setting these in array

5. Job 40:16.

against his adversary, passed through the temptation unscathed. All this was a source of shame to his foe. For he, deeming himself like God, was now mocked by a young man; and he who boasted himself against flesh and blood was being put to flight by a man in the flesh. For the Lord was working with Antony—the Lord who for our sake took flesh and gave the body victory over the devil, so that all who truly fight can say, "not I but the grace of God which was with me." [6]

6. At last when the dragon could not even thus overthrow Antony, but saw himself thrust out of his heart, gnashing his teeth as it is written, and as it were beside himself, he appeared to Antony like a black boy, taking a visible shape in accordance with the colour of his mind. And cringing to him, as it were, he plied him with thoughts no longer, for guileful as he was, he had been worsted, but at last spoke in human voice and said, "Many I deceived, many I cast down; but now attacking thee and thy labours as I had many others, I proved weak." When Antony asked, Who art thou who speakest thus with me? he answered with a lamentable voice, "I am the friend of whoredom, and have taken upon me incitements which lead to it against the young. I am called the spirit of lust. How many have I deceived who wished to live soberly, how many are the chaste whom by my incitements I have over-persuaded! I am he on account of whom also the prophet reproves those who have fallen, saying, 'Ye have been caused to err by the spirit of whoredom.' [7] For by me they have been tripped up. I am he who have so often troubled thee and have so often been overthrown by thee." But Antony having given thanks to the Lord, with good courage said to him, "Thou art very despicable then, for thou art black-hearted and weak as a child. Henceforth I shall have no trouble from thee, 'for the Lord is my helper, and I shall look down on mine enemies.'" [8] Having heard this, the black one straightway fled, shuddering at the words and dreading any longer even to come near the man.

7. This was Antony's first struggle against the devil, or rather this victory was the Saviour's work in Antony, "Who condemned sin in the flesh that the ordinance of the law might be fulfilled in us who walk not after the flesh but after the spirit." [9] But neither did Antony, although the evil one had fallen, henceforth relax his care and despise him; nor did the enemy as though conquered cease to lay snares for him. For again he went round as a lion seeking some occasion against him. But Antony having learned from the Scriptures that the devices of the devil are many, [10] zealously continued the discipline, reckoning that though the devil had not been able to deceive his heart by bodily pleasure, he would endeavour to ensnare him by other

6. 1 Cor. 15:10.   9. Rom. 8:3 and 4.
7. Hosea 4:12.   10. Eph. 6:11.
8. Ps. 118:7.

means. For the demon loves sin. Wherefore more and more he repressed the body and kept it in subjection, lest haply having conquered on one side, he should be dragged down on the other. He therefore planned to accustom himself to a severer mode of life. And many marvelled, but he himself used to bear the labour easily; for the eagerness of soul, through the length of time it had abode in him, had wrought a good habit in him, so that taking but little initiation from others he shewed great zeal in this matter. He kept vigil to such an extent that he often continued the whole night without sleep; and this not once but often, to the marvel of others. He ate once a day, after sunset, sometimes once in two days, and often even in four. His food was bread and salt, his drink, water only. Of flesh and wine it is superfluous even to speak, since no such thing was found with the other earnest men. A rush mat served him to sleep upon, but for the most part he lay upon the bare ground. He would not anoint himself with oil, saying it behoved young men to be earnest in training and not to seek what would enervate the body; but they must accustom it to labour, mindful of the Apostle's words, "when I am weak, then am I strong." [11] "For," said he, "the fibre of the soul is then sound when the pleasures of the body are diminished." And he had come to this truly wonderful conclusion, "that progress in virtue, and retirement from the world for the sake of it, ought not to be measured by time, but by desire and fixity of purpose.". . . And he used to say to himself that from the life of the great Elias the hermit ought to see his own as in a mirror.

8. Thus tightening his hold upon himself, Antony departed to the tombs, which happened to be at a distance from the village; and having bid one of his acquaintances to bring him bread at intervals of many days, he entered one of the tombs, and the other having shut the door on him, he remained within alone. And when the enemy could not endure it, but was even fearful that in a short time Antony would fill the desert with the discipline, coming one night with a multitude of demons, he so cut him with stripes that he lay on the ground speechless from the excessive pain. For he affirmed that the torture had been so excessive that no blows inflicted by man could ever have caused him such torment. But by the Providence of God—for the Lord never overlooks them that hope in Him—the next day his acquaintance came bringing him the loaves. And having opened the door and seeing him lying on the ground as though dead, he lifted him up and carried him to the church in the village, and laid him upon the ground. And many of his kinsfolk and the villagers sat around Antony as round a corpse. But about midnight he came to himself and arose, and when he saw them all asleep and his comrade alone watching, he motioned with his head

11. 2 Cor. 12:10.

for him to approach, and asked him to carry him again to the tombs without waking anybody.

9. He was carried therefore by the man, and as he was wont, when the door was shut he was within alone. And he could not stand up on account of the blows, but he prayed as he lay. And after he had prayed, he said with a shout, Here am I, Antony; I flee not from your stripes, for even if you inflict more nothing shall separate me from the love of Christ. And then he sang, "though a camp be set against me, my heart shall not be afraid." [12] These were the thoughts and words of this ascetic. But the enemy, who hates good, marvelling that after the blows he dared to return, called together his hounds and burst forth, "Ye see," said he, "that neither by the spirit of lust nor by blows did we stay the man, but that he braves us, let us attack him in another fashion." But changes of form for evil are easy for the devil, so in the night they made such a din that the whole of that place seemed to be shaken by an earthquake, and the demons as if breaking the four walls of the dwelling seemed to enter through them, coming in the likeness of beasts and creeping things. And the place was on a sudden filled with the forms of lions, bears, leopards, bulls, serpents, asps, scorpions, and wolves, and each of them was moving according to his nature. The lion was roaring, wishing to attack, the bull seeming to toss with its horns, the serpent writhing but unable to approach, and the wolf as it rushed on was restrained; altogether the noises of the apparitions, with their angry ragings, were dreadful. But Antony, stricken and goaded by them, felt bodily pains severer still. He lay watching, however, with unshaken soul, groaning from bodily anguish; but his mind was clear, and as in mockery he said, "If there had been any power in you, it would have sufficed had one of you come, but since the Lord hath made you weak you attempt to terrify me by numbers: and a proof of your weakness is that you take the shapes of brute beasts." And again with boldness he said, "If you are able, and have received power against me, delay not to attack; but if you are unable, why trouble me in vain? For faith in our Lord is a seal and a wall of safety to us." So after many attempts they gnashed their teeth upon him, because they were mocking themselves rather than him.

10. Nor was the Lord then forgetful of Antony's wrestling, but was at hand to help him. So looking up he saw the roof as it were opened, and a ray of light descending to him. The demons suddenly vanished, the pain of his body straightway ceased, and the building was again whole. But Antony feeling the help, and getting his breath again, and being freed from pain, besought the vision which had appeared to him, saying, "Where wert thou? Why didst thou not appear at the beginning to make my pains to

12. Ps. 27:3.

cease?" And a voice came to him, "Antony, I was here, but I waited to see thy fight; wherefore since thou hast endured, and hast not been worsted, I will ever be a succour to thee, and will make thy name known everywhere." Having heard this, Antony arose and prayed, and received such strength that he perceived that he had more power in his body than formerly. And he was then about thirty-five years old.

11. And on the day following he went forth still more eagerly bent on the service of God, and having fallen in with the old man he had met previously, he asked him to dwell with him in the desert. But when the other declined on account of his great age, and because as yet there was no such custom, Antony himself set off forthwith to the mountain. . . .

12. . . . He hurried to the mountain, and having found a fort, so long deserted that it was full of creeping things, on the other side of the river; he crossed over to it and dwelt there. The reptiles, as though some one were chasing them, immediately left the place. But he built up the entrance completely, having stored up loaves for six months—this is a custom of the Thebans, and the loaves often remain fresh a whole year—and as he found water within, he descended as into a shrine, and abode within by himself, never going forth nor looking at any one who came. Thus he employed a long time training himself, and received loaves, let down from above, twice in the year. . . .

44. While Antony was thus speaking all rejoiced; in some the love of virtue increased, in others carelessness was thrown aside, the self-conceit of others was stopped; and all were persuaded to despise the assaults of the Evil One, and marvelled at the grace given to Antony from the Lord for the discerning of spirits. So their cells were in the mountains, like tabernacles, filled with holy bands of men who sang psalms, loved reading, fasted, prayed, rejoiced in the hope of things to come, laboured in almsgiving, and preserved love and harmony one with another. And truly it was possible, as it were, to behold a land set by itself, filled with piety and justice. For then there was neither the evil-doer, nor the injured, nor the reproaches of the tax-gatherer: but instead a multitude of ascetics; and the one purpose of them all was to aim at virtue. . . .

45. He used, however, when by himself, to eat through bodily necessity, but often also with the brethren; covered with shame on these occasions, yet speaking boldly words of help. And he used to say that it behoved a man to give all his time to his soul rather than his body, yet to grant a short space to the body through its necessities; but all the more earnestly to give up the whole remainder to the soul and seek its profit, that it might not be dragged down by the pleasures of the body, but, on the contrary, the body might be in subjection to the soul. For this is that which was spoken by the Saviour: "Be not anxious for your life what ye shall eat, nor for your body

what ye shall put on. And do ye seek not what ye shall eat, or what ye shall drink, and be not of a doubtful mind. For all these things the nations of the world seek after. But your Father knoweth that ye have need of all these things. Howbeit seek ye first His Kingdom, and all these things shall be added unto you." [13]

46. After this the Church was seized by the persecution which then took place under Maximinus, and when the holy martyrs were led to Alexandria, Antony also followed, leaving his cell, and saying, Let us go too, that if called, we may contend or behold them that are contending. And he longed to suffer martyrdom, but not being willing to give himself up, he ministered to the confessors in the mines and in the prisons. And he was very zealous in the judgment hall to stir up to readiness those who were summoned when in their contest, while those who were being martyred he received and brought on their way until they were perfected. The judge, therefore, beholding the fearlessness of Antony and his companions, and their zeal in this matter, commanded that no monk should appear in the judgment hall, nor remain at all in the city. So all the rest thought it good to hide themselves that day, but Antony gave so little heed to the command that he washed his garment, and stood all next day on a raised place before them, and appeared in his best before the governor. Therefore when all the rest wondered at this, and the governor saw and passed by with his array, he stood fearlessly, shewing the readiness of us Christians. For, as I said before, he prayed himself to be a martyr, wherefore he seemed as one grieved that he had not borne his witness. But the Lord was keeping him for our profit and that of others, that he should become a teacher to many of the discipline which he had learned from the Scriptures. For many only beholding his manner of life were eager to be imitators of his ways. So he again ministered as usual to the confessors, and as though he were their fellow captive he laboured in his ministry.

47. And when at last the persecution ceased, and the blessed Bishop Peter had borne his testimony, Antony departed, and again withdrew to his cell, and was there daily a martyr to his conscience, and contending in the conflicts of faith. And his discipline was much severer, for he was ever fasting, and he had a garment of hair on the inside, while the outside was skin, which he kept until his end. And he neither bathed his body with water to free himself from filth, nor did he ever wash his feet, nor even endure so much as to put them into water, unless compelled by necessity. Nor did any one even see him unclothed, nor his body naked at all, except after his death, when he was buried. . . .

49. But when he saw himself beset by many, and not suffered to with-

13. Matt. 6:31; Luke 12:20.

draw himself according to his intent as he wished, fearing because of the signs which the Lord wrought by him, that either he should be puffed up, or that some other should think of him above what he ought to think, he considered and set off to go into the upper Thebaid, among those to whom he was unknown. . . . he came to a very lofty mountain, and at the foot of the mountain ran a clear spring, whose waters were sweet and very cold; outside there was a plain and a few uncared-for palm trees.

50. Antony then, as it were, moved by God, loved the place, for this was the spot which he who had spoken with him by the banks of the river had pointed out. So having first received loaves from his fellow travellers, he abode in the mountain alone, no one else being with him. And recognising it as his own home, he remained in that place for the future. But the Saracens, having seen the earnestness of Antony, purposely used to journey that way, and joyfully brought him loaves, while now and then the palm trees also afforded him a poor and frugal relish. But after this, the brethren learning of the place, like children mindful of their father, took care to send to him. But when Antony saw that the bread was the cause of trouble and hardships to some of them, to spare the monks this, he resolved to ask some of those who came to bring him a spade, an axe, and a little corn. And when these were brought, he went over the land round the mountain, and having found a small plot of suitable ground, tilled it; and having a plentiful supply of water for watering, he sowed. This doing year by year, he got his bread from thence, rejoicing that thus he would be troublesome to no one, and because he kept himself from being a burden to anybody. But after this, seeing again that people came, he cultivated a few pot-herbs, that he who came to him might have some slight solace after the labour of that hard journey. At first, however, the wild beasts in the desert, coming because of the water, often injured his seeds and husbandry. But he, gently laying hold of one of them, said to them all, "Why do you hurt me, when I hurt none of you? Depart, and in the name of the Lord come not nigh this spot." And from that time forward, as though fearful of his command, they no more came near the place.

51. So he was alone in the inner mountain, spending his time in prayer and discipline. And the brethren who served him asked that they might come every month and bring him olives, pulse and oil, for by now he was an old man. There then he passed his life, and endured such great wrestlings, "Not against flesh and blood," [14] as it is written, but against opposing demons. . . .

54. And once being asked by the monks to come down and visit them and their abodes after a time, he journeyed with those who came to him.

14. Eph. 6:12.

And a camel carried the loaves and the water for them. . . . And when he came to the outer cells all saluted him, looking on him as a father. And he too, as though bringing supplies from the mountain, entertained them with his words and gave them a share of help. And again there was joy in the mountains, zeal for improvement and consolation through their mutual faith. Antony also rejoiced when he beheld the earnestness of the monks, and his sister grown old in virginity, and that she herself was the leader of other virgins.

55. So after certain days he went in again to the mountain. And henceforth many resorted to him, and others who were suffering ventured to go in. . . .

67. Added to this he was tolerant in disposition and humble in spirit. For though he was such a man, he observed the rule of the Church most rigidly, and was willing that all the clergy should be honoured above himself. For he was not ashamed to bow his head to bishops and presbyters, and if ever a deacon came to him for help he discoursed with him on what was profitable, but gave place to him in prayer, not being ashamed to learn himself. . . .

69. And once also the Arians having lyingly asserted that Antony's opinions were the same as theirs, he was displeased and wroth against them. Then being summoned by the bishops and all the brethren, he descended from the mountain, and having entered Alexandria, he denounced the Arians, saying that their heresy was the last of all and a forerunner of Antichrist. . . .

72. And Antony also was exceeding prudent, and the wonder was that although he had not learned letters, he was a ready-witted and sagacious man. At all events two Greek philosophers once came, thinking they could try their skill on Antony. . . . But they departed with wonder, for they saw that even demons feared Antony.

73. And again others such as these met him in the outer mountain and thought to mock him because he had not learned letters. And Antony said to them, "What say ye? which is first, mind or letters? And which is the cause of which—mind of letters or letters of mind?" And when they answered mind is first and the inventor of letters, Antony said, "Whoever, therefore, hath a sound mind hath not need of letters." This answer amazed both the bystanders and the philosophers, and they departed marvelling that they had seen so much understanding in an ignorant man. For his manners were not rough as though he had been reared in the mountain and there grown old, but graceful and polite, and his speech was seasoned with the divine salt, so that no one was envious, but rather all rejoiced over him who visited him.

74. After this again certain others came; and these were men who were

deemed wise among the Greeks, and they asked him a reason for our faith in Christ. . . .

77. But when they were at a loss, turning hither and thither, Antony smiled and said—again through an interpreter—"Sight itself carries the conviction of these things. But as you prefer to lean upon demonstrative arguments, and as you, having this art, wish us also not to worship God, until after such proof, do you tell first how things in general and specially the recognition of God are accurately known. Is it through demonstrative argument or the working of faith? And which is better, faith which comes through the inworking (of God) or demonstration by arguments?" And when they answered that faith which comes through the inworking was better and was accurate knowledge, Antony said, "You have answered well, for faith arises from disposition of soul, but dialectic from the skill of its inventors. Wherefore to those who have the inworking through faith, demonstrative argument is needless, or even superfluous. For what we know through faith this you attempt to prove through words, and often you are not even able to express what we understand. So the inworking through faith is better and stronger than your professional arguments.

78. "We Christians therefore hold the mystery not in the wisdom of Greek arguments, but in the power of faith richly supplied to us by God through Jesus Christ. And to show that this statement is true, behold now, without having learned letters, we believe in God, knowing through His works His providence over all things. And to show that our faith is effective, so now we are supported by faith in Christ, but you by professional logomachies. The portents of the idols among you are being done away, but our faith is extending everywhere. You by your arguments and quibbles have converted none from Christianity to Paganism. We, teaching the faith on Christ, expose your superstition, since all recognise that Christ is God and the Son of God. You by your eloquence do not hinder the teaching of Christ. But we by the mention of Christ crucified put all demons to flight, whom you fear as if they were gods. Where the sign of the Cross is, magic is weak and witchcraft has no strength.

79. "Tell us therefore where your oracles are now? Where are the charms of the Egyptians? Where the delusions of the magicians? When did all these things cease and grow weak except when the Cross of Christ arose?" . . .

86. And a certain general, Balacius by name, persecuted us Christians bitterly on account of his regard for the Arians—that name of ill-omen. And as his ruthlessness was so great that he beat virgins, and stripped and scourged monks, Antony at this time wrote a letter as follows, and sent it to him. "I see wrath coming upon thee, wherefore cease to persecute the

Christians, lest haply wrath catch hold of thee, for even now it is on the point of coming upon thee." But Balacius laughed and threw the letter on the ground, and spit on it, and insulted the bearers, bidding them tell this to Antony: "Since thou takest thought for the monks, soon I will come after thee also." And five days had not passed before wrath came upon him. For Balacius and Nestorius, the Prefect of Egypt, went forth to the first halting-place from Alexandria, which is called Chaereu, and both were on horse-back, and the horses belonged to Balacius, and were the quietest of all his stable. But they had not gone far towards the place when the horses began to frisk with one another as they are wont to do; and suddenly the quieter, on which Nestorius sat, with a bite dismounted Balacius, and attacked him, and tore his thigh so badly with its teeth that he was borne straight back to the city, and in three days died. And all wondered because what Antony had foretold had been so speedily fulfilled. . . .

89. It is worth while that I should relate, and that you, as you wish it, should hear what his death was like. For this end of his is worthy of imitation. . . .

90. But when the brethren were urging him to abide with them and there to die, he suffered it not for many other reasons, as he showed by keeping silence, and especially for this:—The Egyptians are wont to honour with funeral rites, and to wrap in linen cloths at death the bodies of good men, and especially of the holy martyrs; and not to bury them underground, but to place them on couches, and to keep them in their houses, thinking in this to honour the departed. And Antony often urged the bishops to give commandment to the people on this matter. In like manner he taught the laity and reproved the women, saying, "that this thing was neither lawful nor holy at all. For the bodies of the patriarchs and prophets are until now pre-served in tombs, and the very body of the Lord was laid in a tomb, and a stone was laid upon it, and hid it until He rose on the third day." And thus saying, he showed that he who did not bury the bodies of the dead after death transgressed the law, even though they were sacred. For what is greater or more sacred than the body of the Lord? Many therefore having heard, henceforth buried the dead underground, and gave thanks to the Lord that they had been taught rightly.

91. But he, knowing the custom, and fearing that his body would be treated this way, hastened, and having bidden farewell to the monks in the outer mountain entered the inner mountain, where he was accustomed to abide. And after a few months he fell sick. Having summoned those who were there—they were two in number who had remained in the mountain fifteen years, practising the discipline and attending Antony on account of his age—he said to them, ". . . Bury my body, therefore, and hide it underground yourselves, and let my words be observed by you that no one

may know the place but you alone. For at the resurrection of the dead I shall receive it incorruptible from the Saviour. And divide my garments. To Athanasius the bishop give one sheepskin and the garment whereon I am laid, which he himself gave me new, but which with me has grown old. To Serapion the bishop give the other sheepskin, and keep the hair garment yourselves. For the rest fare ye well, my children, for Antony is departing, and is with you no more."

92. Having said this, when they had kissed him, he lifted up his feet, and as though he saw friends coming to him and was glad because of them—for as he lay his countenance appeared joyful—he died and was gathered to the fathers. And they afterward, according to his commandment, wrapped him up and buried him, hiding his body underground. And no one knows to this day where it was buried, save those two only. But each of those who received the sheepskin of the blessed Antony and the garment worn by him guards it as a precious treasure. For even to look on them is as it were to behold Antony; and he who is clothed in them seems with joy to bear his admonitions.

93. This is the end of Antony's life in the body and the above was the beginning of the discipline. Even if this account is small compared with his merit, still from this reflect how great Antony, the man of God, was. Who from his youth to so great an age preserved a uniform zeal for the discipline, and neither through old age was subdued by the desire of costly food, nor through the infirmity of his body changed the fashion of his clothing, nor washed even his feet with water, and yet remained entirely free from harm. For his eyes were undimmed and quite sound and he saw clearly; of his teeth he had not lost one, but they had become worn to the gums through the great age of the old man. He remained strong both in hands and feet; and while all men were using various foods, and washings and divers garments, he appeared more cheerful and of greater strength. And the fact that his fame has been blazoned everywhere; that all regard him with wonder, and that those who have never seen him long for him, is clear proof of his virtue and God's love of his soul. For not from writings, nor from worldly wisdom, nor through any art, was Antony renowned, but solely from his piety towards God. That this was the gift of God no one will deny. For from whence into Spain and into Gaul, how into Rome and Africa, was the man heard of who abode hidden in a mountain, unless it was God who maketh His own known everywhere, who also promised this to Antony at the beginning? For even if they work secretly, even if they wish to remain in obscurity, yet the Lord shows them as lamps to lighten all, that those who hear may thus know that the precepts of God are able to make men prosper and thus be zealous in the path of virtue.

94. Read these words, therefore, to the rest of the brethren that they may

learn what the life of monks ought to be; and may believe that our Lord and Saviour Jesus Christ glorifies those who glorify Him: and leads those who serve Him unto the end, not only to the kingdom of heaven, but here also— even though they hide themselves and are desirous of withdrawing from the world—makes them illustrious and well known everywhere on account of their virtue and the help they render others. And if need be, read this among the heathen, that even in this way they may learn that our Lord Jesus Christ is not only God and the Son of God, but also that the Christians who truly serve Him and religiously believe on Him, prove, not only that the demons, whom the Greeks themselves think to be gods, are no gods, but also tread them under foot and put them to flight, as deceivers and corrupters of mankind, through Jesus Christ our Lord, to whom be glory for ever and ever. Amen.

28. Augustine, *Confessions*, Book 8

<u>6</u>

Now, O Lord, my Helper and my Redeemer, I shall tell and confess to Your name how You delivered me from the chain of that desire of the flesh which held me so bound, and the servitude of worldly things. I went my usual way with a mind ever more anxious, and day after day I sighed for You. I would be off to Your church as often as my business, under the weight of which I groaned, left me free. Alypius was with me, at liberty from his legal office after a third term as Assessor and waiting for private clients, to whom he might sell his legal advice—just as I sold skill in speaking, if indeed this can be bought. Nebridius had yielded to our friendship so far as to teach under Verecundus, a great friend of all of us, a citizen and elementary school teacher of Milan, who had earnestly asked and indeed by right of friendship demanded from our company the help he badly needed. Nebridius was not influenced in the matter by any desire for profit, for he could have done better had he chosen, in a more advanced school; but he was a good and gracious friend and too kindly a man to refuse our requests. But he did it all very quietly, for he did not want to draw the attention of those persons whom the world holds great; he thus avoided distraction of mind, for he wanted to have his mind free and at leisure for as many hours as possible to seek or read or hear truths concerning wisdom.

On a certain day—Nebridius was away for some reason I cannot re-

From *The Confessions of Saint Augustine*, translated by F. J. Sheed (New York: Sheed and Ward, 1942), bk. 8, chaps. 6–7, pp. 136–40.

call—there came to Alypius and me at our house one Ponticianus, a fellow countryman of ours, being from Africa, holder of an important post in the emperor's court. There was something or other he wanted of us and we sat down to discuss the matter. As it happened he noticed a book on a gaming table by which we were sitting. He picked it up, opened it, and found that it was the apostle Paul, which surprised him because he had expected that it would be one of the books I wore myself out teaching. Then he smiled a little and looked at me, and expressed pleasure but surprise too at having come suddenly upon that book, and only that book, lying before me. For he was a Christian and a devout Christian; he knelt before You in church, O our God, in daily prayer and many times daily. I told him that I had given much care to these writings. Whereupon he began to tell the story of the Egyptian monk Antony, whose name was held in high honour among Your servants, although Alypius and I had never heard it before that time. When he learned this, he was the more intent upon telling the story, anxious to introduce so great a man to men ignorant of him, and very much marvelling at our ignorance. But Alypius and I stood amazed to hear of Your wonderful works, done in the true faith and in the Catholic Church so recently, practically in our own times, and with such numbers of witnesses. All three of us were filled with wonder, we because the deeds we were now hearing were so great, and he because we had never heard them before.

From this story he went on to the great groups in the monasteries, and their ways all redolent of You, and the fertile deserts of the wilderness, of all of which we knew nothing. There was actually a monastery at Milan, outside the city walls. It was full of worthy brethren and under the care of Ambrose. And we had not heard of it. He continued with his discourse and we listened in absolute silence. It chanced that he told how on one occasion he and three of his companions—it was at Treves, when the emperor was at the chariot races in the Circus—had gone one afternoon to walk in the gardens close by the city walls. As it happened they fell into two groups, one of the others staying with him, and the other two likewise walking their own way. But as those other two strolled on they came into a certain house, the dwelling of some servants of Yours, poor in spirit, of whom is the kingdom of God. There they found a small book in which was written the life of Antony. One of them began to read it, marvelled at it, was inflamed by it. While he was actually reading he had begun to think how he might embrace such a life, and give up his worldly employment to serve You alone. For the two men were both state officials. Suddenly the man who was doing the reading was filled with a love of holiness and angry at himself with righteous shame. He looked at his friend and said to him: "Tell me, please, what is the goal of our ambition in all these labours of ours? What are we aiming at? What is our motive in being in the public service? Have we any higher hope at court than to be friends of the emperor? And at that level, is not everything uncertain and full of perils? And how many perils must we meet on the way to this greater peril? And how long before we are there? But if I should choose to be a friend of God, I can become one now." He said this, and all troubled with the pain of the new life coming to birth in him, he turned back his eyes to the book. He read on and was changed inwardly, where You alone could see; and the world dropped away from his mind, as soon appeared outwardly. For while he was reading and his heart thus tossing on its own flood, at length he broke out in heavy weeping, saw the better way and chose it for his own. Being now Your servant he said to his friend, "Now I have broken from that hope we had and have decided to serve God; and I enter upon that service from this hour, in this place. If you have no will to imitate me, at least do not try to dissuade me."

The other replied that he would remain his companion in so great a service for so great a prize. So the two of them, now Your servants, built a spiritual tower at the only cost that is adequate, the cost of leaving all things and following You. Then Ponticianus and the man who had gone walking with him in another part of the garden came looking for them in the same place, and when they found them suggested that they should return home as the day was now declining. But they told their decision and their purpose, and how that will had arisen in them and was now settled in them; and asked them not to try to argue them out of their decision, even if they would not also join them. Ponticianus and his friend, though not changed from their former state, yet wept for themselves, as he told us, and congratulated them in God and commended themselves to their prayers. Then with their own heart trailing in the dust they went off to the palace, while the other two, with their heart fixed upon heaven, remained in the hut. Both these men, as it happened, were betrothed, and when the two women heard of it they likewise dedicated their virginity to You.

7

This was the story Ponticianus told. But You, Lord, while he was speaking, turned me back towards myself, taking me from behind my own back where I had put myself all the time that I preferred not to see myself. And You set me there before my own face that I might see how vile I was, how twisted and unclean and spotted and ulcerous. I saw myself and was horrified; but there was no way to flee from myself. If I tried to turn my gaze from myself, there was Ponticianus telling what he was telling; and again You were setting me face to face with myself, forcing me upon my own sight, that I might see my iniquity and loathe it. I had known it, but I had pretended not to see it, had deliberately looked the other way and let it go from my mind.

But this time, the more ardently I approved those two as I heard of their determination to win health for their souls by giving themselves up wholly to Your healing, the more detestable did I find myself in comparison with them. For many years had flowed by—a dozen or more—from the time when I was nineteen and was stirred by the reading of Cicero's Hortensius to the study of wisdom; and here was I still postponing the giving up of this world's happiness to devote myself to the search for that of which not the finding only but the mere seeking is better than to find all the treasures and kingdoms of men, better than all the body's pleasures though they were to be had merely for a nod. But I in my great worthlessness—for it was greater thus early—had begged You for chastity, saying: "Grant me chastity and continence, but not yet." For I was afraid that You would hear my prayer too soon, and too soon would heal me from the disease of lust which I wanted satisfied rather than extinguished. So I had gone wandering in my sacrilegious superstition through the base ways of the Manicheans: not indeed that I was sure they were right but that I preferred them to the Christians, whom I did not inquire about in the spirit of religion but simply opposed through malice.

I had thought that my reason for putting off from day to day the following of You alone to the contempt of earthly hopes was that I did not see any certain goal towards which to direct my course. But now the day was come when I stood naked in my own sight and my conscience accused me: "Why is my voice not heard? Surely you are the man who used to say that you could not cast off vanity's baggage for an uncertain truth. Very well: now the truth is certain, yet you are still carrying the load. Here are men who have been given wings to free their shoulders from the load, though they did not wear themselves out in searching nor spend ten years or more thinking about it."

Thus was I inwardly gnawed at. And I was in the grip of the most horrible and confounding shame, while Ponticianus was telling his story. He finished the tale and the business for which he had come; and he went his way, and I to myself. What did I not say against myself, with what lashes of condemnation did I not scourge my soul to make it follow me now that I wanted to follow You! My soul hung back. It would not follow, yet found no excuse for not following. All its arguments had already been used and refuted. There remained only trembling silence: for it feared as very death the cessation of that habit of which in truth it was dying.

29. Tertullian, *On the Apparel of Women*, Book 1

1. Introduction. Modesty in Apparel Becoming to Women, in Memory of the Introduction of Sin into the World through a Woman.

If there dwelt upon earth a faith as great as is the reward of faith which is expected in the heavens, no one of you at all, best beloved sisters, from the time that she had first "known the Lord," [1] and learned (the truth) concerning her own (that is, woman's) condition, would have desired too gladsome (not to say too ostentatious) a style of dress; so as not rather to go about in humble garb, and rather to affect meanness of appearance, walking about as Eve mourning and repentant, in order that by every garb of penitence she might the more fully expiate that which she derives from Eve,—the ignominy, I mean, of the first sin, and the odium (attaching to her as the cause) of human perdition. "In pains and in anxieties dost thou bear (children), woman; and toward thine husband (is) thy inclination, and he lords it over thee." [2] And do you not know that you are (each) an Eve? The sentence of God on this sex of yours lives in this age: the guilt must of necessity live too. You are the devil's gateway: you are the unsealer of that (forbidden) tree: you are the first deserter of the divine law: you are she who persuaded him whom the devil was not valiant enough to attack. You destroyed so easily God's image, man. On account of your desert—that is, death—even the Son of God had to die. And do you think about adorning yourself over and above your tunics of skins? [3] Come, now; if from the beginning of the world the Milesians sheared sheep, and the Serians spun trees, and the Tyrians dyed, and the Phrygians embroidered with the needle, and the Babylonians with the loom, and pearls gleamed, and onyx-stones flashed; if gold itself also had already issued, with the cupidity (which accompanies it), from the ground; if the mirror, too, already had licence to lie so largely, Eve, expelled from paradise, (Eve) already dead, would also have coveted these things, I imagine! No more, then, ought she now to crave, or be acquainted with (if she desires to live again), what, when she was living, she had neither had nor known. Accordingly these things are all the baggage of woman in her condemned and dead state, instituted as if to swell the pomp of her funeral.

From *On the Apparel of Women*, bk. 1, chaps. 1–2; bk. 2, chaps. 8, 11–13, in *Ante-Nicene Fathers*, vol. 4 (New York: Christian Literature Co., 1890), pp. 14–15, 22, 24–25.

1. Cf. Heb. 8:11; Jer. 31:34 (in the LXX. it is 38:34).

2. Cf. Gen. 3:16, in Eng. ver. and in LXX.

3. See Gen. 3:21.

2. The Origin of Female Ornamentation, Traced Back to the Angels Who Had Fallen.

For they, withal, who instituted them are assigned, under condemnation, to the penalty of death,—those angels, to wit, who rushed from heaven on the daughters of men; so that this ignominy also attaches to woman. For when to an age much more ignorant (than ours) they had disclosed certain well-concealed material substances, and several not well-revealed scientific arts—if it is true that they had laid bare the operations of metallurgy, and had divulged the natural properties of herbs, and had promulgated the powers of enchantments, and had traced out every curious art, even to the interpretation of the stars—they conferred properly and as it were peculiarly upon women that instrumental mean of womanly ostentation, the radiances of jewels wherewith necklaces are variegated, and the circlets of gold wherewith the arms are compressed, and the medicaments of orchil with which wools are coloured, and that black powder itself wherewith the eyelids and eyelashes are made prominent. What is the quality of these things may be declared meantime, even at this point, from the quality and condition of their teachers: in that sinners could never have either shown or supplied anything conducive to integrity, unlawful lovers anything conducive to chastity, renegade spirits anything conducive to the fear of God. If (these things) are to be called teachings, ill masters must of necessity have taught ill; if as wages of lust, there is nothing base of which the wages are honourable. But why was it of so much importance to show these things as well as to confer them? Was it that women, without material causes of splendour, and without ingenious contrivances of grace, could not please men, who, while still unadorned, and uncouth, and—so to say—crude and rude, had moved (the mind of) angels? or was it that the lovers would appear sordid and—through gratuitous use—contumelious, if they had conferred no (compensating) gift on the women who had been enticed into connubial connection with them? But these questions admit of no calculation. Women who possessed angels (as husbands) could desire nothing more; they had, forsooth, made a grand match! Assuredly they who, of course, did sometimes think whence they had fallen, and, after the heated impulses of their lusts, looked up toward heaven, thus requited that very excellence of women, natural beauty, as (having proved) a cause of evil, in order that their good fortune might profit them nothing; but that, being turned from simplicity and sincerity, they, together with (the angels) themselves, might become offensive to God. Sure they were that all ostentation, and ambition, and love of pleasing by carnal means, was displeasing to God. And these are the angels whom we are destined to judge: these are the angels whom in baptism we renounce: these, of course, are the reasons why they have deserved to be judged by man. What business, then, have their things with their judges? What commerce have they who are to condemn with them who are to be condemned? The same, I take it, as Christ has with Belial. With what consistency do we mount that (future) judgment-seat to pronounce sentence against those whose gifts we (now) seek after? For you too, (women as you are,) have the self-same angelic nature promised as your reward, the self-same sex as men: the self-same advancement to the dignity of judging, does (the Lord) promise you. Unless, then, we begin even here to pre-judge, by pre-condemning their things, which we are hereafter to condemn in themselves, they will rather judge and condemn us.

Book 2
8. Men Not Excluded from These Remarks on Personal Adornment.

Of course, now, I, a man, as being envious of women, am banishing them quite from their own (domains). Are there, in our case too, some things which, in respect of the sobriety we are to maintain on account of the fear due to God, are disallowed? If it is true, (as it is,) that in men, for the sake of women (just as in women for the sake of men), there is implanted, by a defect of nature, the will to please; and if this sex of ours acknowledges to itself deceptive trickeries of form peculiarly its own,—(such as) to cut the beard too sharply; to pluck it out here and there; to shave round about (the mouth); to arrange the hair, and disguise its hoariness by dyes; to remove all the incipient down all over the body; to fix (each particular hair) in its place with (some) womanly pigment; to smooth all the rest of the body by the aid of some rough powder or other: then, further, to take every opportunity for consulting the mirror; to gaze anxiously into it:—while yet, when (once) the knowledge of God has put an end to all wish to please by means of voluptuous attraction, all these things are rejected as frivolous, as hostile to modesty. For where God is, there modesty is; there is sobriety, her assistant and ally. How, then, shall we practise modesty without her instrumental mean, that is, without sobriety? How, moreover, shall we bring sobriety to bear on the discharge of (the functions of) modesty, unless seriousness in appearance and countenance, and in the general aspect of the entire man, mark our carriage?

11. Christian Women, Further, Have Not the Same Causes for Appearing in Public, and Hence for Dressing in Fine Array, as Gentiles. On the Contrary, Their Appearance Should Always Distinguish Them from Such.

Moreover, what causes have you for appearing in public in excessive grandeur, removed as you are from the occasions which call for such exhibitions? For you neither make the circuit of the temples, nor demand (to be present at) public shows, nor have any acquaintance with the holy days of the Gentiles. Now it is for the sake of all these public gatherings, and of much seeing and being seen, that all pomps (of dress) are exhibited before the public eye; either for the purpose of transacting the trade of volup-tuousness, or else of inflating "glory." You, however, have no cause of ap-pearing in public, except such as is serious. Either some brother who is sick is visited, or else the sacrifice is offered, or else the word of God is dispensed. Whichever of these you like to name is a business of sobriety and sanctity, requiring no extraordinary attire, with (studious) arrangement and (wanton) negligence. And if the requirements of Gentile friendships and of kindly offices call you, why not go forth clad in your own armour; (and) all the more, in that (you have to go) to such as are strangers to the faith? so that between the handmaids of God and of the devil there may be a differ-ence; so that you may be an example to them, and they may be edified in you; so that (as the apostle says) "God may be magnified in your body."[4] But magnified He is in the body through modesty: of course, too, through attire suitable to modesty. Well, but it is urged by some, "Let not the Name be blasphemed in us, if we make any derogatory change from our old style and dress." Let us, then, not abolish our old vices! let us maintain the same character, if we must maintain the same appearance (as before); and then truly the nations will not blaspheme! A grand blasphemy is that by which it is said, "Ever since she became a Christian, she walks in poorer garb!" Will you fear to appear poorer, from the time that you have been made more wealthy; and fouler, from the time when you have been made more clean? Is it according to the decree of Gentiles, or according to the decree of God, that it becomes Christians to walk?

12. Such Outward Adornments Meretricious, and Therefore Unsuitable to Modest Women.

Let us only wish that we may be no cause for just blasphemy! But how much more provocative of blasphemy is it that you, who are called mod-esty's priestesses, should appear in public decked and painted out after the manner of the immodest? Else, (if you so do,) what inferiority would the poor unhappy victims of the public lusts have (beneath you)? whom, albeit some laws were (formerly) wont to restrain them from (the use of) matri-monial and matronly decorations, now, at all events, the daily increasing depravity of the age has raised so nearly to an equality with all the most honourable women, that the difficulty is to distinguish them. And yet, even the Scriptures suggest (to us the reflection), that meretricious attractive-

4. See Phil. 1:20.

nesses of form are invariably conjoined with and appropriate to bodily prostitution. That powerful state which presides over the seven mountains and very many waters, has merited from the Lord the appellation of a prostitute.[5] But what kind of garb is the instrumental mean of her comparison with that appellation? She sits, to be sure, "in purple, and scarlet, and gold, and precious stone." How accursed are the things without (the aid of) which an accursed prostitute could not have been described! It was the fact that Thamar "had painted out and adorned herself" that led Judah to regard her as a harlot,[6] and thus, because she was hidden beneath her "veil,"—the quality of her garb belying her as if she had been a harlot,—he judged (her to be one), and addressed and bargained with (her as such). Whence we gather an additional confirmation of the lesson, that provision must be made in every way against all immodest associations and suspicions. For why is the integrity of a chaste mind defiled by its neighbour's suspicion? Why is a thing from which I am averse hoped for in me? Why does not my garb pre-announce my character, to prevent my spirit from being wounded by shamelessness through (the channel of) my ears? Grant that it be lawful to assume the appearance of a modest woman: to assume that of an immodest is, at all events, not lawful.

13. It Is Not Enough that God Know Us to Be Chaste: We Must Seem So before Men. Especially in These Times of Persecution We Must Inure Our Bodies to the Hardships Which They May Not Improbably Be Called to Suffer.

Perhaps some (woman) will say: "To me it is not necessary to be approved by men; for I do not require the testimony of men: God is the inspector of the heart." (That) we all know; provided, however, we remember what the same (God) has said through the apostle: "Let your probity appear before men."[7] For what purpose, except that malice may have no access at all to you, or that you may be an example and testimony to the evil? Else, what is (that): "Let your works shine?"[8] Why, moreover, does the Lord call us the light of the world; why has He compared us to a city built upon a mountain;[9] if we do not shine in (the midst of) darkness, and stand eminent amid them who are sunk down? If you hide your lamp beneath a bushel,[10] you must necessarily be left quite in darkness, and be run against by many. The things which make us luminaries of the world are these—our good works.

5. Cf. Rev. 17.

6. Cf. Gen. 38:12–30.

7. See Phil. 4:5, 8; Rom. 12:17; 2 Cor. 8:21.

8. See Matt. 5:16; and cf. *de Idol.*, c. 15 *ad init.*

9. Matt. 5:14.

10. Matt. 5:15; Mark 4:21; Luke 8:16, 11:33.

What is good, moreover, provided it be true and full, loves not darkness: it joys in being seen, and exults over the very pointings which are made at it. To Christian modesty it is not enough to be so, but to seem so too. For so great ought its plenitude to be, that it may flow out from the mind to the garb, and burst out from the conscience to the outward appearance; so that even from the outside it may gaze, as it were, upon its own furniture,—(a furniture) such as to be suited to retain faith as its inmate perpetually. For such delicacies as tend by their softness and effeminacy to unman the manliness of faith are to be discarded. Otherwise, I know not whether the wrist that has been wont to be surrounded with the palmleaf-like bracelet will endure till it grow into the numb hardness of its own chain! I know not whether the leg that has rejoiced in the anklet will suffer itself to be squeezed into the gyve! I fear the neck, beset with pearl and emerald nooses, will give no room to the broadsword! Wherefore, blessed (sisters), let us meditate on hardships, and we shall not feel them; let us abandon luxuries, and we shall not regret them. Let us stand ready to endure every violence, having nothing which we may fear to leave behind. It is these things which are the bonds which retard our hope. Let us cast away earthly ornaments if we desire heavenly. Love not gold; in which (one substance) are branded all the sins of the people of Israel. You ought to hate what ruined your fathers; what was adored by them who were forsaking God. Even then (we find) gold is food for the fire. But Christians always, and now more than ever, pass their times not in gold but in iron: the stoles of martyrdom are (now) preparing: the angels who are to carry us are (now) being awaited! Do you go forth (to meet them) already arrayed in the cosmetics and ornaments of prophets and apostles; drawing your whiteness from simplicity, your ruddy hue from modesty; painting your eyes with bashfulness, and your mouth with silence; implanting in your ears the words of God; fitting on your necks the yoke of Christ. Submit your head to your husbands, and you will be enough adorned. Busy your hands with spinning; keep your feet at home; and you will "please" better than (by arraying yourselves) in gold. Clothe yourselves with the silk of uprightness, the fine linen of holiness, the purple of modesty. Thus painted, you will have God as your Lover!

6
Church Order

The ever-growing number of Christians brought with it need for increasingly elaborate administrative and judicial apparatus in the Church. At the same time, the ferment of theological and mystical reflection produced new ways of thinking about spiritual order in the soul, the Church, and the cosmos. The following texts portray some of the complex issues that arose. The last three documents concern the specific question of Church government. Later they were repeatedly quoted as authoritative statements of rival constitutional doctrines. During the final centuries of the Middle Ages, they played crucial roles in disputes that raged over the question whether the Church were a monarchic or a participatory form of government. Still later, during the seventeenth and eighteenth centuries, doctrines that they inspired were used in conflicts for dominance between kings and parliaments.

In this section, as in section 4, documents are arranged in clusters. Here the clusters concern (1) personal relations and (2) ways of thinking about administrative order in the Church.

From the earliest days of Christianity onward, the faith was portrayed, above all, in its power to change personal relations. The Apostle Paul described that change in words of startling unity and equality: "For as many of you as have been baptised into Christ have put on Christ. There is neither Jew nor Greek: there is neither bond nor free: there is neither male nor female; for ye are all one in Christ Jesus" (*Galat.* 3:27–28). The subject of personal relations runs throughout all the other texts in this anthology. In the following section, I have chosen to focus on the relationships between men and women in the Church.

The *Didaskalia Apostolorum* were written in Syria during the early third century. Evidently the author was a Jewish Christian concerned, as had been the Apostles Peter and Paul, with whether Old Testament law retained binding force on Christian converts. He argued that Christians were freed from the Mosaic law, and yet his argument testifies to the new, and increasing, legalism of the Church. Purporting to be a description of practices handed down from the earliest days of Christianity, the work was widely translated and disseminated throughout the eastern Empire. It is preserved (at least in fragments) in the Greek original and in Syriac, Coptic, Ethiopic, and Arabic translations.

Codex Theodosianus, 16.2.27. This decree, from the year 390, limits the testamentary rights of women consecrated as deaconesses in order to keep family wealth intact. The regulation concerning the ascetic practice of cutting hair should be compared with Tertullian's comments in his treatise *On the Apparel of Women* (document 29, above).

In the excerpts from Augustine of Hippo's *Confessions* (written 397–401), the Church Father described the relationships between husbands and wives in his childhood home, Thagaste, in the North African province of Numidia. The relations between his own parents were complicated by the fact that his mother, Monica (whose memory Augustine greatly revered) was a devout Christian, while his father, Patricius, was not baptised until shortly before his death. (For more on Augustine, see Introductions to topics 2, 3, and 4 above.)

During his troubled episcopate over Constantinople (397–407), John Chrysostom found many faithful supporters, Olympias among them. His letters to her suggest the important, but subordinate, role allowed to women in the patristic Church. (For more on Chrysostom, see Introduction to topic 4 above.)

A professed religious from what is now southern France, Aetheria (or Egeria) went on a pilgrimage to the Holy Land, probably in 393–394. Her account, discovered as late as 1887, provides much valuable information about architecture, hierarchy, and liturgy, and especially about the possibilities and limits of cultural exchanges among travelers from distant parts of the Roman world who met at the geographical source of their common faith.

Four documents have been chosen to illustrate different ways of thinking about Church order.

Eusebius of Caesarea's (263–339) ceremonial address, written for the dedication of a new church in Tyre, sets forth an allegorical order. In a way reminiscent of Scriptural interpretation, Eusebius characterized the material church as an image, or allegorical representation, of the heavenly Jerusalem. The materials that made up the building and its design were regarded as symbols by which believers could pass into the spiritual order that those tangible things both concealed and revealed.

Writers on Church government were likewise constrained to seek an unseen justification for the visible structure of authority in the Church. Again the theme of conflict was dominant. Broadly speaking, three positions emerged.

A native of Asia Minor, Bishop Irenaeus of Lyon (flourished 177), was a disciple of the martyr Polycarp (died 156). Polycarp, in turn, was revered as a disciple of the Apostle John, who appointed him bishop of Smyrna. When, as bishop of a church menaced by persecution and heresy, Irenaeus sought some test of true faith and order, he found it in faithfulness to the teaching of the Apostles: that is, in a common tradition, deposited by the Apostles in churches that they founded and transmitted through the lines of consecration to priestly and episcopal office that they began. Those lines, or "pedigrees," conveyed the sanctification that Christ himself imparted to the Apostles.

Writing from within the as yet undeveloped context of Latin thought, Bishop Cyprian of Carthage (200/210–258) was less well trained as a theologian than Irenaeus. He was educated as a lawyer and rhetorician, and he converted to Christianity relatively late in his life (ca. 246), becoming bishop of Carthage soon after his baptism. His experience of persecution, doctrinal controversy, and ecclesiastical politics (including a jurisdictional dispute with the Bishop of Rome, Pope Stephen I), fused with his legal training. Consequently, before his martyrdom, he set forth an important corporative idea of the Church. Each bishop, he wrote, incorporated his own church, and the whole brotherhood of bishops was united, not by some overarching hierarchic order, but by fraternal charity in the Holy Spirit.

Pope Leo I (440–461) crystallized the thought of many of his predecessors when he declared that the bishop of Rome was the head of the Church. By virtue of Christ's commission, the Apostle Peter had received a principate (a form of monarchic rule) over all other bishops and, indeed, over all who belonged to Christ's flock. Leo's unusually long pontificate gave him many opportunities to assert this monarchic doctrine in his political and legal actions. But the opposition of other bishops, holding to doctrines that resembled Irenaeus' and Cyprian's, the onslaught of the barbarian invasions, and the benign neglect of emperors seated in Constantinople gradually moved Rome itself to the periphery of imperial affairs. Leo's vision was left, unrealized but powerful, to later generations.

30. *Didaskalia Apostolorum*

Chapter 10

. . . But if your judgement be without respect of persons, O bishops, observe him that accuses his brother, whether he be not a false brother, and has brought the accusation out of envy or jealousy, that he may disturb the Church of God and slay him who is accused by him through his expulsion from the Church and his delivery over to the sword of fire. Judge him therefore, thou, sternly, because he has brought evil upon his brother. For as regards his own intent, if he had been able to catch beforehand the judge's ear, he would have slain his brother in fire. It is written: *Whoso sheddeth man's blood, his own blood shall be shed for the blood which he hath shed.* [ii. 43] If then he is found to be such, expel him from the Church with great denunciation as a murderer; and after a time, if he promise to repent, warn him and correct him sternly; and then lay hand upon him and receive him into the Church. And be wary and guard such a one, that he no more disturb any other. But if, after he is come in, you see that he is still contentious and minded to accuse others also, and mischievous and designing, and making false complaints against many: drive him out, that he may no further disturb and trouble the Church. For such a one, though he be within, yet because he is unseemly to the Church, he is superfluous to her, and there is no profit in him. For we see that there are some men born with superfluous members to their bodies, as fingers or other excessive flesh; but these, though they pertain to the body, are a reproach and a disgrace both to the body and to the man, because they are superfluous to him. Yet when they are removed by the surgeon, that man recovers the comeliness and beauty of his body; and he suffers no defect by the removal from it of that which was superfluous, but is even the more conspicuous in his beauty.

In like manner then do you also act, O pastors. For since the Church is a body, and the members are we who believe in God and abide in love in the fear of the Lord, even as we have received command to be perfect: therefore, one who contrives evil against the Church, and troubles her members, and loves the complaints and fault-findings of the Enemy, to wit, disturbances, quarrels, slanders, murmurings, contentions, controversies, accusations, charges, vexations: he that loves and does these things—rather it is the Enemy that works in him—and remains within the Church,

From *Didaskalia Apostolorum*, translated by R. Hugh Connolly (1929; reprint ed., Oxford: Clarendon Press, 1969), chaps. 10, 12–13, 15–16, 18, pp. 106–8, 119–20, 124–28, 133–34, 146–48, 156–60. All footnotes deleted. Reprinted by permission of the publisher, Oxford University Press.

the same is alien to the Church and a domestic of the Enemy; for to him he ministers that he may be working through him and may thwart and harass the Church. Such a one therefore, if he remain within, is a disgrace to the Church by reason of his blasphemies and his manifold disorder; for through him the Church of God comes in danger of being scattered. Deal with him therefore as it is written in Wisdom: *Put forth an evil man from the assembly, and his contention will go out with him; and make an end of strife and ignominy: lest, if (p. 48) he sit in the assembly, he dishonour you all.* For when he has gone forth twice from the Church, he is justly cut off; and the Church is the more beautiful in her proper form, forasmuch as peace has been restored to her, which (before) was wanting to her: for from that hour the Church remains free from blasphemy and disorder.

But if your mind be not pure—whether it be through respect of persons, or the gifts of filthy lucre which you receive—and you endure that an evil person should remain among you; or again, (if) you thrust away and expel from the Church them that are of good conversation, and foster among you many that are evil, contentious persons and scatterers (of the flock) and riotous: you will bring blasphemy upon the assembly of the Church, and will run the risk of scattering her through these persons; and you will have put yourselves in deadly peril of forfeiting eternal life—because you have pleased men, and have turned back from the truth of God, through respect of persons and the habit of receiving empty gifts: and you will have scattered the Catholic Church, the beloved daughter of the Lord God.

Chapter 12
To Bishops: That They Should Be Peaceable

[ii. 57] And you the bishops, be not hard, nor tyrannical, nor wrathful, and be not rough with the people of God which is delivered into your hands. And destroy not the Lord's house nor scatter His people; but convert all, that you may be helpers with God; and gather the faithful with much meekness and long-suffering and patience, and without anger, and with doctrine and exhortation, as ministers of the kingdom everlasting.

And in your congregations in the holy churches hold your assemblies with all decent order, and appoint the places for the brethren with care and gravity. And for the presbyters let there be assigned a place in the eastern part of the house; and let the bishop's throne be set in their midst, and let the presbyters sit with him. And again, let the lay men sit in another part of the house toward the east. For so it should be, that in the eastern part of the house the presbyters sit with the bishops, and next the lay men, and then the women; that when you stand up to pray, the rulers may stand first, and after them the lay men, and then the women also. For it is required that you pray toward the east, as knowing that which is written: *Give ye glory to God, who rideth upon the heaven of heavens toward the east.*

But of the deacons let one stand always by the oblations of the Eucharist; and let another stand without by the door and observe them that come in; and afterwards, when you offer, let them minister together in the Church. And if any one be found sitting out of his place, let the deacon who is within reprove him and make him to rise up and sit in a place that is meet for him. For our Lord likened the Church to a fold; for as we see the dumb animals, oxen and sheep and goats, lie down and rise up, and feed and chew the cud, according to their families, and none of them separate itself from its kind; and (see) the wild beasts also severally range with their like upon the mountains: so likewise in the Church ought those who are young to sit apart, if there be room, and if not to stand up; and those who are advanced in years to sit apart. And let the children stand on one side, or let their fathers and mothers take them to them; and let them stand up. And let the young girls also sit apart; but if there be no room, let them stand up behind the women. And let the young women who are married and have children stand apart, and the aged women and widows sit apart. And let the deacon also see that no one whispers, or falls asleep, or laughs, or makes signs. For so it should be, that with decency and decorum they watch in the Church, with ears attentive to the word of the Lord.

Chapter 13
An Instruction to the People to Be Constant in Assembling in the Church

[ii. 59] Now when thou teachest, command and warn the people to be constant in assembling in the Church, and not to withdraw themselves but always to assemble, lest any man diminish the Church by not assembling, and cause the body of Christ to be short of a member. For let not a man take thought of others only, but of himself as well, hearkening to that which our Lord said: *Every one that gathereth not with me, scattereth.* Since therefore you are the members of Christ, do not scatter yourselves from the Church by not assembling. Seeing that you have Christ for your head, as He promised—for you are partakers with us—be not then neglectful of yourselves, and deprive not our Saviour of His members, and do not rend and scatter His body. And make not your worldly affairs of more account than the word of God; but on the Lord's day leave every thing and run eagerly to your Church; for she is your glory. Otherwise, what excuse have they before God who do not assemble on the Lord's day to hear the word of life and be nourished with the divine food which abides for ever? [ii. 60] For you are eager to receive temporal things and those that are but for a day and an hour, (but) those that are eternal you neglect; and you are anxious about baths, and to be fed with the meat and drink of the belly, and about other things, but for the things eternal you have no care, but neglect your soul and have no zeal for the Church, to hear and receive the word of God.

And in comparison of them that err what excuse have you? For the heathen, when they daily rise from their sleep, go in the morning to worship and minister to their idols; and before all their works and undertakings they go first and worship their idols. Neither at their festivals and their fairs are they wanting, but are constant in assembling: not only they who are of the district, but even those who come from afar; and all likewise assemble and come to the spectacle of their theatre. And so in like manner they who are vainly called Jews, they remain idle one day after six, and assemble in their synagogue; and never do they withdraw themselves or neglect their synagogue, nor disregard their (days of) idleness—even they who by reason of their unbelief are made void of the power of the word, and of the very name by which they call themselves, Jews: for "Jew" is interpreted "confession," but these are no confessors, since they do not confess the passion of Christ, which by transgression of the Law they caused, that they should repent and be saved. If then they who are not saved bestow care at all times on things wherein there is no profit and which avail them nothing, what excuse has he before the Lord God who withdraws himself from the assembly of the Church, and does not even imitate the gentiles, but by reason of his non-attendance grows indifferent and careless, and stands aloof and does evil? to whom the Lord said by Jeremiah [*sic*]: *My laws ye have not kept: but neither have ye conversed after the laws of the gentiles; and ye have well nigh surpassed them in evildoing*; and: *Do the gentiles exchange their gods, which yet be no gods? But my people have exchanged their honour for that which is without profit.* How then shall he excuse himself who is indifferent and has no zeal for the assembly of the Church? But if there be any one who takes occasion of worldly business to withdraw himself, let him know this, that the trades of the faithful are called works of superfluity; for their true work is religion. Pursue your trades therefore as a work of superfluity, for your sustenance, but let your true work be religion. . . .

[ii. 62] And beware of assembling with them that are perishing in the theatre, which is the assembly of the heathen, of error and of destruction. For he who enters an assembly of the gentiles shall be accounted as one of them, and shall receive the Woe. For to such the Lord God said by Isaiah: *Woe, woe to them that come from the spectacle.* And again He saith: *Ye women that come from the spectacle, come: for it is a people without understanding.* "Women," then, He called the Churches, which He called and redeemed and brought forth from the spectacle of the theatre, and took and received; and He taught us from henceforth to go thither no more. For

He saith in Jeremiah: *Ye shall not learn according to the ways of the gentiles.* And He saith again in the Gospel: *In the way of the gentiles ye shall not go; (and into the cities of the Samaritans ye shall not enter.)* Here then He commands and warns us wholly to avoid all heresies, which are *the cities of the Samaritans*; and furthermore, that we should keep far away from the assemblies of the gentiles, and not enter strange congregations; and that we should utterly avoid the theatre, and their fairs which are held for the sake of idols. A believer must not even come near to a fair, except to buy him nourishment for body and soul. Therefore, avoid all vain shows of the idols, and the festivals of their fairs.

Chapter 15

[iii.6] It is neither right nor necessary therefore that women should be teachers, and especially concerning the name of Christ and the redemption of His passion. For you have not been appointed to this, O women, and especially widows, that you should teach, but that you should pray and entreat the Lord God. For He the Lord God, Jesus Christ our Teacher, sent us the Twelve to instruct the People and the Gentiles; and there were with us women disciples, Mary Magdalene and Mary the daughter of James and the other Mary; but He did not send them to instruct the people with us. For if it were required that women should teach, our Master Himself would have commanded these to give instruction with us. But let a widow know that she is the altar of God; and let her sit ever at home, and not stray or run about among the houses of the faithful to receive. For the altar of God never strays or runs about anywhere, but is fixed in one place.

A widow must not therefore stray or run about among the houses. For those who are gadabouts and without shame cannot be still even in their houses; for they are no widows, but wallets, and they care for nothing else but to be making ready to receive. And because they are gossips and chatterers and murmurers, they stir up quarrels; and they are bold and shameless. Now they that are such are unworthy of Him who called them; for neither in the common assembly of rest of the Sunday, when they have come, are such women or men watchful, but they either fall asleep or prate about some other matter: so that through them others also are taken captive by the enemy Satan, who suffers not such persons to be watchful unto the Lord. And they who are such, coming in empty to the Church, go out more empty still, since they hearken not to that which is spoken or read to receive it with the ears of their hearts. Such persons, then, are like those of whom Isaiah said: *Hearing ye shall hear, and shall not understand; and seeing ye shall see, and shall not see. For the heart of this people is waxed gross, and with their ears they hear heavily, and their eyes they have shut:*

lest at any time they should see with their eyes, and hear with their ears.
[iii. 7] So in like manner the ears of such widows' hearts are stopped, because they will not sit beneath the roof of their houses and pray and entreat
the Lord, but are impatient to be running after gain; and by their chattering
they execute the desires of the Enemy. Now such a widow does not con-
form to the altar of Christ; for it is written in the gospel: *If two shall agree
together, and shall ask concerning any thing whatsoever, it shall be given
them. And if they shall say to a mountain that it be removed and fall into
the sea, it shall so be done.*

Chapter 16

[iii. 12] Wherefore, O bishop, appoint thee workers of righteousness as
helpers who may co-operate with thee unto salvation. Those that please
thee out of all the people thou shalt choose and appoint as deacons: a man
for the performance of the most things that are required, but a woman for
the ministry of women. For there are houses whither thou canst not send a
deacon to the women, on account of the heathen, but mayest send a deaconess. Also, because in many other matters the office of a woman deacon
is required. In the first place, when women go down into the water, those
who go down into the water ought to be anointed by a deaconess with the
oil of anointing; and where there is no woman at hand, and especially no
deaconess, he who baptizes must of necessity anoint her who is being baptized. But where there is a woman, and especially a deaconess, it is not
fitting that women should be seen by men: but with the imposition of hand
do thou anoint the head only. As of old the priests and kings were anointed
in Israel, do thou in like manner, with the imposition of hand, anoint the
head of those who receive baptism, whether of men or of women; and afterwards—whether thou thyself baptize, or thou command the deacons or
presbyters to baptize—let a woman deacon, as we have already said,
anoint the women. But let a man pronounce over them the invocation of the
divine Names in the water.

   And when she who is being baptized has come up from the water, let the
deaconess receive her, and teach and instruct her how the seal of baptism
ought to be (kept) unbroken in purity and holiness. For this cause we say
that the ministry of a woman deacon is especially needful and important.
For our Lord and Saviour also was ministered unto by women ministers,
*Mary Magdalene, and Mary the daughter of James and mother of Jose,
and the mother of the sons of Zebedee*, with other women beside. And thou
also hast need of the ministry of a deaconess for many things; for a deaconess is required to go into the houses of the heathen where there are believing women, and to visit those who are sick, and to minister to them in

that of which they have need, and to bathe those who have begun to recover from sickness.

[iii. 13] And let the deacons imitate the bishops in their conversation: nay, let them even be labouring more than he. And let them *not love filthy lucre*; but let them be diligent in the ministry. And in proportion to the number of the congregation of the people of the Church, so let the deacons be, that they may be able to take knowledge (of each) severally and refresh all; so that for the aged women who are infirm, and for brethren and sisters who are in sickness—for every one they may provide the ministry which is proper for him.

But let a woman rather be devoted to the ministry of women, and a male deacon to the ministry of men. And let him be ready to obey and to submit himself to the command of the bishop. And let him labour and toil in every place whither he is sent to minister or to speak of some matter to any one. For it behoves each one to know his office and to be diligent in executing it. And be you (bishop and deacon) of one counsel and of one purpose, and one soul dwelling in two bodies. And know what the ministry is, according as our Lord and Saviour said in the Gospel: *Whoso among you desireth to be chief, let him be your servant: even as the Son of Man came not to be ministered unto, but to minister.*

Chapter 18

[iv. 5] Do you the bishops and the deacons be constant therefore in the ministry of the altar of Christ,—we mean the widows and the orphans,— so that with all care and with all diligence you make it your endeavour to search out concerning the things that are given, (and to learn) of what manner is the conversation of him, or of her, who gives for the nourishment— we say again—of "the altar." For when widows are nourished from (the fruits of) righteous labour, they will offer a holy and acceptable ministry before almighty God through His beloved Son and His holy Spirit: to whom be glory and honour for evermore.

Make it your care and endeavour therefore to minister to widows out of the ministry of a clean conscience, that what they ask and request may be granted them at once upon their praying for it. But if there be bishops who are careless and give no heed to these matters, through respect of persons, or for the sake of filthy lucre, or because they neglect to make inquiry; they shall render no ordinary account. [iv. 6] For they receive, forsooth, to administer for the nourishment of orphans and widows, from rich persons who keep men shut up in prison, or ill-treat their slaves, or behave with cruelty in their cities, or oppress the poor; or from the lewd, and those who abuse their bodies; or from evildoers; or from forgers; or from dishonest advocates, or false accusers; or from hypocritical lawyers; or from painters of pictures; or from makers of idols; or from workers of gold and silver and bronze (who are) thieves; or from dishonest tax-gatherers; or from spectators of shows; or from those who alter weights or measure deceitfully; or from inn-keepers who mingle water (with their wine); or from soldiers who act lawlessly; or from murderers; or from spies who procure condemnations; or from any Roman officials, who are defiled with wars and have shed innocent blood without trial: perverters of judgement who, in order to rob them, deal unjustly and deceitfully with the peasantry and with all the poor; and from idolaters; or from the unclean; or from those who practise usury, and extortioners. Now they who nourish widows from these (sources) shall be found guilty in judgement in the day of the Lord; for the Scripture has said: *Better is a supper of herbs with love and amity than the slaughter of fatted oxen with hatred.* For if a widow be nourished with bread only from the labour of righteousness, it shall even be abundant for her; but if much be given her from (the proceeds) of iniquity it shall be insufficient for her. But again, if she be nourished from (the proceeds) of iniquity, she cannot offer her ministry and her intercession with purity before God; and even though she be righteous and pray for the wicked, her intercession for them will not be heard, but that for herself alone; for God makes trial of the hearts in judgement, and receives intercessions with discernment. But if they pray for those who have sinned and repent, their prayers will be heard. But those who are in sin, and do not repent, not only are they not heard when they pray, but they even call to remembrance their transgressions before the Lord.

[iv. 7] Wherefore, O bishops, fly and avoid such ministrations; for it is written: *There shall not go up upon the altar of the Lord (that which cometh) of the price of a dog, or of the hire of a harlot.* For if widows pray for fornicators and transgressors through your blindness, and be not heard, not receiving their requests, you will perforce bring blasphemy upon the word through your evil management, as though God were not good and ready to give.

Take good heed therefore that you minister not to the altar of God out of the ministrations of transgression. For you have no pretext to say, "We do not know"; for you have heard that which the Scripture saith: *Depart from an evil man, and thou shalt not fear; and trembling shall not come nigh unto thee.* [iv. 8] But if you say: "These are they alone who give alms; and if we receive not of them, from whence shall the orphans and widows and those in distress be provided?" God saith to you: "To this end did you receive the gifts of the Levites, the first fruits and offerings of your people, that you might be sustained and even have over and above, that you might not be constrained to receive from evil persons." But if the Churches are so poor that those in want must needs be supported by such, it were better for you rather to be wasted with famine than to receive from evil persons.

Search out and make trial, therefore, that you may be receiving from the faithful, who communicate with the Churches and conduct themselves well, (wherewithal) to nourish those in distress, and may not receive from those who are expelled from the Church until they are found worthy to be members of the Church. But if you are in want, tell the brethren, and let them treat together and give; and thus perform your ministrations in righteousness. [iv. 9] And teach your people and tell them that it is written: *Honour the Lord with (the fruits of) righteous labour, and with the chiefest of all your increase.* Wherefore, nourish and clothe those in want from the righteous labour of the faithful; and those things which are given by them, as we have already said, bestow for the ransom of the faithful; and redeem slaves and captives and prisoners, and those who are treated with violence, and those condemned by the mob, and those sentenced to fight with beasts, or to the mines, or to exile, and those condemned to the games. And let the deacons go in to those who are in distress, and let them visit each one and provide him with what he lacks.

[iv. 10] But if ever it should happen that you are constrained and receive unwillingly some pieces of money from any evil person, you shall not employ them for (the purchase of) food; but if they be few, spend them on firewood for yourselves and for the widows, lest a widow, receiving of them, be forced to buy her some food with them. And so, unsullied by iniquity, the widows will pray and receive from God all good things for which they ask and make petition, all of them together and each one severally: and you also will not be reproached with these sins.

31. *Codex Theodosianus*, 16.2.27

Emperors Valentinian, Theodosius, and Arcadius Augustuses to Tatianus, Praetorian Prefect.

According to the precept of the Apostle,[1] no woman shall be transferred to the society of deaconesses unless she is sixty years of age and has the desired offspring at home. Then, after she has sought a curator for her children if their age should so require, she shall entrust her goods to suitable persons, to be managed diligently and conscientiously. She herself shall

From *The Theodosian Code and Novels and the Sirmondian Constitutions*, translated by Clyde Pharr (Princeton: Princeton University Press, 1952), p. 444. © 1952 by Clyde Pharr; © renewed 1980 by Roy Pharr. Some footnotes deleted. Reprinted by permission of the publisher.

1. 1 Timothy, 5:9.

receive only the income from her landed estates, which she shall have full power to keep, to alienate, to give, to sell, or to bequeath, as long as she lives or when she is departing to her fate, and her will is unrestricted. She shall expend none of her jewels and ornaments, none of her gold and silver and other embellishments of a sumptuous home, under the pretext of religion. Rather, she shall transfer in writing all her property intact to her children or next of kin or to any other persons whatsoever, according to the judgment of her own free will. However, when she dies, she shall designate as heirs no church, no cleric, or no pauper. For her will shall necessarily lack all force if it should be composed by the decedent contrary to the prohibition concerning the persons specifically mentioned above. Furthermore, if anything should be extorted from the decedent by the aforesaid persons, nothing shall be bestowed on clerics, to the fraud of Our venerable sanction, by secret trust, through cunning artifice or the disgraceful connivance of any person. Rather, they shall be deprived of all the goods which they had coveted. Moreover, if anything is revealed to have been transferred in writing through a letter, codicil, gift, or testament, or finally, in any way whatsoever, to those persons whom We have excluded by this sanction, such deed of transfer shall not be cited in court. On the contrary, according to the limitation prescribed by this statute, that person shall succeed as heir through intestacy who understands that he is entitled to the goods, provided that he acknowledges that he is a child or proves that he is a near kinsman; or finally, if either by chance or by will he is found to be an heir, a legatee, or a beneficiary of a trust for all or for a portion of the goods, by an open codicil; he shall enjoy the gift of his fortune, the reward of his knowledge, and, after the above-mentioned persons have been disqualified and rejected, he shall assume the authority of an heir over the hereditary substance.

1. Women who cut off their hair, contrary to divine and human laws, at the instigation and persuasion of some professed belief, shall be kept away from the doors of the churches. It shall be unlawful for them to approach the consecrated mysteries, nor shall they be granted, through any supplications, the privilege of frequenting the altars which must be venerated by all. Moreover, if a bishop should permit a woman with shorn head to enter a church, even the bishop himself shall be expelled from his position and kept away, along with such comrades. Not only if he should recommend that this be done, but even if he should learn that it is being accomplished by any persons, or finally, that it has been done in any way whatsoever, he shall understand that nothing will exonerate him. This shall indisputably serve as a law for those who deserve correction and as a customary practice for those who have already received correction, so that the latter may have a witness, and the former may begin to fear judgment.

Given on the eleventh day before the kalends of July at Milan in the year
of the fourth consulship of Valentinian Augustus and the consulship of the
Most Noble Neoterius. [June 21, 390.]

32. Augustine, *Confessions*, Book 9

8

You, Lord, who make men of one mind to dwell in one house brought to
our company a young man of our own town, Evodius. He had held office in
the civil service, had been converted and baptised before us, had resigned
from the state's service, and given himself to Yours. We kept together, meaning to live together in our devout purpose. We thought deeply as to the
place in which we might serve You most usefully. As a result we started
back for Africa. And when we had come as far as Ostia on the Tiber, my
mother died. I pass over many things, for I must make haste. Do You, O my
God, accept my confessions and my gratitude for countless things of which
I say nothing. But I will not omit anything my mind brings forth concerning her, Your servant, who brought me forth—brought me forth in the flesh
to this temporal light, and in her heart to light eternal. Not of her gifts do I
speak but of Your gifts in her. For she did not bring herself into the world or
educate herself in the world: it was You who created her, nor did her father
or mother know what kind of being was to come forth from them. It was
the scepter of Your Christ, the discipline of your Only-Begotten, that
brought her up in holy fear, in a Catholic family which was a worthy member of Your church. Yet it was not the devotion of her mother in her upbring-
ing that she talked most of, but of a certain aged servant, who had indeed
carried my mother's father on her back when he was a baby, as little ones
are accustomed to be carried on the backs of older girls. Because of this,
because also of her age and her admirable character, she was very much
respected by her master and mistress in their Christian household. As a
result she was given charge of her master's daughters. This charge she fulfilled most conscientiously, checking them sharply when necessary with
holy severity and teaching them soberly and prudently. Thus, except at the
times when they ate—and that most temperately—at their parents' table,
she would not let them even drink water, no matter how tormenting their
thirst. By this she prevented the forming of a bad habit, and she used to
remark very sensibly: "Now you drink water because you are not allowed
to have wine; but when you are married, and thus mistresses of food-stores

From *The Confessions of Saint Augustine*, translated by F. J. Sheed (New York: Sheed &
Ward, 1942), bk. 9, chaps. 8–9, pp. 160–63.

and wine-cellars, you will despise water, but the habit of drinking will still remain." By this kind of teaching and the authority of her commands she moderated the greediness that goes with childhood and brought the little girls' thirst to such a control that they no longer wanted what they ought not to have.

Yet, as Your servant told me, her son, there did steal upon my mother an inclination to wine. For when, in the usual way, she was sent by her parents, as a well-behaved child, to draw wine from the barrel, she would dip the cup in, but before pouring the wine from the cup into the flagon, she would sip a little with the very tip of her lips, only a little because she did not yet like the taste sufficiently to take more. Indeed she did it not out of any craving for wine, but rather from the excess of childhood's high spirits, which tend to boil over in absurdities, and are usually kept in check by the authority of elders. And so, adding to that daily drop a little more from day to day—for he that despises small things, falls little by little—she fell into the habit, so that she would drink off greedily cups almost full of wine. Where then was that wise old woman with her forceful prohibitions? Could anything avail against the evil in us, unless Your healing, O Lord, watched over us? When our father and mother and nurses are absent, You are present, who created us, who call us, who can use those placed over us for some good unto the salvation of our souls. What did You do then, O my God? How did You cure her, and bring her to health? From another soul You drew a harsh and cutting sarcasm, as though bringing forth a surgeon's knife from Your secret store, and with one blow amputated that sore place. A maidservant with whom she was accustomed to go to the cellar, one day fell into a quarrel with her small mistress when no one else chanced to be about, and hurled at her the most biting insult possible, calling her a drunkard. My mother was pierced to the quick, saw her fault in its true wickedness, and instantly condemned it and gave it up. Just as the flattery of a friend can pervert, so the insult of an enemy can sometimes correct. Nor do You, O God, reward men according to what You do by means of them, but according to what they themselves intended. For the girl being in a temper wanted to enrage her young mistress, not to amend her, for she did it when no one else was there, either because the time and place happened to be thus when the quarrel arose, or because she was afraid that elders would be angry because she had not told it sooner. But You, O Lord, Ruler of heavenly things and earthly, who turn to Your own purposes the very depths of rivers as they run and order the turbulence of the flow of time, did by the folly of one mind bring sanity to another; thus reminding us not to attribute it to our own power if another is amended by our word, even if we meant to amend him.

9

My mother, then, was modestly and soberly brought up, being rather made obedient to her parents by You than to You by her parents. When she reached the age for marriage, and was bestowed upon a husband, she served him as her lord. She used all her effort to win him to You, preaching You to him by her character, by which You made her beautiful to her husband, respected and loved by him and admirable in his sight. For she bore his acts of unfaithfulness quietly, and never had any jealous scene with her husband about them. She awaited Your mercy upon him, that he might grow chaste through faith in You. And as a matter of fact, though generous beyond measure, he had a very hot temper. But she knew that a woman must not resist a husband in anger, by deed or even by word. Only, when she saw him calm again and quiet, she would take the opportunity to give him an explanation of her actions, if it happened that he had been roused to anger unreasonably. The result was that whereas many matrons with much milder husbands carried the marks of blows to disfigure their faces, and would all get together to complain of the way their husbands behaved, my mother—talking lightly but meaning it seriously—advised them against their tongues: saying that from the day they heard the matrimonial contract read to them they should regard it as an instrument by which they became servants; and from that time they should be mindful of their condition and not set themselves up against their masters. And they often expressed amazement—for they knew how violent a husband she had to live with— that it had never been heard, and there was no mark to show, that Patricius had beaten his wife or that there had been any family quarrel between them for so much as a single day. And when her friends asked her the reason, she taught them her rule, which was as I have just said. Those who followed it, found it good and thanked her; those who did not, went on being bullied and beaten.

Her mother-in-law began by being angry with her because of the whispers of malicious servants. But my mother won her completely by the respect she showed, and her unfailing patience and mildness. She ended by going to her son, telling him of the tales the servants had bandied about to the destruction of peace in the family between herself and her daughter-in-law, and asking him to punish them for it. So he, out of obedience to his mother and in the interests of order in the household and peace among his womenfolk, had the servants beaten whose names he had been given, as she had asked when giving them. To which she added the promise that anyone must expect a similar reward from her own hands who should think to please her by speaking ill of her daughter-in-law. And as no one had the courage to do so, they lived together with the most notable degree of kindness and harmony.

This great gift also, O my God, my Mercy, You gave to Your good servant, in whose womb You created me, that she showed herself, wherever possible, a peacemaker between people quarreling and minds at discord. For swelling and undigested discord often belches forth bitter words when in the venom of intimate conversation with a present friend hatred at its rawest is breathed out upon an absent enemy. But when my mother heard bitter things said by each of the other, she never said anything to either about the other save what would help to reconcile them. This might seem a small virtue, if I had not had the sorrow of seeing for myself so many people who—as if by some horrible widespreading infection of sin—not only tell angry people the things their enemies said in anger, but even add things that were never said at all. Whereas, on the contrary, ordinary humanity would seem to require not merely that we refrain from exciting or increasing wrath among men by evil speaking, but that we study to extinguish wrath by kind speaking. Such a one was she: and You were the master who taught her most secretly in the school of her heart.

The upshot was that towards the very end of his life she won her husband to You; and once he was a Christian she no longer had to complain of the things she had had to bear with before he was a Christian. Further, she was a servant of Your servants. Such of them as knew her praised and honoured and loved You, O God, in her; for they felt Your presence in her heart, showing itself in the fruit of her holy conversation. She had been the wife of one husband, had requited her parents, had governed her house piously, was well reported of for good works. She had brought up her children, being in labour of them as often as she saw them swerving away from You. Finally of all of us Your servants, O Lord—since by Your gift You suffer us to speak—who before her death were living together after receiving the grace of baptism, she took as much care as if she had been the mother of us all, and served us as if she had been the daughter of us all.

33. John Chrysostom, *Letter to Olympias*

Having risen from the very gates of death I address this letter to the discreet lady; and I am very glad that thy servants have met me just as I am anchoring at last in harbour. For had they met me when I was still tossing on the open sea, and experiencing the cruel waves of bodily sickness, it

From *Nicene and Post-Nicene Fathers*, vol. 9 (New York: Christian Literature Co., 1889), pp. 297–98.

would not have been easy for me to deceive your cautious spirit, by sending good tidings instead of sorrowful.

For the winter, which has become more than commonly severe, brought on a storm of internal disorder even more distressing, and during the last two months I have been no better than one dead, nay worse. For I had just enough life to be sensible of the horrors which encircled me, and day and dawn and noon were all one night to me as I spent all my time closely confined to my bed, and in spite of endless contrivances I could not shake off the pernicious effects of the cold; but although I kept a fire burning, and endured a most unpleasant amount of smoke, and remained cooped up in one chamber, covered with any quantity of wraps, and not daring to set a foot outside the threshold I underwent extreme sufferings, perpetual vomiting supervening on headache, loss of appetite, and constant sleeplessness. Thus restlessly did I pass through my long dark sea of troubles.

But not to distress thy mind by dwelling upon my miseries, from all of them I am now relieved. For as soon as spring approached, and a little change in the temperature took place, all my troubles spontaneously vanished. Nevertheless I still require great care as regards diet; therefore I put only a light load on my stomach, so that it may be able to digest it easily. But it has occasioned me no little concern to learn that my discreet mistress was brought to the verge of death. Nevertheless in consideration of my great affection, and anxiety, and solicitude for your welfare I was relieved from this care, even before the arrival of your letters, many persons having come from thence who brought me tidings of your restoration to health.

And now I am exceedingly glad and delighted to hear, not only that you have been released from your infirmity, but above all that you bear the things which befall you so bravely, calling them all but an idle tale; and, which is indeed a greater matter, that you have applied this name even to your bodily infirmity, which is an evidence of a robust spirit, rich in the fruit of courage. For not only to bear misfortunes bravely but to be actually insensible to them, to overlook them, and with such little exertion to wreathe your brows with the garland prize of patience, neither labouring, nor toiling, neither feeling distress nor causing it to others, but as it were leaping and dancing for joy all the while, this is indeed a proof of the most finished philosophy.

Therefore I rejoice, and leap for joy, I am in a flutter of delight, I am insensible to my present loneliness, and the other troubles which surround me, being cheered, and brightened, and not a little proud on account of your greatness of soul, and the repeated victories which you have won, and this, not only for your own sake, but also for the sake of that large and populous city, where you are like a tower, a haven, and a wall of defence, speaking in the eloquent voice of example, and through your sufferings instructing either sex to strip readily for these contests, and descend into the lists with all courage, and cheerfully bear the toils which such contests involve.

And the wonder is that without thrusting yourself into the forum, or occupying the public centres of the city, but sitting all the while in a small house and confined chamber you serve and anoint the combatants for the contest, and whilst the sea is thus raging round you, and the billows are rising to a crest, and crags and reefs, and rocky ledges and fierce monsters appear on every side, and everything is shrouded in the most profound darkness you, setting the sails of patience, float on with great serenity, as if it was noonday, and calm weather, and a favourable breeze wafting you on, and so far from being overwhelmed by this grievous tempest are not even sprinkled by the spray; and very naturally so; such is the force of virtue as a rudder.

Now merchants and pilots, and sailors and voyagers when they see clouds gathering up, or fierce winds rushing down upon them, or the breakers seething with an abundance of foam keep their vessels moored inside harbour; and if they chance to be tempest-tossed in the open sea they do their best, and devise every means to bring their ship to some anchorage, or island or shore. But you, although such innumerable winds, and fierce waves burst upon you together, and the sea is heaved up from its very depths owing to the severity of the storm, and some are submerged, others floating dead upon the water, others drifting naked upon planks, you plunging into the mid ocean of calamities call all these things an idle tale, sailing on with a favourable breeze in the midst of the tempest; and naturally so; for pilots, even if they are infinitely wise in that science, nevertheless have not skill sufficient to withstand every kind of storm; consequently they often shrink from doing battle with the waves.

But the science which you have is superior to every kind of storm—the power of a philosophic soul—which is stronger than ten thousand armies, more powerful than arms, and more secure than towers and bulwarks. For the arms, and bulwarks, and towers which soldiers have, are serviceable for the security of the body only, and this not always, nor in every way; but there are times when all these resources are baffled, and leave those who fly to them for refuge destitute of protection. But thy powers do not repel the weapons of barbarians, nor the devices of hostile men, nor any assaults and stratagems of that kind, but they have trampled under foot the constraining forces of nature, put down their tyranny and levelled their citadel.

And whilst ceaselessly contending with demons, you have won countless victories, yet have not received a single blow, but stand unwounded in the midst of a storm of darts and turn the spears which are hurled at you back upon those who discharge them. Such is the wisdom of your art; by the sufferings which you undergo you take vengeance on those who inflict them; by the plots of which you are the subject you put your enemies to pain, possessing in their malice the best foundation for the materials of fame. And you, knowing these things well yourself, and having gained perception by experience, naturally call them all an idle tale. For how, pray, should you not call them by that name, possessing as you do a mortal body, and yet despising death as if you were hastening to quit a foreign country, and return to your own land; a chronic sufferer from the most severe infirmity, and yet more cheerfully disposed than the thriving and robust, not depressed by insults, nor elated by honours and glory, the latter being a cause of infinite mischief to many who after an illustrious career in the priesthood, and after reaching extreme old age, and the most venerable hoar hairs, have fallen into disgrace on this account, and become a common spectacle of derision for those who wish to make merry.

But you on the contrary, woman as you are, clothed with a fragile body, and subject to these severe attacks, have not only avoided falling into such a condition yourself, but have prevented many others from so doing. They indeed before they had advanced far in the contest, even at the very outset and starting point, have been overthrown; whereas you, after having gone countless times round the farther turning post, have won a prize in every course, after playing your part in manifold kinds of wrestling and combats. And very naturally so; for the wrestlings of virtue do not depend upon age, or bodily strength, but only on the spirit and the disposition.

Thus women have been crowned victors, while men have been upset; so also boys have been proclaimed conquerors, while aged men have been put to shame. It is indeed always fitting to admire those who pursue virtue, but especially when some are found to cling to it at a time when many are deserting it. Therefore, my sweet lady, you deserve superlative admiration, inasmuch as after so many men, women, and aged persons who seemed to enjoy the greatest reputation have been turned to flight, all lying prostrate before the eyes of the world, and this not after a severe onslaught, nor any alarming muster of the enemy's force, but overthrown before the encounter and worsted before the struggle, you on the contrary after so many battles and such large muster of the enemy are so far from being unstrung, or dismayed by the number of your adversities, that you are all the more vigorous, and the increase of the contest gives you an increase of strength. For the recollection of what has been already achieved becomes the ground of cheerfulness, and joy, and greater zeal.

Therefore I rejoice, and leap for joy; for I will not cease repeating this, and taking about with me everywhere the material of my joy; so that although my separation from you distresses you, yet you have this very great consolation arising from your successful exploits; for I also who am banished to so great a distance gain no small cheerfulness from this cause,—I mean your courage.

34. Aetheria, *The Pilgrimage of Etheria*

Edessa

Then, journeying through certain stations, I came to a city whose name we read recorded in the Scriptures—Batanis, which city exists to-day: it has a church with a truly holy bishop, both monk and confessor, and certain martyr-memorials. The city has a teeming population, and the soldiery with their tribune are stationed there. Departing thence, we arrived at Edessa in the Name of Christ our God, and, on our arrival, we straightway repaired to the church and memorial of saint Thomas. There, according to custom, prayers were made and the other things that were customary in the holy places were done; we read also some things concerning saint Thomas himself. The church there is very great, very beautiful and of new construction, well worthy to be the house of God, and as there was much that I desired to see, it was necessary for me to make a three days' stay there. Thus I saw in that city many memorials, together with holy monks, some dwelling at the memorials, while others had their cells in more secluded spots farther from the city. Moreover, the holy bishop of the city, a truly devout man, both monk and confessor, received me willingly and said: "As I see, daughter, that for the sake of devotion you have undertaken so great a labour in coming to these places from far-distant lands, if you are willing, we will show you all the places that are pleasant to the sight of Christians." Then, first thanking God, I besought the bishop much that he would deign to do as he said. He thereupon led me first to the palace of King Abgar, where he showed me a great marble statue of him—very much like him, as they said—having a sheen as if made of pearl. From the face of Abgar it seemed that he was a very wise and honourable man. Then the holy bishop said to me: "Behold King Abgar, who before he saw the Lord believed in Him that He was in truth the Son of God." There was another statue near, made of the same marble, which he said was that of his son Magnus; this also had something gracious in the face. Then we entered the inner part of the palace, and there were fountains full of fish such as I never saw before, of so great size, so bright and of so good a flavour were they. The city has

From *The Pilgrimage of Etheria*, translated by M. L. McClure, edited by C. L. Feltoe (New York: SPCK, n.d. [1919]), pp. 32–41, 52–54, 90–94.

no water at all other than that which comes out of the palace, which is like a great silver river.

The Story of King Abgarus

Then the holy bishop told me about the water, saying: "At some time, after that King Abgar had written to the Lord, and the Lord had answered King Abgar by Ananias the courier—as it is written in the letter itself—when some time had passed, the Persians came against the city and surrounded it. And straightway Abgar, bearing the letter of the Lord to the gate, with all his army, prayed publicly. And he said: 'O Lord Jesus, Thou hadst promised us that none of our enemies should enter this city, and lo! the Persians now attack us.' And when the king had said this, holding the open letter in his uplifted hands, suddenly there came a great darkness outside the city before the eyes of the Persians, as they were approaching the city at a distance of about three miles, and they were so baffled by the darkness that they could hardly form their camp and surround the whole city about three miles off. So baffled were the Persians that they could never afterwards see the way to enter the city, but they surrounded it and shut it in with their hostile forces, at a distance of about three miles, for several months. Then, when they saw that they could by no means enter, they wished to slay those within the city by thirst. Now that little hill which you see, my daughter, over against the city, supplied it with water at that time, and the Persians, perceiving this, diverted the water from the city and made it to run near that place where they had made their camp. And on that day and at that hour when the Persians diverted the water, the fountains which you see in this place burst forth at once at God's bidding, and by the favour of God they remain here from that day to this. But the water which the Persians had diverted was dried up at that hour, so that they who were besieging the city had nothing to drink for even one day; which thing is plain to the present time, for no moisture of any sort has ever been seen there from that day to this. So, at God's bidding, Who had promised that this should come to pass, they were obliged to return to their own home in Persia. Moreover afterwards, as often as enemies determined to come and take the city, this letter was brought out and read in the gate, and straightway all enemies were driven back by the will of God." The holy Bishop also told me that the place where these fountains broke forth had previously been open ground within the city, lying under the palace of King Abgar, which same palace had been situated on somewhat higher ground, as was plainly visible. For the custom was at that time that, whenever palaces were built, they should always stand on higher ground. But after that these fountains had burst forth here, then Abgar built this palace for his son Magnus, whose statue I saw near that of his father, so that the fountains should be included in the palace. And when the holy bishop had told me all these things, he said to me: "Let us now go to the gate by which Ananias the courier entered with the letter of which I spoke." So when we had come to the gate, the bishop, standing, made a prayer and read us the letters; then, after he had blessed us, another prayer was made. Moreover the holy man told us that from the day on which Ananias the courier entered it with the letter of the Lord, the gate is kept to this day, that no one who is unclean, nor any mourner, should pass through nor should any dead body be borne out through it. The holy bishop also showed us the memorial of Abgar and of his whole family, very beautiful, but made in the ancient style. He took us also to the palace which King Abgar had at first, on the higher ground, and if there were any other places he showed them to us. It was very pleasant to me to receive from the holy man himself the letters of Abgar to the Lord and of the Lord to Abgar, which the holy bishop had read to us there. For although I have copies at home, yet it seemed to me more pleasant to receive them from him, lest perhaps something less might have reached us at home, and indeed that which I received here is fuller. So if Jesus our God bids it, and I come home, you too shall read them, ladies, my own souls.

Charrae (Haran)

Then, after three days spent there, it was necessary for me to go still farther, to Charrae, as it is now called. In holy Scripture it is called Charran, where holy Abraham dwelt, as it is written in Genesis when the Lord said unto Abram: *Get thee out of thy country, and from thy father's house, and go to Charran* and the rest.[1] And when I arrived at Charrae I went straightway to the church which is within the city, and soon I saw the bishop of the place, a truly holy man of God, both monk and confessor, who deigned to show us all the places there that we desired. He took us at once to the church, which is without the city on the spot where stood the house of holy Abraham; it stands on the same foundations, and it is made of the same stone, as the holy bishop said. When we had come to the church, prayer was made, the passage from Genesis was read, one psalm was said, and after a second prayer the bishop blessed us and we came out. Then he deigned to take us to the well whence holy Rebecca used to fetch water,[2] and the holy bishop said to us: "Behold the well whence holy Rebecca watered the camels of holy Abraham's servant Eleazar"; thus he deigned to show us each thing. Now at the church, which is outside the city, as I said, ladies, reverend sisters, where Abraham's house was originally, there is

---

1. Gen. 12:1.   2. Gen. 24:15, etc.

now the martyr-memorial of a certain holy monk named Helpidius. It happened very pleasantly for us that we arrived on the day before the martyr's
feast of saint Helpidius, which is on the twenty-third of April. On that day
it was of obligation that all the monks from all parts and from all the borders of Mesopotamia should come down to Charrae, even the greater ones
who dwelt in solitude, whom they call ascetics. For this day is observed
with great dignity there on account of the memorial of holy Abraham,
whose house stood where the church now is, in which the body of the holy
martyr is laid. So it happened to us very pleasantly beyond our expecta-
tions that we should see these holy monks of Mesopotamia, truly men of
God, as well as those whose good report and manner of life had reached
men's ears far and wide, whom I thought that I could not by any means see,
not because it was impossible for God to give me this, Who had deigned to
give me all things, but because I had heard that they never come down from
their dwellings except on Easter Day and on this day. For they are men who
do many wonders, and, moreover, I did not know in what month was the
day of the martyr's feast which I have mentioned; but at God's bidding it
came about that I arrived on the day that I had not hoped for. We stayed
there two days, for the memorial day and for the sake of seeing those holy
men, who deigned to receive me very willingly for the sake of salutation,
and to speak with me, of which I was not worthy. Nor were they seen there
after the memorial day, for they sought the desert without delay in the
night, each one returning to his own cell. In that city I found scarcely a
single Christian excepting a few clergy and holy monks—if any such dwell
in the city; all are heathen. And in like manner, as we gazed with great
reverence at the place where the house of holy Abraham was at first for the
sake of his memorial, so do those heathen gaze with great reverence at a
place about a mile from the city, where are the memorials of Nahor and
Bethuel. And since the bishop of that city is very learned in the Scriptures,
I asked him, saying: "I beg of you, my lord, to tell me that which I desire to
hear." And he said: "Tell me, daughter, what you wish, and I will tell it
you, if I know it." Then I said: "I know by the Scriptures[3] that holy Abraham came to this place with his father Terah and with Sarah his wife, and
with Lot his brother's son, but I have not read when Nahor and Bethuel
came here; I know only that afterwards Abraham's servant came to Charrae
that he might seek Rebecca, the daughter of Bethuel, the son of Nahor, for
Isaac the son of his master Abraham."[4] Then the holy bishop said to me:
"Truly, daughter, it is written as you say, in Genesis, that holy Abraham
came here with his relatives, but canonical Scripture does not say when
Nahor and his relatives and Bethuel came here, but it is plain that they did

3. Gen. 11:31.   4. Gen. 24:10, 15.

come here afterwards, since their memorials are here at about a mile from the city. The Scripture does indeed relate[5] how holy Abraham's servant came here to take holy Rebecca, and how holy Jacob came here when he took to himself the daughters of Laban the Syrian." Then I asked where was the well where holy Jacob watered the flocks which Rachel, the daughter of Laban the Syrian, was feeding. The bishop said to me: "The place is six miles hence, near the village which then was the farm of Laban the Syrian, and if you wish to go there, we will go with you and show it to you; there are also many very holy monks and ascetics, and a holy church." I also asked the holy bishop where was that place of the Chaldees where Terah lived at first with his family,[6] and the holy bishop said to me: "The place, daughter, of which you ask, is at the tenth station hence, as you go into Persia. There are five stations from here to Nisibis, and five stations thence to Ur, which was a city of the Chaldees, but there is now no access for Romans, for the Persians hold the whole country. This district is specially called the Eastern; it is on the borders of the Romans, the Persians and the Chaldees." And many other things he deigned to tell me, as did also the other holy bishops and holy monks, but all they told us was from the Scriptures of God or of the acts of holy men, that is of monks, either the wonderful things that those already departed had done, or what those who are still in the body do daily, at any rate those who are ascetics. For I would not that your affection should think that the monks ever told me any other stories except from the Scriptures of God or else those of the acts of the greater monks.

Rachel's Well. The Return to Antioch

Now after two days which I spent there, the bishop took us to the well where holy Jacob had watered holy Rachel's flocks;[7] the well is six miles from Charrae, and in its honour a very great and beautiful holy church has been built hard by. When we had come to the well, prayer was made by the bishop, the passage from Genesis was read, one psalm suitable to the place was said and, after a second prayer, the bishop blessed us. We saw also, lying on a spot near the well, that very great stone which holy Jacob had moved away from the well, and which is shown to-day. No one dwells there around the well, except the clergy of the church which is there and the monks who have their cells near at hand, whose truly unheard-of mode of life the bishop described to us. Then, after prayer had been made in the church, I visited, in company with the bishop, the holy monks in their

5. Gen. 29:1, 2, 4.
6. Gen. 11:28.
7. Gen. 29:10.

cells, giving thanks both to God and to them, who deigned with willing mind to receive me in their cells wherever I entered, and to address me in such words as were fitting to proceed out of their mouth. They deigned also to give me and all who were with me *eulogiae*, such as is the custom for monks to give those whom they receive with willing mind into their cells.

And the place being in a large plain, a great village over against us was pointed out to me by the holy bishop, about five hundred paces from the well, through which village our route lay. This village, as the bishop said, was once the farm of Laban the Syrian, and is called Fadana; in the village the memorial of Laban the Syrian, Jacob's father-in-law, was shown to me; the place was also shown to me where Rachel stole her father's images. So, having seen everything in the Name of God, and bidding farewell to the holy bishop and the holy monks who had deigned to conduct us to the place, we returned by the route and by the stations through which we had come from Antioch. . . .

Festivals at Epiphany

1. Night Station at Bethlehem

. . . *Blessed is he that cometh in the Name of the Lord*, and the rest which follows.[8] And since, for the sake of the monks who go on foot, it is necessary to walk slowly, the arrival in Jerusalem thus takes place at the hour when one man begins to be able to recognize another, that is, close upon but a little before daybreak. And on arriving there, the bishop and all with him immediately enter the Anastasis, where an exceedingly great number of lights are already burning. There a psalm is said, prayer is made, first the catechumens and then the faithful are blessed by the bishop; then the bishop retires, and every one returns to his lodging to take rest, but the monks remain there until daybreak and recite hymns.

2. Morning Services at Jerusalem

But after the people have taken rest, at the beginning of the second hour they all assemble in the greater church, which is in Golgotha.

Now it would be superfluous to describe the adornment either of the church, or of the Anastasis, or of the Cross, or in Bethlehem on that day; you see there nothing but gold and gems and silk. For if you look at the veils, they are made wholly of silk striped with gold, and if you look at the curtains, they too are made wholly of silk striped with gold. The church vessels too, of every kind, gold and jewelled, are brought out on that day, and indeed, who could either reckon or describe the number and weight of

8. Matt. 21:9.

the *cereofala*, or of the *cicindelae*, or of the *lucernae*, or of the various vessels? And what shall I say of the decoration of the fabric itself, which Constantine, at his mother's instigation, decorated with gold, mosaic, and costly marbles, as far as the resources of his kingdom allowed him, that is, the greater church as well as the Anastasis, at the Cross, and the other holy places in Jerusalem? But to return to the matter in hand: the dismissal takes place on the first day in the greater church, which is in Golgotha, and when they preach or read the several lessons, or recite hymns, all are appropriate to the day. And afterwards when the dismissal from the church has been made, they repair to the Anastasis with hymns, according to custom, so that the dismissal takes place about the sixth hour. And on this day *lucernare* also takes place according to the daily use. . . .

Baptism

1. The Inscribing of the Competents

Moreover, I must write how they are taught who are baptised at Easter. Now he who gives in his name, gives it in on the day before Quadragesima, and the priest writes down the names of all; this is before the eight weeks which I have said are kept here at Quadragesima. And when the priest has written down the names of all, after the next day of Quadragesima, that is, on the day when the eight weeks begin, the chair is set for the bishop in the midst of the great church, that is, at the martyrium, and the priests sit in chairs on either side of him, while all the clergy stand. Then one by one the competents are brought up, coming, if they are males (*viri*) with their fathers, and if females (*feminae*), with their mothers. Then the bishop asks the neighbours of every one who has entered concerning each individual, saying: "Does this person lead a good life, is he obedient to his parents, is he not given to wine, nor deceitful?" making also inquiry about the several vices which are more serious in man. And if he has proved him in the presence of witnesses to be blameless in all these matters concerning which he has made inquiry, he writes down his name with his own hand. But if he is accused in any matter, he orders him to go out, saying: "Let him amend, and when he has amended then let him come to the font (*lavacrum*)." And as he makes inquiry concerning the men, so also does he concerning the women. But if any be a stranger, he comes not so easily to Baptism, unless he has testimonials from those who know him.

2. Preparation for Baptism—Catechisings

This also I must write, reverend sisters, lest you should think that these things are done without good reason. The custom here is that they who come to Baptism through those forty days, which are kept as fast days, are first exorcised by the clergy early in the day, as soon as the morning dismissal has been made in the Anastasis. Immediately afterwards the chair is placed for the bishop at the martyrium in the great church, and all who are to be baptised sit around, near the bishop, both men and women, their fathers and mothers standing there also. Besides these, all the people who wish to hear come in and sit down—the faithful however only, for no catechumen enters there when the bishop teaches the others the Law. Beginning from Genesis he goes through all the Scriptures during those forty days, explaining them, first literally, and then unfolding them spiritually. They are also taught about the Resurrection, and likewise all things concerning the Faith during those days. And this is called the catechising.

3. "Traditio" of the Creed

Then when five weeks are completed from the time when their teaching began, (the Competents) are then taught the Creed. And as he explained the meaning of all the Scriptures, so does he explain the meaning of the Creed; each article first literally and then spiritually. By this means all the faithful in these parts follow the Scriptures when they are read in church, inasmuch as they are all taught during those forty days from the first to the third hour, for the catechising lasts for three hours. And God knows, reverend sisters, that the voices of the faithful who come in to hear the catechising are louder (in approval) of the things spoken and explained by the bishop than they are when he sits and preaches in church. Then, after the dismissal of the catechising is made, it being already the third hour, the bishop is at once escorted with hymns to the Anastasis. So the dismissal takes place at the third hour. Thus are they taught for three hours a day for seven weeks, but in the eighth week of Quadragesima, which is called the Great Week, there is no time for them to be taught, because the things that are [described] above must be carried out.

4. "Redditio" [Recitation] of the Creed

And when the seven weeks are past, [and] the Paschal week is left, which they call here the Great Week, then the bishop comes in the morning into the great church at the martyrium, and the chair is placed for him in the apse behind the altar, where they come one by one, a man with his father and a woman with her mother, and recite the Creed to the bishop. And when they have recited the Creed to the bishop, he addresses them all, and says: "During these seven weeks you have been taught all the law of the Scriptures, you have also heard concerning the Faith, and concerning the resurrection of the flesh, and the whole meaning of the Creed, as far as you were able, being yet catechumens. But, lest you should think that anything is done without good reason, these, when you have been baptised in the Name of God, you shall hear in the Anastasis, during the eight Paschal days, after the dismissal from the church has been made. You, being as yet catechumens, cannot be told the more secret mysteries of God."

5. Mystic Catechisings

But when the days of Easter have come, during those eight days, that is, from Easter to the Octave, when the dismissal from the church has been made, they go with hymns to the Anastasis. Prayer is said anon, the faithful are blessed, and the bishop stands, leaning against the inner rails which are in the cave of the Anastasis, and explains all things that are done in Baptism. In that hour no catechumen approaches the Anastasis, but only the neophytes and the faithful, who wish to hear concerning the mysteries, enter there, and the doors are shut lest any catechumen should draw near. And while the bishop discusses and sets forth each point, the voices of those who applaud are so loud that they can be heard outside the church. And truly the mysteries are so unfolded that there is no one unmoved at the things that he hears to be so explained.

Now, forasmuch as in that province some of the people know both Greek and Syriac, while some know Greek alone and others only Syriac; and because the bishop, although he knows Syriac, yet always speaks Greek, and never Syriac, there is always a priest standing by who, when the bishop speaks Greek, interprets into Syriac, that all may understand what is being taught. And because all the lessons that are read in the church must be read in Greek, he always stands by and interprets them into Syriac, for the people's sake, that they may always be edified. Moreover, the Latins here, who understand neither Syriac nor Greek, in order that they be not disappointed, have (all things) explained to them, for there are other brothers and sisters knowing both Greek and Latin, who translate into Latin for them. But what is above all things very pleasant and admirable here, is that the hymns, the antiphons, and the lessons, as well as the prayers which the bishop says, always have suitable and fitting references, both to the day that is being celebrated and also to the place where the celebration is taking place.

35. Eusebius of Caesarea, *The Ecclesiastical History*, Book 10

The Peace Bestowed on Us by God

1. Thanks be to God, the Almighty, the King of the universe, for all His mercies; and heartfelt thanks to the Saviour and Redeemer of our souls,

From Eusebius, *The History of the Church*, translated by G. A. Williamson (Baltimore: Penguin Books, 1965), portions of bk. 10, pp. 380–414. © 1965 by Penguin Books. Reprinted by permission of the publisher.

Jesus Christ, through whom we pray that peace from troubles outside and troubles in the heart may be kept for us stable and unshaken for ever.

Together with my prayers I now add Book 10 of the *History of the Church* to its predecessors. This I shall dedicate to you, my most worshipful Paulinus, calling on you to set the seal on the entire work; and it is appropriate that in a perfect number I should here set out the perfect account in celebration of the re-establishment of the churches, obeying the Divine spirit when He exhorts us thus:

> Sing to the Lord a new song, for he has done marvellous things;
> His right hand and His holy arm have wrought salvation for Him.
> The Lord has made known His salvation;
> In the sight of the heathen He has revealed His righteousness.[1]

As these inspired lines command me, let me now obediently sing aloud the new song, because after those terrifying darksome sights and stories I was now privileged to see and celebrate such things as in truth many righteous men and martyrs of God before us desired to see on earth and did not see, and to hear and did not hear.[2] But they, hastening with all speed, attained far better things in the heavens, caught up in a paradise of divine pleasure;[3] whereas I, acknowledging that even my present lot is better than I deserve, have been more than amazed at the bountiful grace of its Author, and am duly filled with wonder, worshipping Him with my whole soul's strength, and testifying to the truth of the written prophecies which declare:

> Come hither and behold the works of the Lord,
> What wonders He has wrought in the world,
> Making wars cease to the ends of the world:
> The bow He will break and will shatter the weapon,
> And the shields He will burn up with fire.[4]

Happy that all this has been clearly fulfilled in my own time let me proceed with the next part of my story.

Destruction, in the way described, had overtaken the whole brood of God's enemies, and at one stroke had blotted them out from human sight. Thus yet another inspired saying had been fulfilled:

> I saw the wicked high exalted,
> And lifted up like the cedars of Lebanon.
> And I passed by, and lo, he was not;
> And I sought his place, and it was not found.[5]

From that time on a day bright and radiant, with no cloud overshadowing it, shone down with shafts of heavenly light on the churches of Christ

---

1. Ps. 98:1–2.
2. Adapted from Matt. 13:17.
3. See 2 Cor. 12:4.

4. Ps. 46:8–9.
5. Ps. 37:33–6.

throughout the world, nor was there any reluctance to grant even those outside our community the enjoyment, if not of equal blessings, at least
of an effluence from and a share in the things that God had bestowed on us.

Re-establishment of the Churches

2. Thus all men living were free from oppression by the tyrants; and released from their former miseries, they all in their various ways acknowledged as the only true God the Defender of the godly. Above all for us who
had fixed our hopes on the Christ of God there was unspeakable happiness,
and a divine joy blossomed in all hearts as we saw that every place which a
little while before had been reduced to dust by the tyrants' wickedness was
now, as if from a prolonged and deadly stranglehold, coming back to life;
and that cathedrals were again rising from their foundations high into the
air, and far surpassing in magnificence those previously destroyed by the
enemy.

Emperors too, the most exalted, by a succession of ordinances in favour
of the Christians, confirmed still further and more surely the blessings that
God showered upon us; and a stream of personal letters from the emperor
reached the bishops, accompanied by honours and gifts of money. I shall
take the opportunity at the proper place in my account to inscribe in
this book as on a sacred tablet these communications, translated from
Latin into Greek, in order that all who come after us may bear them in
remembrance.

Dedication Ceremonies Everywhere

3. The next stage was the spectacle prayed and longed for by us all—dedication festivals in the cities and consecrations of the newly built places of
worship, convocations of bishops, gatherings of representatives from far
distant lands, friendly intercourse between congregation and congregation,
unification of the members of Christ's body conjoint in one harmony. In
accordance with a prophet's prediction, which mystically signified beforehand what was to be, there came together bone to bone[6] and joint to
joint, and all that in riddling oracles the scripture infallibly foretold. There
was one power of the divine Spirit coursing through all the members, one
soul in them all,[7] the same enthusiasm for the faith, one hymn of praise on
all their lips. Yes, and our leaders performed ceremonies with full pomp,
and ordained priests the sacraments and majestic rites of the Church, here

---

6. Ez. 37:7. Eusebius has added the   7. Acts 4:32.
"joints" to secure the play upon words.

with the singing of psalms and intoning of the prayers given us from God, there with the carrying out of divine and mystical ministrations; while over all were the ineffable symbols of the Saviour's Passion. And together, the people of every age, male and female alike, with all their powers of mind, rejoicing in heart and soul, gave glory through prayers and thanksgiving to the Author of their happiness, God Himself.

Every one of the dignitaries of the Church present delivered a public oration according to his ability, inspiring the great audience. 4. One of the moderately capable came forward into their midst with a prepared discourse. It was a church assembly, and the many pastors present gave him a quiet and orderly hearing. Addressing himself personally to a single bishop, an admirable man and one dear to God, through whose initiative and enthusiasm the most magnificent cathedral in Phoenicia had been built at Tyre, he delivered the following address.

Festival Oration on the Building of the Churches, Addressed to Paulinus, Bishop of Tyre

Friends of God, and priests clothed with the sacred vestments and the heavenly crown of glory, the divine unction and priestly garments of the Holy Spirit; and you, so young and yet the pride of the holy temple of God, honoured with ripe wisdom from God yet renowned for the precious works and deeds of virtue in its youthful prime, on whom the God who holds the entire universe in His hand has Himself bestowed the supreme honour of building His house upon earth and re-establishing it for Christ, His only begotten and firstborn Word, and for Christ's holy and majestic bride— shall I call you a new Bezalel,[8] the master builder of a divine tabernacle, or a Solomon, king of a new and far nobler Jerusalem, or a new Zerubbabel, who adorned the temple of God with the glory that was far greater than the old?[9] And you too, nurslings of the sacred flock of Christ, home of good words, school of self-discipline, and university of true religion, earnest and dear to God.

Long ago, as the inspired records of miraculous signs from God and the wonders performed by the Lord in the service of men were read aloud in our hearing, we might well send up hymns and songs to God; for we were taught to say:

O God, with our ears have we heard, our fathers have told us,
The work which Thou didst in their days, in ancient days.[10]

8. Ex. 35:30.   10. Ps. 44:1.
9. Hag. 2:9.

But now it is no longer by hearing the spoken word that men learn of the uplifted arm and the heavenly right hand of our God, All-gracious and King of all; but by deeds, if we may put it so, and with our very eyes we see that the traditions of an earlier age were trustworthy and true. And so we may raise our voices in a second hymn of victory and cry aloud:

> As we have heard, so also we have seen
> In the city of the Lord of Hosts, in the city of our God.[11]

And in what city but this new-made city built by God? It is the Church of the Living God, the pillar and basis of truth,[12] and of it another inspired saying joyously declares:

> Glorious things have been spoken of thee,
> O city of God.[13]

And since in this city God the All-Gracious has brought us together through the grace of His Only-Begotten, let each of the invited guests sing, nay shout,

> I was glad when they said to me
> "Into the house of the Lord we will go"

and

> Lord, I have loved the beauty of Thy house,
> And the dwelling-place of Thy glory.[14]

It is not only for each by himself, but for all of us together with one spirit and one soul, to give glory and praise, saying:

> Great is the Lord and highly to be praised
> In the city of our God, in His holy mountain.[15]

For great He is in truth, and great is His house, lofty and stretching far, and lovely in beauty beyond the sons of men.[16] Great is the Lord, who alone does wondrous things; great is He who does things great and unsearchable, glorious and marvellous things of which there is no number;[17] great is He who changes times and seasons, removing kings and setting them up, raising the poor man from the ground and from the dunghill lifting up the needy.[18] He has pulled down princes from their thrones and exalted the humble from the ground; the hungry He has filled with good things and the arms of the proud He has broken.[19] Not only for believers but also for

11. Ps. 48:8.
12. 1 Tim. 3:15.
13. Ps. 87:3.
14. Ps. 122:1 and 26:8.
15. Ps. 48:1.

16. Baruch 3:24 and Ps. 45:2.
17. Ps. 72:18 and Job 9:10.
18. Dan. 2:21 and Ps. 113:7.
19. Luke 1:52–3 and Job 38:15.

unbelievers has He proved true·the record of the ancient narratives, He the Doer of wonders, the Doer of great things, the Master of the universe, the Fashioner of the whole world, the almighty, the All-Gracious, the one and only God. To Him then let us sing the new song with this as the background to our thought:

> To Him who alone does wondrous things
> (For everlasting is His mercy);
> To Him who smote great kings,
> And slew mighty kings
> (For everlasting is His mercy).
> For in our low estate He remembered us,
> And redeemed us from our adversaries.[20]

The Father of the universe may we praise aloud in such strains without ceasing. The second source of our blessings, our Guide to the knowledge of God, the Teacher of true religion, the Destroyer of the wicked, the Tyrannicide, the Reformer of our life, our Deliverer from despair, Jesus, let us glorify, His name ever on our lips. For He alone, being an All-Gracious Father's unique, All-Gracious Son, in fulfilment of His Father's love for man, most willingly put on the nature of us men who lay far below, doomed to perish. A devoted physician, to save the lives of the sick, sees the horrible danger yet touches the infected place, and in treating another man's troubles brings suffering on himself: but we were not merely sick, or afflicted with horrible ulcers and wounds already festering, but actually lying among the dead, when He by his own efforts saved us from the very abyss of death, because no one else in heaven was strong enough to minister unscathed to the salvation of so many. Alone He took hold of our most painful perishing nature; alone endured our sorrows; alone He took upon Him the retribution for our sins.[21] When we were not half dead, but lying in tombs and graves and by now altogether foul and stinking,[22] He raised us up; and as He did long ago, so now in His eager love for men He surpasses all the hopes of ourselves or anyone else, saving us and giving us His Father's blessings without stint—He the Lifegiver, the Lightbringer, our great Physician and King and Lord, the Christ of God. Then, once for all, seeing that the entire human race was buried in gloomy night and deep darkness through the deceitfulness of wicked demons and the activities of accursed spirits, by nothing but His appearing He tore asunder—as easily as the sun's rays melt wax—the imprisoning bonds of our sins.

And now, as a result of this wonderful grace and bounty, the envy that hates good, the demon that loves evil, bursting with rage, lined up all his

20. Ps. 136:4, 17–18, 23–4.
21. Adapted from Is. 53:4–5.

22. A reminiscence of John 5:28 and 11:39.

lethal forces against us. At first he was like a mad dog that closes his jaws on the stones thrown at him and vents on the inanimate missiles his fury against those who are trying to keep him away: he directed his ferocious madness against the stones of the places of worship and the inanimate timbers of the buildings, bringing, as he himself imagined, ruin on the churches. Then he uttered terrible hissings and his own serpent-like sounds, at one time in the threats of godless tyrants, at another in the blasphemous decrees of impious rulers. Again, he vomited forth his own deadly venom, and by his noxious, soul-destroying poisons he paralysed the souls enslaved to him, almost annihilating them by his death-bringing sacrifices to dead idols, and letting loose against us every beast in human shape and every kind of savagery.

But once again the Angel of great counsel, God's great Commander-in-Chief, after the thoroughgoing training of which the greatest soldiers in His kingdom gave proof by their patience and endurance in all trials, appeared suddenly and thereby swept all that was hostile and inimical into oblivion and nothingness, so that its very existence was forgotten. But all that was near and dear to Him He advanced beyond glory in the sight of all, not men only but the heavenly powers as well—sun, moon, and stars, and the entire heaven and earth. So now as never before the most exalted emperors of all, aware of the honour they have been privileged to receive from Him, spit in the faces of dead idols, trample on the lawless rites of demons, and laugh at the old lies handed down by their fathers. But as the one only God they recognize the common Benefactor of themselves and all men, and Christ they acknowledge as Son of God and sovereign Lord of the universe, naming Him "Saviour" on monuments, and inscribing in royal characters in the middle of the city that is queen of the cities on earth an indelible record of His triumphs and His victories over the wicked. So it is that alone since time began Jesus Christ our Saviour is not acknowledged as an ordinary human king—even by the most exalted on earth—but worshipped as the true Son of the God of the universe and as Himself God.

And no wonder. For which of the kings who ever lived achieved such greatness as to fill the ears and mouths of all men on earth with his name? What king established laws so just and impartial, and was strong enough to have them proclaimed in the hearing of all mankind from the ends of the earth and to the furthest limit of the entire world? Who made the barbarous, uncivilized customs of uncivilized races give place to his own civilized and most humane laws? Who was for whole ages attacked on every side, yet displayed such super-human greatness as to be for ever in his prime and to remain young throughout his life? Who so firmly established a people unheard-of from the beginning of time that it is not hidden in some corner of the earth but is found in every place under the sun? Who so armed his soldiers with the weapons of true religion that their souls proved tougher than steel in their battles with their opponents? Which of the kings wields such power, leads his armies after death, sets up trophies over his enemies, and fills every place, district, and city, Greek or non-Greek, with votive offerings—his own royal houses and sacred temples, like this cathedral with its exquisite ornaments and offerings?

These things are indeed awe-inspiring and overwhelming, astonishing and amazing, and serve as clear proofs that our Saviour is King; for now too

> He spoke, and they were made;
> He commanded, and they were created.[23]

What indeed could withstand the will of the sovereign Lord and Ruler, the Word of God Himself? These things, again, call for a lengthy exposition of their own, if we are to examine them carefully and interpret them. But less importance attaches to the efforts of those who have laboured, in the eyes of Him whom we name God, when He looks at the live temple consisting of us all, and views the house of living and immovable stones,[24] well and securely based on the foundation of the apostles and prophets, Jesus Christ Himself being the chief cornerstone.[25] This stone was rejected by the master builders not only of that old building which no longer exists, but also of the building that still stands and consists of most of mankind—bad builders of bad buildings. But it was accepted by the Father, who laid it then to be for all time the head of the corner of this our common Church. This temple built of you yourselves, a living temple of a living God, the greatest truly majestic sanctuary, I say, whose innermost shrines are hidden from the mass of men and are in truth a Holy Place and a Holy of Holies, who would dare to examine and describe? Who could ever look inside the surrounding temple buildings, except the Great High Priest of the universe, who alone is permitted to search out the secrets of every rational soul?

But perhaps there is one other for whom, alone among equals, it is possible to take the second place after Him. I mean the commander at the head of this army, whom the first and great High Priest[26] Himself has honoured with second place in the priestly offices here performed, the shepherd of your spiritual flock, who by the allotment and judgement of the Father was set over your people, as if He had Himself appointed him His votary and interpreter, the new Aaron or Melchizedek, made like the Son of God,[27] abiding and guarded by Him continually through the common prayers of

23. Ps. 33:9 and 148:5.
24. 1 Peter 2:4.
25. Eph. 2:20–1.

26. Heb. 4:14.
27. Heb. 7:1, 3.

you all. Let him then be permitted alone after the first and greatest High Priest, if not in the first place at any rate in the second, to see and examine the innermost recesses of your souls; for through long experience he has made a thorough test of every man, and by his enthusiasm and attentiveness he has disposed you all in the order and teaching of true religion; and of all men he is best able to give an account to match his deeds of all that by divine power he has accomplished.

Our first and great High Priest tells us that whatever He sees the Father doing, that the Son does likewise.[28] This one looks to the First as to a teacher, with the pure eyes of the mind, and whatever he sees Him doing, that he takes as an archetype and pattern, and like an artist he has moulded its image, to the best of his ability, into the closest likeness. In no respect is he inferior to that Bezalel whom God Himself filled with a spirit of wisdom and understanding, and with technical and scientific knowledge, and chose to be architect of the temples that symbolized the heavenly types. In the same way this man, having the whole Christ, the Word, the Wisdom, the Light, impressed upon his soul, has built this magnificent shrine for God Most High, resembling in its essence the pattern of the better one as the visible resembles the invisible. Words cannot do justice to his generosity, to his liberal hand, so insatiable in its determination, or to the eagerness of you all, to the generous scale of your contributions, as in splendid rivalry you strove to be in no way behind him in this same purpose.

This site, to put first things first, which by the machinations of our opponents had been buried under a heap of filthy rubbish, he did not disregard or abandon to the malignity of those responsible, though he could have gone to any of the innumerable sites that abounded in the city, and so found an easy solution of the problem and a means of avoiding trouble. Instead, he first braced himself to his task, then roused all Christian people by his enthusiasm, gathered them all together in one great body, and launched his first campaign; for he felt that the church which had been assailed by her enemies, which had suffered before the rest and had endured the same persecutions as we, but before they came to us, and which was like a mother bereft of her children, should be the first to share the enjoyment of the All-Gracious God's munificence. For when the Great Shepherd[29] had driven away the wild beasts and wolves and every kind of savage creature, and had, as the word of God declares, broken the teeth of the lions,[30] deeming it good that His sons should again come together, it was most proper that he should erect the fold of the flock, in order to shame the

---

28. John 5:19.   30. Ps. 58:6.
29. Heb. 13:20.

enemy and avenger and publicly condemn the crimes of the sacrilegious enemies of God.

Now these men no longer exist, these enemies of God—in fact they never did; for after bringing distress on other people and on themselves too, they paid to justice a penalty not to be laughed at, utterly ruining themselves, their friends, and their families. Thus the predictions inscribed so long ago on sacred tablets have been proved trustworthy by events. In them the voice of God speaks the truth throughout, but listen to these declarations about them.

> A sword have the wicked drawn, they have bent their bow,
> To cast down the poor and needy,
> To slay the upright in heart.
> May their sword enter their own hearts,
> And may their bows be broken.[31]

And again:

> Their memorial has perished with a resounding crash,
> And their name Thou hast blotted out for ever and for ever and ever.[32]

For indeed, when they were in trouble,

> They cried, and there was none to save;
> To the Lord, and He did not listen to them.
> They were bound hand and foot and fell;
> But we have risen and have been set upright.[33]

And listen to this prophecy:

> Lord, in Thy city Thou shalt set their image at nought.[34]

The truth of that statement has been established for all to see.

These men, like the giants of old, joined battle with God and have brought their lives to this miserable end. By contrast, the Church that was desolate and rejected by men has by her inspired endurance won the victory we have seen, so that the prophetic voice of Isaiah calls aloud to her thus:

> Be glad, thirsty desert;
> Let the desert rejoice, and blossom as a lily;
> The desert places shall blossom forth and rejoice.
> Be strong, weak hands and feeble knees:
> Take courage, you that are timid at heart;

31. Ps. 37:13–14.   33. Ps. 18:41, 20:8.
32. Ps. 9:6, 5.   34. Ps. 73:20.

Be strong, do not fear.
Lo, our God dispenses justice and will dispense;
He will come and save us.
For (says he) in the desert water broke out,
And a channel in thirsty soil;
And the dry ground shall become lush meadows,
And on the thirsty soil shall be a spring of water.[35]

These things were foretold in words long ago, and set down in sacred books; but the fulfilment has reached us no longer by hearsay but in fact. This desert, this dry ground, this defenceless widow—they cut down her gates with axes as in a thicket of trees, together breaking her down with hatchet and stonemason's hammer; they destroyed her books and set on fire the sanctuary of God; they profaned to the ground the dwelling-place of His name; all that passed by the way plucked her fruit, having first broken down her fences; the boar from the thicket ravaged her and the solitary wild beast devoured her—yet by the miraculous power of Christ, now when He wills it, she has become like a lily. At that time by His command, as of a father who cares, she was disciplined:

For whom the Lord loves, He disciplines,
And He whips every son whom He acknowledges.[36]

In moderation, then, she was suitably corrected; and now once more she is commanded to rejoice again, and she blossoms like a lily and breathes her sweet divine odour on all mankind; for, as the Scripture says, in the desert water broke out, the stream of the divine regeneration by the saving baptism; and now what a little while ago was desert has become lush meadows, and on the thirsty soil has gushed a spring of living water. Strength has indeed come to hands that before were weak; and to the strength of those hands these great and splendid works bear witness. The once diseased and sagging knees have recovered their normal movement, and march straight forward along the road to the knowledge of God, in haste to rejoin the flock of the All-Gracious Shepherd. If the tyrants' threats have reduced some souls to torpor, even they are not passed over by the Saving Word as incurable: to them He freely gives the healing medicine, urging them on towards the divine comfort:

Take courage, you that are timid at heart;
Be strong, do not fear.

The word which foretold that she whom God had allowed to become desolate should enjoy these blessings was heard and readily understood by this new and splendid Zerubbabel of ours, after that bitter captivity and the

35. Is. 35:1–7.   36. Prov. 3:12 and Heb. 12:6.

abomination of desolation.[37] He did not pass the body over as dead, but he made it his very first task, by means of entreaties and prayers, to propitiate the Father, with the warm approval of you all. Taking the only Quickener of the dead as ally and co-worker, he raised up the fallen church, after first cleansing her and curing her sickness; and he clothed her with a garment— not the old one she had had from the first, but one that accorded with the further instructions of the divine oracles which emphatically declare: "The final glory of this house shall be greater than the former."[38]

Accordingly, the whole area that he took in was much larger, and he gave the outer enclosure the protection of a wall surrounding the whole, to provide the maximum safety for the entire structure. Then he opened up a gateway, wide and towering high, to receive the rays of the rising sun, thus providing even those who stood outside the sacred precincts with an unlimited view of the interior, and as it were turning the eyes even of strangers to the Faith towards the first entrances, so that no one should hurry past without being profoundly moved by the thought of the former desolation and the miraculous transformation now: he hoped that perhaps emotion at the mere sight would turn people and propel them towards the entrance.

He does not permit a man who has passed inside the gates to go at once with unhallowed and unwashed feet into the holy places within; he has left a very wide space between the church proper and the first entrances, adorning it all round with four colonnades at right angles, so that the outer walls turn the site into a quadrangle and pillars rise on every side. The space between these he has filled with wooden screens of trellis work to a proportionate height. In the middle he left a clear space where the sky can be seen so that the air is bright and open to the sun's rays. There he placed symbols of sacred purifications, constructing fountains exactly in front of the cathedral: these with their ample flow of fresh water enable those who are proceeding towards the centre of the sacred precincts to purify themselves. For all who enter, this is the first stopping-place, lending beauty and splendour to the whole and at the same time providing those still in need of elementary instruction with the station they require.

Passing beyond this wonderful sight, he opened passages to the cathedral through still more numerous gateways inside the court. In the full blaze of the sun once more, he sited three gates on one side: the centre one he dignified with height and breadth far exceeding those of the outside pair, and by providing bronze plates bound with iron, and elaborate reliefs, he gave it breathtaking loveliness, so that it looks like a queen between two humble bodyguards. In the same way he determined the number of the gateways to the colonnades along both sides of the whole edifice: over the

37. Dan. 12:11 and Matt. 24:15.   38. Hag. 2:9.

colonnades, to admit still more light, he designed separate openings into the buildings; and these he ornamented elaborately with exquisite wood-carvings.

The basilica itself he built solidly of still richer materials in abundance, never for a moment counting the cost. This is not, I think, the time to state the precise measurements of the building, or to describe in full its dazzling beauty, the incredible vastness, the brilliant appearance of the workmanship, the towering walls that reach for the sky, and the costly cedars of Lebanon that form the ceiling. Even about them the inspired word has something to tell us.

> The trees of the Lord shall be glad,
> The cedars of Lebanon which He planted.[39]

I need not go into details now about the perfection of the overall design and the superlative beauty of the individual parts, for the evidence of our eyes makes instruction through the ears unnecessary. But I will say this: after completing the great building I have described, he furnished it with thrones high up, to accord with the dignity of the prelates, and also with benches arranged conveniently throughout. In addition to all this, he placed in the middle the Holy of Holies—the altar—excluding the general public from this part too by surrounding it with wooden trellis-work wrought by the craftsmen with exquisite artistry, a marvellous sight for all who see it.

Not even the floor was overlooked by him. This he made bright with marble laid in wonderful patterns, going on next to the outside of the building, where he constructed halls and chambers along both sides on a great scale, skilfully uniting them with the fabric of the basilica so that they share the openings that let light into the central building. These, too, were provided for those still in need of cleansing and sprinkling with water and the Holy Ghost, and were the work of our most peaceful Solomon, who built the temple of God, so that the prophecy I quoted earlier is no longer mere words but plain fact; for the final glory of this house has become and now in truth is greater than the former.

It was natural and right that—as her Shepherd and Lord had once for all accepted death on her behalf, and after His Passion had changed the foul body which for her sake He had put on into His dazzling glorious body, and brought the very flesh that was dissolved from perishability to imperishability[40]—so in her turn the Church should reap the benefit of the Saviour's labours. For having received from Him the promise of much better things than these,[41] she longs to receive permanently and for all time the

---

39. Ps. 104:16.
40. 1 Cor. 15:42.

41. An allusion to Heb. 11:39–40.

much greater glory of the regeneration in the resurrection of an imperishable body, with the choir of the angels of light in the kingdom of God beyond the skies, and with Christ Jesus Himself, the great Benefactor and Saviour. Meanwhile, in the present she who was once widowed and desolate has by God's grace been wreathed with these blossoms, and has become in truth like a lily, as the prophecy declares; and having donned her bridal dress and put on the garland of loveliness, she is taught by Isaiah to dance, so to speak, offering her thanks to God the King in words of praise. Listen to what she says:

> Let my soul rejoice in the Lord;
> For He has clothed me with the mantle of salvation and the tunic of gladness;
> He has wreathed me like a bridegroom with a chaplet,
> And like a bride He has adorned me with ornaments,
> And like the ground that grows its blossom,
> And as a garden will cause what is sown in it to spring up,
> So the Lord, the LORD, has caused righteousness and rejoicing to spring up
>   before all the heathen.[42]

With such words on her lips she dances. And how does the Bridegroom, the heavenly Word, Jesus Christ Himself, answer her? Listen to His words:

> Do not fear because you have been put to shame,
> Or tremble because you have been reproached;
> For your everlasting shame you will forget,
> And the reproach of your widowhood you will remember no more.
> Not as a wife forsaken and without hope has the Lord called you,
> Nor as a woman hated from her youth, says your God.
> For a little while I forsook you,
> And with great mercy will I comfort you.
> With a little wrath I turned my face from you,
> And with everlasting mercy will I comfort you,
> Says your Deliverer, the Lord.
> Awake, awake!
> You who have drunk from the hand of the Lord the cup of His wrath;
> For the cup of staggering, the bowl of my wrath, you have drained and
>   emptied.
> There was none to comfort you out of all the children whom you bore,
> And there was none to take your hand.
> Lo, I have taken from your hand the cup of staggering, the bowl of my wrath;
> And never again shall you drink it:
> I will put it into the hands of those who wronged you and humbled you.
> Awake, awake! put on your strength, put on your glory:
> Shake off the dust and stand up.

---

42. Is. 61:10–11.

Sit down: loose the band from your neck.
Raise your eyes and look about you, and see your children gathered together:
Lo, they are gathered together and have come to you.
As I live, says the Lord, you will put them all on as an ornament,
And wrap them about you like the ornaments of a bride.
For your desolate, destroyed, and ruined places will be too narrow for your
  inhabitants,
And those who swallow you up will be removed far from you.
For the sons you have lost will say in your ears,
"The place is too narrow for me: give me a place where I may dwell."
And you will say in your heart, "Who has begotten me these?
I am childless and a widow: who has brought these up for me?
I was left alone: these my children, whence came they?" [43]

These things Isaiah foretold, these things had long ago been set down about us in sacred books, but it was necessary, was it not, that their truth should one day be shown by facts. And since this is the way in which the Bridegroom, the Word, speaks to His Bride, the Sacred and Holy Church, it was with good reason that this escort of the Bride stretched out her hands in the common prayers of you all, and woke and raised up the desolate one who lay dead, despaired of by men, by the will of God the universal King and by the manifestation of the power of Jesus Christ; and when he had raised her he made her such as the precepts of the sacred oracles taught him she should be.

This cathedral is a marvel of beauty, utterly breathtaking, especially to those who have eyes only for the appearance of material things. But all marvels pale before the archetypes, the metaphysical prototypes and heavenly patterns of material things—I mean the re-establishment of the divine spiritual edifice in our souls. This edifice the Son of God Himself created in His own image, and in every way and in every respect He endowed it with the divine likeness, an imperishable nature, a non-physical spiritual essence, remote from any earthly matter and actively intelligent. Once for all, at the first He transformed it from non-existence to existence, making it a holy bride and a most sacred temple for Himself and the Father. This He Himself plainly reveals in this confession:

I will dwell in them and walk in them;
And I·will be their God, and they shall be my people. [44]

Such is the perfect and cleansed soul, begotten from the beginning so as to bear the image of the heavenly Word.

But when, through the envy and jealousy of the demon that loves evil,

43. Is. 54:4–8, 51:17–23, 52:1–2, 49:18–21.

44. 2 Cor. 6:16; a conflation of Lev. 26:12 and Ez. 37:27.

she became by her own free choice a lover of sensuality and evil, the Deity withdrew from her, and bereft of a protector, she was soon captured, proving an easy prey to the inveiglements of those so long bitter against her. Overthrown by the battering-rams and engines of her unseen and spiritual foes, she came crashing to the ground, so that not even one stone of her virtue remained standing on another in her; she lay full length on the ground dead, her natural thoughts about God gone without trace. As she lay prostrate, made as she was in the image of God,[45] she was ravaged not by that boar out of the wood[46] visible to us, but by some destroying demon and spiritual beasts of the field, who inflamed her with sensual passions as if with blazing arrows of their own wickedness,[47] and set on fire the truly divine sanctuary of God, profaning to the ground the dwelling-place of His name.[48] Then they buried the unfortunate under a great heap of earth, and robbed her of the last hope of salvation.

But when she had paid the just penalty of her sins, the Protector, the Word, the divinely bright and saving One, restored her once more, obedient to the benevolent spirit of His Father, the All-Gracious. First He chose the souls of the supreme emperors, most dear to Him, and by their means He purged the whole world of all the wicked and pernicious people, and of the terrible God-hating tyrants themselves. Then He brought out into the open His own disciples, who all their lives had been dedicated to Him but, as in a storm of evils, secretly concealed under His sheltering wings, and with His Father's munificence He gave them a worthy reward. Again by their means He purged the souls which a little while before were fouled and heaped with rubbish of every sort and the debris of impious decrees: He cleansed them with pickaxes and two-pronged hoes—the penetrating lessons that He taught; and when He had made the place of the understanding of you all bright and shining, thenceforth He entrusted it to this leader, so wise and dear to God. An acute and discriminating judge of other matters, he is well able to appreciate and evaluate the character of the souls entrusted to his care; and from almost the first day he has never yet ceased to build, finding the right place, now for the shining gold, now for the tested, pure silver and the precious, costly stones among you all. So once more a sacred, mystic prophecy is fulfilled in what he has done for you—the prophecy that says:

> Lo, I prepare for you the carbuncle for your stone,
> And for your foundations the sapphire,
> And for your battlements the jasper,
> And for your gates stones of crystal,

45. Gen. 1:27.
46. Ps. 80:13.

47. A reminiscence of Eph. 6:16.
48. Ps. 74:7.

And for your enclosing wall choice stones,
And all your sons taught of God,
And in perfect peace your children;
And in righteousness shall you be built.[49]

Building truly in righteousness, he equitably divided the whole people in accordance with their powers. With some, he walled round the outer enclosure—that was enough for them—making unwavering faith the protective barrier. This accounted for far the greater part of the people, who were not strong enough to support a greater edifice. To some he entrusted the entrances to the church proper, giving them the task of waiting at the doors to guide those entering, since he justifiably regarded them as gateways to the house of God. Others he made under-props to the first outer pillars that form a quadrangle round the court, bringing them for the first time into touch with the letter of the four gospels. Others he joined to the basilica along both sides, still under instruction and in process of advancing, but not very far removed from the divine vision that the faithful enjoy of what is innermost. From these last he chooses the undefiled souls, purified like gold by divine washing; these he makes under-props to pillars much grander than the outer ones, drawing on the innermost mystic teaching of Holy Writ, while others he illumines with openings towards the light. With one huge gateway, consisting of the praise of our Sovereign Lord, the one only God, he adorns the whole cathedral; and on both sides of the Father's supreme power he supplies the secondary beams of the light of Christ, and the Holy Ghost. As to the rest, from end to end of the building he reveals in all its abundance and rich variety the clear light of the truth in every man, and everywhere and from every source he has found room for the living, securely-laid, and unshakable stones of human souls. In this way he is constructing out of them all a great and kingly house, glowing and full of light within and without, in that not only their heart and mind, but their body too, has been gloriously enriched with the many-blossomed adornment of chastity and temperance.

There are also in this shrine thrones and an infinite number of benches and seats, all the souls, on which rest the Holy Spirit's gifts, just as in olden time, they appeared to the holy apostles, and others with them, to whom were revealed dividing tongues like flames of fire, fire which rested on each one of them.[50] In the ruler of them all[51] we may say that the entire Christ Himself has found a resting-place, and in those who take second place to him proportionately, according to each man's capacity to receive the power of Christ and the Holy Spirit divided among them.[52] The souls of some

49. Is. 54:11–14.
50. Acts 2:3.

51. Paulinus.
52. Heb. 2:4.

might be benches for the angels assigned to each man with a view to his instruction and protection. As to the solemn, great, and unique altar, what could it be if not the spotless Holy of Holies of the common Priest of them all—His soul? Standing beside it on the right-hand side,[53] the great High Priest of the universe,[54] Jesus Himself, the only begotten of God, receives with shining eyes and upturned hands the sweet-smelling incense of all the worshippers, and the bloodless and immaterial prayer-sacrifices, and transmits them to the Father in heaven, the God of the universe. He Himself first adores the Father, and alone renders Him the honour due; then He beseeches Him to continue favourable and propitious towards us for ever.[55]

Such is the great cathedral which throughout the whole world under the sun the great Creator of the universe, the Word, has built, Himself again fashioning this spiritual image on earth of the vaults beyond the skies, so that by the whole creation and by rational beings on earth His Father might be honoured and worshipped. As for the realm above the skies and the patterns there of things here on earth, the Jerusalem above, as it is called,[56] the heavenly Mount Zion and the celestial city of the Living God, in which countless hosts of assembled angels and the church of the first-born enrolled in heaven give glory with praises beyond our utterance or understanding to their Maker, the supreme Ruler of the universe—these things no mortal can worthily hymn; for indeed eye has not seen and ear has not heard, and into the heart of man there have not entered, these very things which God has prepared for those that love Him.[57] Of these things we have now in part been found worthy; so let us all—men, women, and children, small and great together, with one spirit and one soul—everlastingly give thanks and praise to the Author of all the blessings we enjoy. He is very merciful to all our iniquities, He cures all our diseases, He redeems our life from destruction, He crowns us with pity and compassion, He satisfies our desire with good things. He has not dealt with us according to our sins or rewarded us according to our iniquities; for as far as the east is from the west, He has removed our iniquities from us. Just as a father pities his sons, the Lord has pitied those who fear Him.

Let us now and for all time to come rekindle the memory of these things; and let the Author of the present assembly and of this joyous and most glorious day, the Lord of the festival Himself, be before the eyes of our mind night and day at every hour and, may I say, at every breath. Let us love and reverence Him with all the power of our soul; and let us now stand up and with a loud voice of supplication beseech Him to shelter us in His

---

53. Luke 1:11.
54. Heb. 4:14.
55. Rom. 8:34 and Heb. 7:25.

56. Gal. 4:26.
57. 1 Cor. 2:9, slightly modified.

fold and preserve us to the end, bestowing on us His own unbreakable, unshakable, and everlasting peace in Christ Jesus our Saviour, through whom be glory to Him for ever and ever. Amen.

36. Irenaeus of Lyon, *Against Heresies*, Book 3

2. The Heretics Follow Neither Scripture Nor Tradition

1. When, however, they are confuted from the Scriptures, they turn round and accuse these same Scriptures, as if they were not correct, nor of authority, and [assert] that they are ambiguous, and that the truth cannot be extracted from them by those who are ignorant of tradition. For [they allege] that the truth was not delivered by means of written documents, but *viva voce*: wherefore also Paul declared, "But we speak wisdom among those that are perfect, but not the wisdom of this world." [1] And this wisdom each one of them alleges to be the fiction of his own inventing, forsooth; so that, according to their idea, the truth properly resides at one time in Valentinus, at another in Marcion, at another in Cerinthus, then afterwards in Basilides, or has even been indifferently in any other opponent, who could speak nothing pertaining to salvation. For every one of these men, being altogether of a perverse disposition, depraving the system of truth, is not ashamed to preach himself.

2. But, again, when we refer them to that tradition which originates from the apostles, [and] which is preserved by means of the successions of presbyters in the Churches, they object to tradition, saying that they themselves are wiser not merely than the presbyters, but even than the apostles, because they have discovered the unadulterated truth. For [they maintain] that the apostles intermingled the things of the law with the words of the Saviour; and that not the apostles alone, but even the Lord Himself, spoke as at one time from the Demiurge, at another from the intermediate place, and yet again from the Pleroma, but that they themselves, indubitably, unsulliedly, and purely, have knowledge of the hidden mystery: this is, indeed, to blaspheme their Creator after a most impudent manner! It comes to this, therefore, that these men do now consent neither to Scripture nor to tradition.

3. Such are the adversaries with whom we have to deal, my very dear friend, endeavouring like slippery serpents to escape at all points. Wherefore they must be opposed at all points, if perchance, by cutting off their

---

From *Against Heresies*, bk. 3, chaps. 2.1–4, 3, in *Ante-Nicene Fathers*, vol. 1 (New York: Christian Literature Co., 1890), pp. 415–17.

1. 1 Cor. 2:6.

retreat, we may succeed in turning them back to the truth. For, though it is not an easy thing for a soul under the influence of error to repent, yet, on the other hand, it is not altogether impossible to escape from error when the truth is brought alongside it.

3. A Refutation of the Heretics, from the Fact That, in the Various Churches, a Perpetual Succession of Bishops Was Kept Up

1. It is within the power of all, therefore, in every Church, who may wish to see the truth, to contemplate clearly the tradition of the apostles manifested throughout the whole world; and we are in a position to reckon up those who were by the apostles instituted bishops in the Churches, and [to demonstrate] the succession of these men to our own times; those who neither taught nor knew of anything like what these [heretics] rave about. For if the apostles had known hidden mysteries, which they were in the habit of imparting to "the perfect" apart and privily from the rest, they would have delivered them especially to those to whom they were also committing the Churches themselves. For they were desirous that these men should be very perfect and blameless in all things, whom also they were leaving behind as their successors, delivering up their own place of government to these men; which men, if they discharged their functions honestly, would be a great boon [to the Church], but if they should fall away, the direst calamity.

2. Since, however, it would be very tedious, in such a volume as this, to reckon up the successions of all the Churches, we do put to confusion all those who, in whatever manner, whether by an evil self-pleasing, by vainglory, or by blindness and perverse opinion, assemble in unauthorized meetings; [we do this, I say,] by indicating that tradition derived from the apostles, of the very great, the very ancient, and universally known Church founded and organized at Rome by the two most glorious apostles, Peter and Paul; as also [by pointing out] the faith preached to men, which comes down to our time by means of the successions of the bishops. For it is a matter of necessity that every Church should agree with this Church, on account of its preeminent authority, that is, the faithful everywhere, inasmuch as the apostolical tradition has been preserved continuously by those [faithful men] who exist everywhere.

3. The blessed apostles, then, having founded and built up the Church, committed into the hands of Linus the office of the episcopate. Of this Linus, Paul makes mention in the Epistles to Timothy. To him succeeded Anacletus; and after him, in the third place from the apostles, Clement was allotted the bishopric. This man, as he had seen the blessed apostles, and had been conversant with them, might be said to have the preaching of the apostles still echoing [in his ears], and their traditions before his eyes. Nor

was he alone [in this], for there were many still remaining who had received instructions from the apostles. In the time of this Clement, no small dissension having occurred among the brethren at Corinth, the Church in Rome despatched a most powerful letter to the Corinthians, exhorting them to peace, renewing their faith, and declaring the tradition which it had lately received from the apostles, proclaiming the one God, omnipotent, the Maker of heaven and earth, the Creator of man, who brought on the deluge, and called Abraham, who led the people from the land of Egypt, spake with Moses, set forth the law, sent the prophets, and who has prepared fire for the devil and his angels. From this document, whosoever chooses to do so, may learn that He, the Father of our Lord Jesus Christ, was preached by the Churches, and may also understand the apostolical tradition of the Church, since this Epistle is of older date than these men who are now propagating falsehood, and who conjure into existence another god beyond the Creator and the Maker of all existing things. To this Clement there succeeded Evaristus. Alexander followed Evaristus; then, sixth from the apostles, Sixtus was appointed; after him, Telephorus, who was gloriously martyred; then Hyginus; after him, Pius; then after him, Anicetus. Soter having succeeded Anicetus, Eleutherius does now, in the twelfth place from the apostles, hold the inheritance of the episcopate. In this order, and by this succession, the ecclesiastical tradition from the apostles, and the preaching of the truth, have come down to us. And this is most abundant proof that there is one and the same vivifying faith, which has been preserved in the Church from the apostles until now, and handed down in truth.

4. But Polycarp also was not only instructed by apostles, and conversed with many who had seen Christ, but was also, by apostles in Asia, appointed bishop of the Church in Smyrna, whom I also saw in my early youth, for he tarried [on earth] a very long time, and, when a very old man, gloriously and most nobly suffering martyrdom, departed this life, having always taught the things which he had learned from the apostles, and which the Church has handed down, and which alone are true. To these things all the Asiatic Churches testify, as do also those men who have succeeded Polycarp down to the present time,—a man who was of much greater weight, and a more steadfast witness of truth, than Valentinus, and Marcion, and the rest of the heretics. He it was who, coming to Rome in the time of Anicetus caused many to turn away from the aforesaid heretics to the Church of God, proclaiming that he had received this one and sole truth from the apostles,—that, namely, which is handed down by the Church. There are also those who heard from him that John, the disciple of the Lord, going to bathe at Ephesus, and perceiving Cerinthus within, rushed out of the bath-house without bathing, exclaiming, "Let us fly, lest

even the bath-house fall down, because Cerinthus, the enemy of the truth, is within." And Polycarp himself replied to Marcion, who met him on one occasion, and said, "Dost thou know me?" "I do know thee, the first-born of Satan." Such was the horror which the apostles and their disciples had against holding even verbal communication with any corrupters of the truth; as Paul also says, "A man that is an heretic, after the first and second admonition, reject; knowing that he that is such is subverted, and sinneth, being condemned of himself." [2] There is also a very powerful Epistle of Polycarp written to the Philippians, from which those who choose to do so, and are anxious about their salvation, can learn the character of his faith, and the preaching of the truth. Then, again, the Church in Ephesus, founded by Paul, and having John remaining among them permanently until the times of Trajan, is a true witness of the tradition of the apostles.

4. The Truth Is to Be Found Nowhere Else but in the Catholic Church, the Sole Depository of Apostolical Doctrine. Heresies Are of Recent Formation, and Cannot Trace Their Origin up to the Apostles

1. Since therefore we have such proofs, it is not necessary to seek the truth among others which it is easy to obtain from the Church; since the apostles, like a rich man [depositing his money] in a bank, lodged in her hands most copiously all things pertaining to the truth: so that every man, whosoever will, can draw from her the water of life. [3] For she is the entrance to life; all others are thieves and robbers. On this account are we bound to avoid *them*, but to make choice of the things pertaining to the Church with the utmost diligence, and to lay hold of the tradition of the truth. For how stands the case? Suppose there arise a dispute relative to some important question among us, should we not have recourse to the most ancient Churches with which the apostles held constant intercourse, and learn from them what is certain and clear in regard to the present question? For how should it be if the apostles themselves had not left us writings? Would it not be necessary, [in that case,] to follow the course of the tradition which they handed down to those to whom they did commit the Churches?

2. To which course many nations of those barbarians who believe in Christ do assent, having salvation written in their hearts by the Spirit, without paper or ink, and, carefully preserving the ancient tradition, believing in one God, the Creator of heaven and earth, and all things therein, by means of Christ Jesus, the Son of God; who, because of His surpassing love towards His creation, condescended to be born of the virgin, He Himself uniting man through Himself to God, and having suffered under

2. Tit. 3:10.   3. Rev. 22:17.

Pontius Pilate, and rising again, and having been received up in splendour, shall come in glory, the Saviour of those who are saved, and the Judge of those who are judged, and sending into eternal fire those who transform the truth, and despise His Father and His advent. Those who, in the absence of written documents, have believed this faith, are barbarians, so far as regards our language; but as regards doctrine, manner, and tenor of life, they are, because of faith, very wise indeed; and they do please God, ordering their conversation in all righteousness, chastity, and wisdom. If any one were to preach to these men the inventions of the heretics, speaking to them in their own language, they would at once stop their ears, and flee as far off as possible, not enduring even to listen to the blasphemous address. Thus, by means of that ancient tradition of the apostles, they do not suffer their mind to conceive anything of the [doctrines suggested by the] portentous language of these teachers, among whom neither Church nor doctrine has ever been established.

3. For, prior to Valentinus, those who follow Valentinus had no existence; nor did those from Marcion exist before Marcion; nor, in short, had any of those malignant-minded people, whom I have above enumerated, any being previous to the initiators and inventors of their perversity. For Valentinus came to Rome in the time of Hyginus, flourished under Pius, and remained until Anicetus. Cerdon, too, Marcion's predecessor, himself arrived in the time of Hyginus, who was the ninth bishop. Coming frequently into the Church, and making public confession, he thus remained, one time teaching in secret, and then again making public confession; but at last, having been denounced for corrupt teaching, he was excommunicated from the assembly of the brethren. Marcion, then, succeeding him, flourished under Anicetus, who held the tenth place of the episcopate. But the rest, who are called Gnostics, take rise from Menander, Simon's disciple, as I have shown; and each one of them appeared to be both the father and the high priest of that doctrine into which he has been initiated. But all these (the Marcosians) broke out into their apostasy much later, even during the intermediate period of the Church.

37. Cyprian of Carthage, *Letter 68 (64): To Florentius Pupianus, On Calumniators*

1. Cyprian, who is also called Thascius, to Florentius, who is also Pupianus, his brother, greeting. I had believed, brother, that you were now at length turned to repentance for having either rashly heard or believed in time past

From *Ante-Nicene Fathers*, vol. 5 (New York: Christian Literature Co., 1890), pp. 372–75.

things so wicked, so disgraceful, so execrable even among Gentiles, concerning me. But even now in your letter I perceive that you are still the same as you were before—that you believe the same things concerning me, and that you persist in what you did believe, and, lest by chance the dignity of your eminence and your martyrdom should be stained by communion with me, that you are inquiring carefully into my character; and after God the Judge who makes priests, that you wish to judge—I will not say of me, for what am I?—but of the judgment of God and of Christ. This is not to believe in God—this is to stand forth as a rebel against Christ and His Gospel; so that although He says, "Are not two sparrows sold for a farthing? and neither of them falls to the ground without the will of my Father," [1] and His majesty and truth prove that even things of little consequence are not done without the consciousness and permission of God, you think that God's priests are ordained in the Church without His knowledge. For to believe that they who are ordained are unworthy and unchaste, what else is it than to believe that his priests are not appointed in the Church by God, nor through God?

2. Think you that my testimony of myself is better than that of God? when the Lord Himself teaches, and says that testimony is not true, if any one himself appears as a witness concerning himself, for the reason that every one would assuredly favour himself. Nor would any one put forward mischievous and adverse things against himself, but there may be a simple confidence of truth if, in what was announced of us, another is the announcer and witness. "If," He says, "I bear witness of myself, my testimony is not true; but there is another who beareth witness of me." [2] But if the Lord Himself, who will by and by judge all things, was unwilling to be believed on His own testimony, but preferred to be approved by the judgment and testimony of God the Father, how much more does it behove His servants to observe this, who are not only approved by, but even glory in the judgment and testimony of God! But with you the fabrication of hostile and malignant men has prevailed against the divine decree, and against our conscience resting upon the strength of its faith, as if among lapsed and profane persons placed outside the Church, from whose breasts the Holy Spirit has departed, there could be anything else than a depraved mind and a deceitful tongue, and venomous hatred, and sacrilegious lies, which whosoever believes, must of necessity be found with them when the day of judgment shall come.

3. But with respect to what you have said, that priests should be lowly, because both the Lord and His apostles were lowly; both all the brethren and Gentiles also well know and love my humility; and you also knew and

1. Matt. 10:29.   2. John 5:31, 32.

loved it while you were still in the Church, and were in communion with me. But which of us is far from humility: I, who daily serve the brethren, and kindly receive with good-will and gladness every one that comes to the Church; or you, who appoint yourself bishop of a bishop, and judge of a judge, given for the time by God? Although the Lord God says in Deuteronomy, "And the man that will do presumptuously, and will not hearken unto the priests or unto the judge who shall be in those days, even that man shall die; and all the people, when they hear, shall fear, and do no more presumptuously."[3] And again He speaks to Samuel, and says, "They have not despised thee, but they have despised me."[4] And moreover the Lord, in the Gospel, when it was said to Him, "Answerest thou the high priest so?" guarding the priestly dignity, and teaching that it ought to be maintained, would say nothing against the high priest, but only clearing His own innocence, answered, saying, "If I have spoken evil, bear witness of the evil; but if well, why smitest thou me?"[5] The blessed apostle also, when it was said to him, "Revilest thou God's high priest?" spoke nothing reproachfully against the priest, when he might have lifted up himself boldly against those who had crucified the Lord, and who had already sacrificed God and Christ, and the temple and the priesthood; but even although in false and degraded priests, considering still the mere empty shadow of the priestly name, he said, "I wist not, brethren, that he was the high priest; for it is written, Thou shalt not speak evil of the ruler of thy people."[6]

4. Unless perchance I was a priest to you before the persecution, when you held communion with me, and ceased to be a priest after the persecution! For the persecution, when it came, lifted you to the highest sublimity of martyrdom. But it depressed me with the burden of proscription, since it was publicly declared, "If any one holds or possesses any of the property of Caecilius Cyprian, bishop of the Christians;" so that even they who did not believe in God appointing a bishop, could still believe in the devil proscribing a bishop. Nor do I boast of these things, but with grief I bring them forward, since you constitute yourself a judge of God and of Christ, who says to the apostles, and thereby to all chief rulers, who by vicarious ordination succeed to the apostles: "He that heareth you, heareth me; and he that heareth me, heareth Him that sent me; and he that despiseth you, despiseth me, and Him that sent me."[7]

5. For from this have arisen, and still arise, schisms and heresies, in that the bishop who is one and rules over the Church is contemned by the

---

3. Deut. 17:12, 13.
4. 1 Sam. 8:7.
5. John 18:23.

6. Acts 23:4, 5.
7. Luke 10:16.

haughty presumption of some persons; and the man who is honoured by God's condescension, is judged unworthy by men. For what swelling of pride is this, what arrogance of soul, what inflation of mind, to call prelates and priests to one's own recognition, and unless I may be declared clear in your sight and absolved by your judgment, behold now for six years the brotherhood has neither had a bishop, nor the people a prelate, nor the flock a pastor, nor the Church a governor, nor Christ a representative, nor God a priest! Pupianus must come to the rescue, and give judgment, and declare the decision of God and Christ accepted, that so great a number of the faithful who have been summoned away, under my rule, may not appear to have departed without hope of salvation and of peace; that the new crowd of believers may not be considered to have failed of attaining any grace of baptism and the Holy Spirit by my ministry; that the peace conferred upon so many lapsed and penitent persons, and the communion vouchsafed by my examination, may not be abrogated by the authority of your judgment. Condescend for once, and deign to pronounce concerning us, and to establish our episcopate by the authority of your recognition, that God and His Christ may thank you, in that by your means a representative and ruler has been restored as well to their altar as to their people.

6. Bees have a king, and cattle a leader, and they keep faith to him. Robbers obey their chief with an obedience full of humility. How much more simple and better than you are the brute cattle and dumb animals, and robbers, although bloody, and raging among swords and weapons! The chief among them is acknowledged and feared, whom no divine judgment has appointed, but on whom an abandoned faction and a guilty band have agreed.

7. You say, indeed, that the scruple into which you have fallen ought to be taken from your mind. You have fallen into it, but it was by your irreligious credulity. You have fallen into it, but it was by your own sacrilegious disposition and will in easily hearkening to unchaste, to impious, to unspeakable things against your brother, against a priest, and in willingly believing them; in defending other men's falsehoods, as if they were your own and your private property; and in not remembering that it is written, "Hedge thine ears with thorns, and hearken not to a wicked tongue;" [8] and again: "A wicked doer giveth heed to the tongue of the unjust; but a righteous man regards not lying lips." [9] Wherefore have not the martyrs fallen into this scruple, full of the Holy Ghost, and already by their passion near to the presence of God and of His Christ; martyrs who, from their dungeon, directed letters to Cyprian the bishop, acknowledging the priest of God, and bearing witness to him? Wherefore have not so many bishops,

8. Ecclus. 28:24 (Vulg. 28).   9. Prov. 17:4, LXX.

my colleagues, fallen into this scruple, who either, when they departed from the midst of us, were proscribed, or being taken were cast into prison and were in chains; or who, sent away into exile, have gone by an illustrious road to the Lord; or who in some places, condemned to death, have received heavenly crowns from the glorification of the Lord? Wherefore have not they fallen into this scruple, from among that people of ours which is with us, and is by God's condescension committed to us—so many confessors who have been put to the question and tortured, and glorious by the memory of illustrious wounds and scars; so many chaste virgins, so many praiseworthy widows; finally, all the churches throughout the whole world who are associated with us in the bond of unity? Unless all these, who are in communion with me, as you have written, are polluted with the pollution of my lips, and have lost the hope of eternal life by the contagion of my communion. Pupianus alone, sound, inviolate, holy, modest, who would not associate himself with us, shall dwell alone in paradise and in the kingdom of heaven.

8. You have written also, that on my account the Church has now a portion of herself in a state of dispersion, although the whole people of the Church are collected, and united, and joined to itself in an undivided concord: they alone have remained without, who even, if they had been within, would have had to be cast out. Nor does the Lord, the protector of His people, and their guardian, suffer the wheat to be snatched from His floor; but the chaff alone can be separated from the Church, since also the apostle says, "For what if some of them have departed from the faith? shall their unbelief make the faith of God of none effect? God forbid; for God is true, but every man a liar." [10] And the Lord also in the Gospel, when disciples forsook Him as He spoke, turning to the twelve, said, "Will ye also go away?" then Peter answered Him, "Lord, to whom shall we go? Thou hast the word of eternal life; and we believe, and are sure, that Thou art the Son of the living God." [11] Peter speaks there, on whom the Church was to be built, teaching and showing in the name of the Church, that although a rebellious and arrogant multitude of those who will not hear and obey may depart, yet the Church does not depart from Christ; and they are the Church who are a people united to the priest, and the flock which adheres to its pastor. Whence you ought to know that the bishop is in the Church, and the Church in the bishop; and if any one be not with the bishop, that he is not in the Church, and that those flatter themselves in vain who creep in, not having peace with God's priests, and think that they communicate secretly with some; while the Church, which is Catholic and one, is not cut nor

10. Rom. 3:3, 4.   11. John 6:67–69.

divided, but is indeed connected and bound together by the cement of priests who cohere with one another.

9. Wherefore, brother, if you consider God's majesty who ordains priests, if you will for once have respect to Christ, who by His decree and word, and by His presence, both rules prelates themselves, and rules the Church by prelates; if you will trust, in respect of the innocence of bishops, not human hatred, but the divine judgment; if you will begin even a late repentance for your temerity, and pride, and insolence; if you will most abundantly make satisfaction to God and His Christ whom I serve, and to whom with pure and unstained lips I ceaselessly offer sacrifices, not only in peace, but in persecution; we may have some ground for communion with you, even although there still remain among us respect and fear for the divine censure; so that first I should consult my Lord whether He would permit peace to be granted to you, and you to be received to the communion of His Church by His own showing and admonition.

10. For I remember what has already been manifested to me, nay, what has been prescribed by the authority of our Lord and God to an obedient and fearing servant; and among other things which He condescended to show and to reveal, He also added this: "Whoso therefore does not believe Christ, who maketh the priest, shall hereafter begin to believe Him who avengeth the priest." Although I know that to some men dreams seem ridiculous and visions foolish, yet assuredly it is to such as would rather believe in opposition to the priest, than believe the priest. But it is no wonder, since his brethren said of Joseph, "Behold, this dreamer cometh; come now therefore, let us slay him." [12] And afterwards the dreamer attained to what he had dreamed; and his slayers and sellers were put to confusion, so that they, who at first did not believe the words, afterwards believed the deeds. But of those things that you have done, either in persecution or in peace, it is foolish for me to pretend to judge you, since you rather appoint yourself a judge over us. These things, of the pure conscience of my mind, and of my confidence in my Lord and my God, I have written at length. You have my letter, and I yours. In the day of judgment, before the tribunal of Christ, both will be read.

12. Gen. 37:19, 20; Matt. 2:20, 23; Ps. 89:19, Vulgate.

38. Leo I, *Sermon 3: On the Anniversary of His Elevation to the Pontificate*

1. The Honour of Being Raised to the Episcopate Must Be Referred Solely to the Divine Head of the Church

As often as God's mercy deigns to bring round the day of His gifts to us, there is, dearly-beloved, just and reasonable cause for rejoicing, if only our appointment to the office be referred to the praise of Him who gave it. For though this recognition of God may well be found in all His priests, yet I take it to be peculiarly binding on me, who, regarding my own utter insignificance and the greatness of the office undertaken, ought myself also to utter that exclamation of the Prophet, "Lord, I heard thy speech and was afraid: I considered Thy works and was dismayed." [1] For what is so unwonted and so dismaying as labour to the frail, exaltation to the humble, dignity to the undeserving? And yet we do not despair nor lose heart, because we put our trust not in ourselves but in Him who works in us. And hence also we have sung with harmonious voice the psalm of David, dearly beloved, not in our own praise, but to the glory of Christ the Lord. For it is He of whom it is prophetically written, "Thou art a priest for ever after the order of Melchizedeck," [2] that is, not after the order of Aaron, whose priesthood descending along his own line of offspring was a temporal ministry, and ceased with the law of the Old Testament, but after the order of Melchizedeck, in whom was prefigured the eternal High Priest. And no reference is made to his parentage because in him it is understood that He was portrayed, whose generation cannot be declared. And finally, now that the mystery of this divine priesthood has descended to human agency, it runs not by the line of birth, nor is that which flesh and blood created, chosen, but without regard to the privilege of paternity and succession by inheritance, those men are received by the Church as its rulers whom the Holy Ghost prepares: so that in the people of God's adoption, the whole body of which is priestly and royal, it is not the prerogative of earthly origin which obtains the unction, but the condescension of Divine grace which creates the bishop.

From *Nicene and Post-Nicene Fathers*, 2d ser., vol. 12 (New York: Christian Literature Co., 1895), pp. 116–18.

1. Hab. 3:2 (LXX.).   2. Ps. 110:4.

2. From Christ and through S. Peter the Priesthood Is Handed On in Perpetuity

Although, therefore, dearly beloved, we be found both weak and slothful in fulfilling the duties of our office, because, whatever devoted and vigorous action we desire to do, we are hindered by the frailty of our very condition; yet having the unceasing propitiation of the Almighty and perpetual Priest, who being like us and yet equal with the Father, brought down His God-head even to things human, and raised His Manhood even to things Divine, we worthily and piously rejoice over His dispensation, whereby, though He has delegated the care of His sheep to many shepherds, yet He has not Himself abandoned the guardianship of His beloved flock. And from His overruling and eternal protection we have received the support of the Apostles' aid also, which assuredly does not cease from its operation: and the strength of the foundation, on which the whole superstructure of the Church is reared, is not weakened by the weight of the temple that rests upon it. For the solidity of that faith which was praised in the chief of the Apostles is perpetual: and as that remains which Peter believed in Christ, so that remains which Christ instituted in Peter. For when, as has been read in the Gospel lesson, the Lord had asked the disciples whom they believed Him to be amid the various opinions that were held, and the blessed Peter had replied, saying, "Thou art the Christ, the Son of the living God," the Lord says, "Blessed art thou, Simon Bar-Jona, because flesh and blood hath not revealed it to thee, but My Father, which is in heaven. And I say to thee, that thou art Peter, and upon this rock will I build My church, and the gates of Hades shall not prevail against it. And I will give unto thee the keys of the kingdom of heaven. And whatsoever thou shalt bind on earth, shall be bound in heaven; and whatsoever thou shalt loose on earth, shall be loosed also in heaven." [3]

3. S. Peter's Work Is Still Carried Out by His Successors

The dispensation of Truth therefore abides, and the blessed Peter persevering in the strength of the Rock, which he has received, has not abandoned the helm of the Church, which he undertook. For he was ordained before the rest in such a way that from his being called the Rock, from his being pronounced the Foundation, from his being constituted the Doorkeeper of the kingdom of heaven, from his being set as the Umpire to bind and to loose, whose judgments shall retain their validity in heaven, from all these

3. Matt. 16:16–19.

mystical titles we might know the nature of his association with Christ. And still to-day he more fully and effectually performs what is entrusted to him, and carries out every part of his duty and charge in Him and with Him, through Whom he has been glorified. And so if anything is rightly done and rightly decreed by us, if anything is won from the mercy of God by our daily supplications, it is of his work and merits whose power lives and whose authority prevails in his See. For this, dearly-beloved, was gained by that confession, which, inspired in the Apostle's heart by God the Father, transcended all the uncertainty of human opinions, and was endued with the firmness of a rock, which no assaults could shake. For throughout the Church Peter daily says, "Thou art the Christ, the Son of the living God," and every tongue which confesses the Lord, accepts the instruction his voice conveys. This Faith conquers the devil, and breaks the bonds of his prisoners. It uproots us from this earth and plants us in heaven, and the gates of Hades cannot prevail against it. For with such solidity is it endued by God that the depravity of heretics cannot mar it nor the unbelief of the heathen overcome it.

4. This Festival Then Is in S. Peter's Honour, and the Progress of His Flock Redounds to His Glory

And so, dearly beloved, with reasonable obedience we celebrate to-day's festival by such methods, that in my humble person he may be recognized and honoured, in whom abides the care of all the shepherds, together with the charge of the sheep commended to him, and whose dignity is not abated even in so unworthy an heir. And hence the presence of my venerable brothers and fellow-priests, so much desired and valued by me, will be the more sacred and precious, if they will transfer the chief honour of this service in which they have deigned to take part to him whom they know to be not only the patron of this see, but also the primate of all bishops. When therefore we utter our exhortations in your ears, holy brethren, believe that he is speaking whose representative we are: because it is his warning that we give, nothing else but his teaching that we preach, beseeching you to "gird up the loins of your mind,"[4] and lead a chaste and sober life in the fear of God, and not to let your mind forget his supremacy and consent to the lusts of the flesh. Short and fleeting are the joys of this world's pleasures which endeavour to turn aside from the path of life those who are called to eternity. The faithful and religious spirit, therefore, must desire the things which are heavenly, and being eager for the Divine promises, lift itself to the love of the incorruptible Good and the hope of the true

4. 1 Pet. 1:13.

Light. But be sure, dearly-beloved, that your labour, whereby you resist vices and fight against carnal desires, is pleasing and precious in God's sight, and in God's mercy will profit not only yourselves but me also, because the zealous pastor makes his boast of the progress of the Lord's flock. "For ye are my crown and joy," [5] as the Apostle says; if your faith, which from the beginning of the Gospel has been preached in all the world, has continued in love and holiness. For though the whole Church, which is in all the world, ought to abound in all virtues, yet you especially, above all people, it becomes to excel in deeds of piety, because founded as you are on the very citadel of the Apostolic Rock, not only has our Lord Jesus Christ redeemed you in common with all men, but the blessed Apostle Peter has instructed you far beyond all men. Through the same Christ our Lord.

5. 1 Thess. 2:20.

Index of Names